PATHWAYS TO PARTICIPATION

PATHWAYS TO PARTICIPATION

Reflections on PRA

EDITED BY ANDREA CORNWALL AND GARETT PRATT

ITDG
PUBLISHING

Published by ITDG Publishing
103–105 Southampton Row, London WC1B 4HL, UK
www.itdgpublishing.org.uk

© Institute of Development Studies 2003

First published in 2003

ISBN 1 85339 569 2

ISBN 1 85339 584 6
(for sale only in Africa, the Caribbean and Asia excluding Japan)

A catalogue record for this book is available from the British Library.

ITDG Publishing is the publishing arm of the Intermediate Technology
Development Group. Our mission is to build the skills and capacity of people
in developing countries through the dissemination of information in all forms,
enabling them to improve the quality of their lives and that of future generations.

Printed in Great Britain by Antony Rowe Ltd, Wiltshire.

Contents

Contents

Preface

Over the course of a decade, the rapid spread of Participatory Rural Appraisal (PRA) has taken it from being a marginal, innovative practice to a globally familiar way to think about and practise mainstream development. As PRA came to be used by people and organizations across the spectrum of development practice, for an ever-expanding range of purposes, champions of the approach began to raise their concerns. Some celebrated the adoption of PRA by mainstream development organizations after struggling on the margins to promote it. But for many others the cacophony of versions of PRA that resulted from its widespread uptake led to concerns about the quality of much of the work being labelled PRA. The need to push and promote PRA waned in the late 1990s, as it became for many a taken-for-granted part of 'doing participation'. This provided more space for concerned practitioners to openly voice concerns and reservations, which might have been saved previously for discussion among trusted friends and colleagues.

In the late 1990s, the Participation Group at the Institute of Development Studies (IDS) was hearing more calls from the loose international network of professionals working with PRA to work with this new reflective mood. What was needed, people said, were spaces to think critically about PRA in a constructive and more public way, and to help practitioners continue innovating and moving forward their thinking about participation. The Pathways to Participation project was initiated by IDS in 1999 to create opportunities for PRA practitioners to reflect on their own experience and the trends they saw in the application of PRA in their wider working contexts.

The Pathways to Participation project encouraged people to look back at experiences to date with PRA, to build on reflections on the past, to develop an analysis of the present and to look forward for new directions. The project supported research, workshops, video making, and reflective documentation by practitioners about their diverse experiences with PRA, collaborating with researchers, development organizations and networks in China, the Gambia, India, Kenya, Mexico, Nepal and Vietnam.[1]

Bringing together different generations of PRA practitioners from across the world and from a diversity of institutional and sectoral contexts, a three-day retreat was held in April 2000. The retreat was facilitated in a very open-ended way, led by different participants at different moments. Through individual reflection, diagramming, small group discussions, open space, forum theatre, informal chats and video interviews, people shared their analysis of the promise, achievements, disappointments and dilemmas of PRA with one another. As a preparatory exercise, people were asked to prepare short, reflective pieces of writing on PRA and participation, choosing whatever entry point they felt would be most fruitful. The contributions to this book are expanded and refined versions of those papers, and reflect some of the diversity of contexts and possibilities that PRA has come to represent in development practice.

Andrea Cornwall and Garett Pratt

Note

[1] A number of outputs from this work are featured on the IDS Participation website (www.ids.ac.uk/particip/), and include a series of IDS working papers and publications produced locally in Nepal, Kenya and Mexico.

Acknowledgements

The Pathways to Participation project was funded by the Swedish International Development Agency, the UK Department for International Development and Swiss Development Co-operation, through support to the Participation Group at the Institute of Development Studies (IDS). We are extremely grateful for this funding. We should like to thank all those people who took part in project activities, and especially those who were part of the International Workshop and who were unable to contribute to this collection. We are grateful to all the members of the Participation Group at IDS for their engagement with and support for our work, but should like to single out a few people for their specific contributions. Kamal Singh was key to conceptualizing and launching the whole project, and for the spirit of the retreat. We owe a special debt to Robert Chambers for his encouragement, insight, generosity and enthusiasm. Alexandra Hughes, Kelly Greene and Laura Hutchings provided valuable assistance in preparing the manuscript. And special thanks to Jane Stevens for guiding us through the publishing process.

Acronyms and abbreviations

AAPk	ActionAid Pakistan
ADB	Asian Development Bank
AEA	Agroecosystems Analysis
AISCO	Agricultural and Industries Supplies Company Ltd.
AKRSP	Aga Khan Rural Support Programme India
AMREF	African Medical and Research Foundation
ARHEP	Adolescent Reproductive Health Project
BATMAN	Barangay Administrator's Trainings on Management consortium, now the Barangay–Bayan Governance Consortium
BCDP	Banda Community Development Program
BDC	Barangay Development Committee
BRALUP	Bureau of Resource Development and Land Use Planning, Tanzania
CCF	Christian Children's Fund
CEDHA	Centre for Educational Development for Health, Arusha
CIE	Centre for International Education, University of Massachusetts
CSOs	civil society organizations
DFID	Department for International Development, UK
DILG	Department of Interior and Local Government
DIPs	Deliberative and Inclusive Processes
DPID	Department of Research and Development Projects, Nur University
FAO	Food and Agriculture Organization
FUNDESIB	Fundación para el Desarrollo Integral de Bolivia
HIV/AIDS	human immunodeficiency virus/acquired immune deficiency syndrome
HDR	Human Development Report
HRD	human resource development
ICAE	International Council for Adult Education
IDS	Institute of Development Studies, University of Sussex
ILO	International Labour Organization
IIED	International Institute for Environment and Development, UK
IPID	Institute for Participatory Interaction in Development
IRA	internal revenue allotment

ISEM	Information and Skills Exchange Meeting
JV	Neighbourhood Councils (*Junta Vecinales*)
LFA	Logical Framework Approach
LGU	Local Government Unit
LPP	Law of Popular Participation
MPA	Member of Provincial Assembly, Pakistan
MP	Member of Parliament
ODA	Overseas Development Agency, now the Department for International Development, UK
OTB	Local Territorial Organizations
PAR	Participatory Action Research
PakPLAN	Pakistan Participatory Learning and Action Network
PAMFORK	Participatory Methodologies Forum of Kenya
PDM	Plan for Municipal Development
PDO	project development officer
PLA	Participatory Learning and Action
PM&E	Participatory Monitoring and Evaluation
PO	people's organization
POA	Annual Operating Plan
PPA	Participatory Poverty Assessment
PRA	Participatory Rural Appraisal
PRAP	Participatory Rural Appraisal and Planning
PRIA	Society for Participatory Research in Asia
PRRA	Participatory Rapid Rural Appraisal
PRSP	Poverty Reduction Strategy Paper
PTD	Participatory Technology Development
RC	regional commissioner
REFLECT	Regenerated Freirean Literacy through Empowering Community Techniques
RILA	Research, Information, Learning and Advocacy approach
RIPS	Rural Integrated Project Support program
RRA	Rapid Rural Appraisal
SSP-IC	Swiss Inter-co-operation
STDs	sexually transmitted diseases
TARSC	Training and Research Support Centre
UNDP	United Nations Development Program
UNICEF	United Nations Children's Fund
UNV	United Nations Volunteers
VDC	Village Development Committee
ZOPP	Objectives Oriented Project Planning

Contributors' biographical notes

John Kennedy Alumasa, the former network co-ordinator of the Participatory Methodologies Forum of Kenya (PAMFORK), is a participatory development practitioner and facilitator, currently based in UNICEF, Kenya. He has wide experience in research using participatory learning and action techniques, and recently served as the assistant team leader for the Participatory Poverty Assessments in the Kenyan Poverty Reduction Strategy Paper process.

Eloy Anello is the director of the Center of Excellence for Teacher Training at Nur University in Santa Cruz, Bolivia. He has worked in countries throughout Latin America as a consultant and trainer in the areas of institutional strengthening of NGOs, the training of personnel for primary healthcare and the training of rural schoolteachers as community development agents.

Qais Anwar has been practising participatory approaches in Pakistan since 1991. He has used PRA in community organizing, programme auditing, monitoring and evaluation, child protection and education. He led the team that piloted Reflect-action in Pakistan. Currently, he is using PRA in child-led governance and advocacy programmes.

Karen Brock works in the Participation Group at the Institute of Development Studies at the University of Sussex, UK, and is currently working with partners in Uganda and Nigeria on policy processes and poverty reduction. She has also done research on the methodologies and impacts of participatory poverty assessment, and the sustainability of agropastoral livelihoods in sub-Saharan Africa.

Robert Chambers is a research associate at the Institute of Development Studies at the University of Sussex, UK. He has worked in Kenya, India and other countries of sub-Saharan Africa and South Asia.

Rene D. Clemente is a senior training officer of the *KAISAHAN tungo sa Kaunlaran ng Kanayunan* at Repormang Pansakahan, a Manila-based NGO working for agrarian reform, local governance and sustainable integrated area development. He is an agriculturist working to promote democratic participation in governance in the Philippines. He is interested in PRA and other participatory approaches to development, training and travel.

Andrea Cornwall is a fellow of the Institute of Development Studies at the University of Sussex, UK. A social anthropologist by training, she has been involved with PRA since the early 1990s. Her current interests include the history and ethnography of participation in development, and the politics of citizen participation in governance.

Chandan Datta has a postgraduate degree in geography and regional planning. For 17 years, he has specialized in decentralization, local self-governance, and participatory development and research. His current duties as a programme director for the Society for Participatory Research in Asia (PRIA) include work with new tribal and women's leadership in the new Indian state of Jharkhand.

Michael Drinkwater is located in Johannesburg as a regional programme co-ordinator with CARE International's regional office for Southern and West Africa. In his work for CARE, Michael has promoted programming with a much stronger emphasis on participation and empowerment, based initially around a household livelihoods perspective, and now increasingly, a human rights perspective. During the 1990s, Michael spent eight years in Zambia, initially working as a sociologist in the field of farming systems research, where he gained much of his early experience with participatory practice.

Marc Fiedrich is studying for a DPhil in development studies at the Institute of Development Studies at the University of Sussex, UK. His thesis is titled 'Paths to modernity: gender, literacy, and social change in Uganda'. He was formerly with ActionAid Uganda, working on participatory adult education (REFLECT), both as a researcher and as a trainer of trainers. His background is in social work, in particular with disabled children and adults.

Bara Gueye is a trainer and researcher working for the International Institute for Environment and Development. Over the past nine years, he has been co-ordinating the Sahel office of the IIED Drylands Programme, whose main activities focus on promoting participatory training and research methods in Francophone West Africa.

Irene Guijt is a freelance consultant specializing in collective monitoring for learning-oriented natural resource management. She is working on her PhD on the same topic at Wageningen University and Research Centre, the Netherlands. Prior to this she was a research associate for the Sustainable Agriculture and Rural Livelihoods Programme at the International Institute for Environment and Development and a visiting fellow at the Department of Forestry, Australian National University in Canberra. As a tropical land and water use engineer, she worked on diverse aspects of participatory resource management in Brazil, eastern and West Africa, south Asia and Australia. Key publications include *Participatory Learning and Action: a learner's guide* and *The Myth of Community: gender issues in participatory development*.

Regis M. Gwaba has an MSc in national development and project planning from the University of Bradford, and a BSc in agricultural sciences from University of Zambia. She is the monitoring, evaluation and research sector co-ordinator and the Gender Point person for CARE International in Zambia.

Katja Jassey is a socio-cultural adviser at the Swedish International Development Cooperation Agency (Sida). For the past decade her main interest and work has been within the field of participatory development and communication, with a strong focus on equity for all.

Barbara Kaim co-ordinates a programme on adolescent reproductive health in Zimbabwe through a local civic organization, the Training and Research Support Centre. She uses participatory approaches extensively in her work, especially around issues related to reproductive and sexual health, HIV/AIDS, gender, and participatory monitoring and evaluation.

Humera Malik is an anthropologist presently working with the International Union for Conservation of Nature (IUCN) on environmental issues. She is a founding member of two national NGOs, Sungi Development Foundation and Cavish Development Foundation. Her experience is mostly with community development work and the promotion of participatory approaches, especially PRA.

Mwajuma Saiddy Masaiganah is a freelance participatory planning and rural development worker. She is well known for her involvement and work in the area of social and organizational change through participatory approaches, and has worked extensively on gender, environment protection (especially marine), participatory media, poverty assessments, sustainable livelihoods, HIV/AIDS, education and integrated health.

Jessica Nalwoga first came across participatory methods while at Makerere University pursuing her undergraduate degree. She then applied these methods while doing research for the University, and then with ActionAid Uganda on their adult literacy programme using the REFLECT approach.

She is now working with the Church of Uganda on a peace and human rights programme, where she continues to use participatory methods.

Koos Neefjes was with Oxfam Great Britain for eight years and since May 2000 has been the representative of Oxfam Hong Kong for Vietnam and Laos, based in Hanoi. His interests include analysis of questions of poverty and environment, facilitating learning of development professionals, and developing methodology to uncover the impact of development processes and to enable deprived people to take part in decision making.

Bardolf Paul has a general background in communication media and forestry in development. He is interested in experiences, processes and approaches that foster the release and development of full human potential in individuals and organizations.

Wilhelmina R. Pelegrina has worked with Southeast Asia Regional Initiatives for Community Empowerment (SEARICE) since 1998, and currently co-ordinates the regional Biodiversity Use and Conservation in Asia Program (BUCAP). The programme aims at increasing agricultural biodiversity; strengthening farmers' management systems and control over their agrobiodiversity; and building capacities of local institutions to support farmers' agrobiodiversity management systems. She previously worked in development for 11 years in the Philippines.

Kamal Phuyal is a freelance participatory planning and rural development worker. He learned development work through a decade of experience as a community facilitator in rural areas. Since 1990, he has been promoting participatory approaches as a route to social transformation. He advocates for attitudinal change among development workers, as only good human beings can be effective agents for social transformation.

Michel Pimbert is a principal researcher at the International Institute for Environment and Development and a visiting fellow at the Institute of Development Studies at the University of Sussex, UK. Michel previously worked in agricultural research, focusing on the agro-ecology of small farms, and has done policy research on the links between biodiversity, livelihoods and cultural diversity. He co-ordinates the joint IIED-IDS programme on Institutionalizing Participation in Natural Resource Management and is currently involved in action research on sustaining local food systems, agricultural biodiversity and livelihoods.

Rajendra Prasad is a programme co-ordinator in SPEECH, an Indian

NGO, and is now concentrating on the integrated child development programme in Sivakasi, Tamil Nadu. He co-ordinates participatory research in SPEECH, and is also a renowned international trainer in participatory methods. He has worked as a short-term consultant in both Africa and Asia.

Garett Pratt is a research officer in the Participation Group, Institute of Development Studies at the University of Sussex, UK. He co-ordinated the Pathways to Participation project. He is now working on participation and organizational learning issues, mainly with Sida in Kenya.

Jules Pretty is professor of the environment and society at the University of Essex. He was formerly at the International Institute for Environment and Development in London, where he was director of their Sustainable Agriculture Programme between 1989 and 1997. He has published widely (more than 150 papers, articles and chapters), and his books include *The Living Land* (1998) and *Regenerating Agriculture* (1995).

Mallika R. Samaranayake is chairperson of the Institute for Participatory Interaction in Development Sri Lanka. She is well known in Sri Lanka and internationally for her work in promoting and training in participatory approaches and its application to research in various sectors, including the environment, gender, education, poverty, and social and impact assessments.

Tilly Sellers has worked in both the North and the South, using the principles and practice of PRA to assist organizations and community groups to develop, implement and monitor sexual health and other projects. She currently works for the International HIV/AIDS Alliance providing technical support in Southeast Asia.

Meera Kaul Shah is a development consultant and trainer. She is involved in developing and promoting participatory approaches in natural resources management, local institution development, post-conflict and disaster rehabilitation, policy research and advocacy, gender analysis, and monitoring and evaluation.

Marja-Liisa Swantz is a senior anthropologist and scholar in development studies. She pioneered Participatory Action Research in the University of Dar es Salaam and in the Institute of Development Studies in the University of Helsinki in the 1970s, where she served as director, using participatory approaches for action and research, and training many doctoral students. She has also developed participatory evaluation methods and guided ways of analysing local conflict situations. She has been a visiting professor at the University of Madison and a visiting professor in the WIDER Institute in Helsinki. She acted as senior sociologist in the RIPS support programme in southern Tanzania. She has published extensively, and has most recently contributed to the *Handbook of Participatory Action Research* together with her Tanzanian women partners.

John Thompson is a resource geographer and a specialist on human–environment interactions, who joined the International Institute for Environment and Development in 1991. As director of IIED's Sustainable Agriculture and Rural Livelihoods Programme, his work focuses on the political ecology of food and agricultural systems, institutionalizing participation for natural resource management and water policy issues. Previously, he has worked as a research associate at the National Environment Secretariat, Kenya, a research fellow at Clark and Harvard Universities, USA, and a fellow at the International Institute for Applied Systems Analysis, Austria.

Andreas Wilkes is a British citizen who worked in Yunnan, China, from 1997 to 2000, where he was an adviser to the Management Committee of the Yunnan PRA Network. His work has mainly involved training and other forms of capacity building related to participatory approaches to rural development. He is now pursuing a PhD in anthropology at the University of Kent.

INTRODUCTION
Andrea Cornwall and Garett Pratt

Participation may have become the buzzword of the 1990s, but the pathways of current enthusiasm for participatory methods stretch back over decades (Wright and Nelson 1995; Cornwall 2000). Perhaps the most popularly recognized and most widely used participatory approach in the current development scene, Participatory Rural Appraisal (PRA) had its genesis in the late 1980s in India and Kenya (McCracken et al. 1988; Kabutha and Ford 1988; Mascarenhas et al. 1991; Chambers 1992, 1994). Since then, it has come to be used in countless communities, in dozens of countries and in a huge variety of contexts. Once a marginal practice battling for recognition, it has now become an instrument used by the most powerful of global development institutions.

As PRA has spread and been taken up by actors and institutions across the spectrum of development practice, it has taken on a diversity of forms and meanings. In some settings, it has enabled development workers and activists to engage poor and marginalized people in shaping plans, projects and policies intended for their benefit. In others, it has provoked those working in development agencies and government bureaucracies to rethink and seek to transform their practice. In yet others still, it has become a routinized ritual, a form of legitimization, and a substitute for longer-term enquiry and engagement.

Pathways to Participation brings together the reflections of a diversity of development professionals from different generations and arenas of development work, cultural and political contexts, and professional backgrounds. All have engaged with PRA in one way or another, whether as practitioners, trainers, donors, academics or activists. Their pathways to participation have taken different directions, influenced by their personal, political and professional backgrounds, as well as by the forms of PRA which they were introduced to and helped to evolve. Embracing a range of entry points and experiences, their stories speak of moments of frustration and revelation, of dilemmas and discoveries; of pathways in which encounters

1

with participation shaped their perspectives on PRA, as well as vice versa. Together, their accounts speak of and about the sheer variety of the forms of practice that have come to be called 'PRA'.

In this introduction, we seek neither to editorialize nor to expound on the papers in this collection. Each speaks for itself. Rather, our intention is to provide a backdrop to complement and contextualize some of the stories told here.

Sharing concerns

The challenges and dilemmas that the rapid growth and spread of PRA have provoked have been a concern among practitioners since the early 1990s (see Cornwall et al. 1993; Chambers 1994; Guijt and Cornwall 1995). International gatherings of practitioners have given rise to statements of principle and concerns about 'bad practice' (Absalom et al. 1995; Adhikari et al. 1997). Yet these debates and critical concerns have remained largely internal, barely visible to a wider development community. Convincing the mainstream to adopt PRA took precedence over exposing shortcomings; and promoting participatory approaches sat uneasily with honest critical reflection. Critiques of PRA and participatory development directed at a wider audience have tended to be written by people not closely identified with the loose, informal network of people promoting PRA (Mosse 1995; Richards 1995; Stirrat 1996; Brown 1998; Cooke and Kothari 2001).

The enthusiasm of the mid-1990s, as international organizations began to incorporate PRA into their procedures and practices and produce statements and guidelines on participation, has given way in recent years to a more cautious appraisal of the effects of efforts to institutionalize the use of PRA (Thompson 1995; Blackburn with Holland 1998; Guijt and Kaul Shah 1998; Holmes 2001; Speight et al. 2001). With this, a new mood of critical reflection is emerging: one marked less by defensiveness and more by a desire to bring greater congruence between the rhetoric and realities of participation in development and the place PRA occupies within it. Concerns are beginning to converge on issues of ethics and values, moving beyond earlier, more methodological, debates.

Defying definition? Versions of PRA

For both those new to and familiar with PRA, there is no easy answer to the question, what is PRA? Absalom et al. (1995) define PRA as:

> A family of approaches and methods to enable rural people to share, enhance and analyse their knowledge of life and conditions, to plan and to act.

2

But empirical research shows that practitioners around the globe under-stand PRA very differently (Cornwall et al. 2001; Pratt 2001; Moya and Way 2003). People draw boundaries about what they consider to be 'PRA' in a variety of ways. For many, PRA is primarily identified with its distinc-tive visualization methods – maps, calendars, matrices and so on. PRA is widely known for the use of these kinds of visual representations with and by groups of people in poor communities, often using local materials on the ground, and symbols rather than writing. Sequences of tools are often applied to create general analyses of the life and conditions of people, but methods can also be applied in a more focused way to explore a particular sector or issue, whether it is views on a planned irrigation project, or people's parenting styles. As groups of people create representations of their knowledge together, they discuss the topic at hand and share views and ideas. For some, PRA ought to culminate in making action plans in which people define what they would like to change and how they would go about it. But not everyone views the use of visual representations as essential to PRA. There are practitioners who hold focus group discussions or commu-nity meetings and do not use any diagrams, but describe their practice as PRA. There are also professionals who use semi-structured interviews or short questionnaires and also refer to their practice as PRA, even if few PRA practitioners would regard this as legitimate.

Others regard PRA as a wider approach to the way in which development is and should be done, which suggests ways of going about any task, from creating a system of information management for NGOs to managing pro-grammes. For them, PRA is more than techniques; it is about underlying values and about the attitudes and behaviour of professionals towards those they work with, within as well as beyond the organizations they work for. For some, PRA is a way of life: an entry point for changing the ways in which development work is done because it directly addresses relationships of power which subordinate local people and local knowledge. Practitioners who subscribe to this view commonly complain that the attitudes and behaviour of many PRA practitioners fall short of their ideal – that profes-sionals are simply substituting PRA for the tools they used to use without changing the ways in which they think about local people, and without changing the way they conceive their own role as people working for social change.

The definition above makes reference to 'rural people' as participants, the ones doing the analysis, planning and acting, and suggests that it is PRA, not a person or organization, that enables them to do these activities. In reality, 'rural people', or whoever the non-professionals are who participate in PRA, exercise different degrees of power to analyse, decide and act in rela-tion to the professionals who usually initiate it. This is not just a question of the attitudes and behaviour of the professional during PRA processes. Most – if not all – PRA is initiated by 'outsiders', be they donors funding PRA for project appraisal or policy research, or local organizations using PRA as part of their development activities. The choice of PRA as a methodology is one made prior to engagement; and the form that PRA takes is often determined by the frame of reference of those who fund, commission and use it, something to which participants may make limited contributions.

Many practitioners complain that participants' involvement often stops at the analysis stage, as the right to make final decisions is reserved by professionals in development organizations. This can happen subtly through professional 'facipulating' (facilitating + manipulating) the direction or conclusions of the analysis. Or it can happen when professionals take the analysis away and make their own judgements, given their position in a development organization with both the associated power and constraints, as to what should be done. While the definition of PRA above emphasizes the importance of participants themselves taking action, many would argue that the organization that initiates and convenes PRA carries an ethical responsibility for what happens thereafter.

These days, the practice of PRA has spread well beyond the kinds of application conveyed in the definition above. It has developed along myriad pathways, leading to and coming from diverse directions. Defying definition, the label 'PRA' has come to be used to describe a bewildering array of concepts and practices. PRA has come to be used for a diversity of purposes, spilling beyond the project cycle and beyond community-level work to influence the management practices of organizations and the ways in which staff relate to one another as well as to those they work with and for. Contributors in this volume alone have brought versions of PRA into a diversity of settings: work on sexual and reproductive health, agricultural research, local government planning, research on poverty, activism over fishing rights, community activism on child rights, influencing development research, behaviour change on nutrition, and more besides.

From margin to mainstream

The debate around PRA has changed as it has moved from the margin to the mainstream and from applications in rural development to other sectors and contexts, over the past decade. Many of the authors became involved in the loose international network of PRA practitioners through their excitement over the tools and techniques they were using at community level; their journeys with PRA have taken them in other directions. For many, frustration with what Chambers (1997) has called 'normal professionalism' led them to embrace PRA as an alternative that offered them the space to realize another kind of development. For those working in agricultural development, PRA served to affirm the value of farmers' own agro-ecological knowledge and transform top-down extension practice, building on earlier work with agro-ecosystems analysis and farmer participatory research (Conway 1985; Scoones and Thompson 1994). For those involved in conventional social and economic research, PRA promised a new way of finding out, one that worked with rather than on people, and one that was action oriented, building on people's capabilities for learning and change. For activists, PRA offered new possibilities for engagement and the tools with which to build collective consciousness and collective action (Jones and SPEECH 2001).

In the early 1990s, a fairly small and close-knit international network of people became actively involved in promoting PRA globally, some of whom share their reflections in this book. Networking and sharing was largely around methodological innovation, and the focus was spread: how to communicate the ideas and practices of PRA to more people quickly, to start influencing and changing 'normal' development practice. As practitioners began to introduce PRA methods into government and into the programmes of large non-governmental organizations (NGOs), the challenges of working in a way that fulfilled the principles and promises associated with PRA when working within established development organizations started to emerge. Strategies for spread raised challenges for quality, as 'second generation' institutional questions came to the fore. As PRA has come to be used in ever-broadening areas of development work, from policy research to participatory monitoring, and evaluation to local government planning, so many people are using PRA and making claims about 'participation' that 'third generation' questions – about politics, ethics and power – have become increasingly important.

The popularization – and, in some contexts, the marketization – of PRA has given rise to a proliferation of practitioners, with differing versions and visions of PRA and participation. For some contributors to this book, 'PRA' no longer captures what they see themselves as doing; for others, the struggle to reframe and reclaim PRA defines their continued engagement with it. For many practitioners, PRA continues to offer the potential for doing development differently, but on a terrain that has changed substantially since they first became involved with it. New concerns with governance, policy and rights form a new focus for participatory work, and with it a series of potent new challenges for the use of PRA. The reflections in this collection show the personal dilemmas people using PRA in their work face as they make their own pathways through organizations and projects, and with different people in changing times.

Many practitioners who entered PRA as reformist 'outsiders' began to feel alienated from PRA as it was 'mainstreamed' by organizations whose purposes and actions they otherwise found politically objectionable, such as the World Bank. For example, the assumptions underlying Participatory Poverty Assessments (PPAs) that were meant to introduce public participation into poverty reduction policies were quietly questioned by some, at the same time as they were being enthusiastically promoted by others (Holland and Blackburn 1998; Brock and McGee 2002). As PRA training and consultancies became big business rather than marginal activism, decisions around engagement with powerful organizations versus distance and critique have become highly charged. The financial incentives for practitioners as carriers of a newly valuable and scarce commodity – 'expertise' in PRA – has introduced layers of uncertainty among practitioners in thinking about their own role, and into their judgement of the motivations and actions of others.

Now that the early days of innovating tools and discovering that 'they can do it' is past for many, doing some version of PRA is not enough for most people to feel a strong sense of identification with one another. Instead, people find themselves in networks of people working on local governance, gender issues, democratizing policy making or changing government bureaucracies to be more people-centred, and using PRA becomes one tool in their strategy. Although values have always been at the centre of discussions among PRA practitioners, and people have long criticized others for adopting 'only the tools', more recently internal debates have shifted even further away from methods to engage more directly with the politics of participation.

A number of the contributors to this collection reflect on, and provide examples of, the links between participation and governance, and the broader political dimensions of participatory development work. Many emphasize the personal politics of engagement in processes that seek to transform the ways in which development is practised. From stories of institutional dilemmas and transformations, to reflection on realizing the principles and values that underpin a commitment to participation, they offer rich food for thought about the dilemmas of participatory development as practice. For the contributors here, issues of ethics and questions of power are overriding concerns.

Tracks and traces

The papers in this collection speak of such a diversity of experiences that it would be hard to summarize or synthesize the rich lessons that can be drawn from them. As editors, we want to celebrate this diversity, not smooth over it. In this introduction, we have sought to avoid drawing any conclusions or highlighting more than the broader span of issues that the papers address. Each contributor has chosen their own entry point and narrative form for their reflections, from biographical accounts to instances of practice to the exploration of particular episodes or cases.

Putting these contributions together, we experimented with sequences and clusters: none adequately captured the extent to which tracks and traces cut across and complement each other. Instead, we have chosen to present these reflections in alphabetical order by author's surname, to be dipped into rather than read from beginning to end. For those looking for some guidance when they first 'dip in', we have created a matrix indicating some of the themes addressed in the papers. Some readers may choose to read clusters of papers touching on a topic particularly relevant to their own current interests.

Theme	Sub-themes	Papers
Starting and spreading	Origins; networks; promotion; creativity; innovation	Alumasa, Anello, Anwar, Chambers, Clemente, Cornwall, Gueye, Guijt, Kaim, Kaul Shah, Malik, Neefjes, Pelegrina, Pretty, Samaranayake, Sellers, Swantz, Thompson, Wilkes
Mainstreaming		Alumasa, Anwar, Brock, Clemente, Gueye, Jassey, Malik, Sellers, Thompson, Wilkes
Meanings and practices	Contrasts with conventional research, different interpretations of PRA	Alumasa, Anwar, Brock, Cornwall, Datta, Drinkwater, Fiedrich, Gueye, Guijt, Gwaba, Jassey, Kaul Shah, Malik, Nalwoga, Pelegrina, Pimbert, Prasad, Pratt, Pretty, Samaranayake, Sellers, Thompson, Wilkes
Policy	Changing policies through participation; participatory poverty assessments (PPAs)	Alumasa, Anello, Brock, Chambers, Clemente, Gueye, Jassey, Neefjes, Pimbert, Pratt
Governance	Local government; participatory governance	Anello, Clemente, Datta, Drinkwater, Pimbert, Swantz

Theme	Sub-themes	Papers
The politics of participation	Political activism; the politics of change	Anwar, Clemente, Cornwall, Malik, Masaiganah, Pimbert
Issues of difference	Gender	Drinkwater, Guijt, Gwaba, Jassey, Kaim, Kaul Shah, Masaiganah, Prasad
Issues of quality	Dilemmas and contradictions; ethical and political choices	Brock, Chambers, Cornwall, Drinkwater, Guijt, Gueye, Malik, Pimbert, Pratt, Pretty, Sellers, Thompson
Personal ethics and changing behaviour	Hypocrisy; motivation of practitioners; personal dimensions of change	Alumasa, Anello, Anwar, Brock, Chambers, Clemente, Drinkwater, Gueye, Prasad, Wilkes

We hope that this collection will inspire people who are new to PRA to begin their own journey of learning and exploration about participatory methodologies. And we hope that readers who have been engaged with PRA in the past will see the value of their own experiences anew, revisiting the pathways they have travelled with PRA, and sharpening their perspective on the directions in which they will take their own participatory development work in the future.

References

Absalom, E., Chambers, R., Francis, S., Gueye, B., Guijt, I., Joseph, S., Johnson, D., Kabutha, C., Rahman Khan, M., Leurs, R., Mascarenhas, J., Norrish, P., Pimbert, M., Pretty, J., Samaranyake, M., Scoones, I., Kaul Shah, M., Shah, P., Tamang, D., Thompson, J., Tym, G. and Welbourn, A., 'Sharing our concerns and looking to the future', *PLA Notes*, vol. 22, 1995, pp.5–10.

Adhikari, G.B., Chambers, R., Chatterjee, M., Chitrakar, S., Gopalakrishnan, N., Hettiarachchi, L., Jare, R., Jayakaran, R., Joseph, S., Kar, K., Kudaliyanage, G., Kumar, S., Lama, M.S., Murlidhar, G., Muthucumarana, P.S., Naser, A., Paul, S., Prabhakar, R., Salman, A., Samaranyake, M., Satheesh, P.V., Sheelu, Singh, H.B., Vashishta, H., Verma, A. and Wajih, S., 'Going to scale with PRA: Reflections and Recommendations', mimeo, 1997.

Blackburn, J. and Holland, J. (eds) (1998) *Who Changes?: institutionalizing participation in development*, ITDG Publishing, London.

Brock, K. and McGee, R. (eds) (2002) *Knowing Poverty: critical reflections on participatory research and policy*, Earthscan, London.

Brown, D. (1998) 'Professionalism, participation and the public good: issues of arbitration in development management and a critique of the neo-populist approach', in Minogue,

M., Polidano, C. and Hulme, D. (eds.), *Modern Public Management: changing ideas and practices in governance*, Edward Elgar, London.

Chambers, R., 'Rural appraisal: rapid, relaxed and participatory', *IDS Discussion Paper* 311, 1992, IDS, Brighton.

Chambers, R., 'The origins and practice of participatory rural appraisal', *World Development*, vol. 22(7), 1994, pp.953–69.

Chambers, R. (1997) *Whose Reality Counts? Putting the first last*, ITDG Publishing, London.

Conway, G., 'Agro-ecosystem analysis', *Agricultural Administration*, vol. 20, 1985, pp.31–55.

Cooke, B. and Kothari, U. (2001) *The Tyranny of Participation*, Zed, London.

Cornwall, A., 'Beneficiary, consumer, citizen: perpectives on participation for poverty reduction,' *Sida Studies*, vol. 2, 2000, Sida, Stockholm.

Cornwall, A., Guijt, I. and Welbourn, A., 'Acknowledging process: challenges for agricultural research and extension methodology', *IDS Discussion Paper* 333, 1993, IDS, Brighton.

Cornwall, A., Musyoki, S. and Pratt, G., 'In search of a new impetus: practioners' reflections on PRA and participation in Kenya', *IDS Working Paper* 131, 2001, IDS, Brighton.

Guijt, I. and Cornwall, A., 'Editorial: Critical reflections on the practice of PRA', *PLA Notes*, vol. 24, 1995, pp.2–7.

Guijt, I. and Kaul Shah, M. (eds) (1998) *Myth of Community: gender issues in participatory development*, ITDG Publishing, London.

Holland, J. and Blackburn, J. (1998) *Whose Voice?: participatory research and policy change*, ITDG Publishing, London.

Holmes, T., 'A participatory approach in practice: understanding fieldworkers' use of participatory rural appraisal in ActionAid The Gambia', *IDS Working Paper* 123, 2001, IDS, Brighton.

Jones, E. and SPEECH, 'Of other spaces' situating participatory practices: a case study from South India', *IDS Working Paper* 137, 2001, IDS, Brighton.

Kabutha, C. and Ford, R., 'Using RRA to formulate a village resources management plan, Mbusanyi, Kenya', *RRA Notes*, vol. 2, 1988, pp.4–11.

McCracken, J., Pretty, J. and Conway, G. (1988) *An Introduction to Rapid Rural Appraisal for Agricultural Development*, IIED, London.

Mascarenhas, J., Shah, P., Joseph, S., Jayakaran, R., Devavaram, J., Ramachandran, V., Fernandez, A., Chambers, R. and Pretty, J. (eds), 'Participatory Rural Appraisal: proceedings of the February 1991 Bangalore PRA Trainers' Workshop', *RRA Notes*, vol. 13, 1991.

Mosse, D., 'Authority, gender and knowledge: theoretical reflections on Participatory Rural Appraisal', *ODI Agricultural Administration –Research and Extension Network Paper*, vol. 44, 1995, pp.569–78.

Moya, X. and Way, S-A., 'Winning spaces: participatory methodologies in rural processes in Mexico', *IDS Working Paper*, 2003, IDS, Brighton.

Pratt, G., 'Practitioners' critical reflections on PRA and participation in Nepal', *IDS Working Paper* 122, 2001, IDS, Brighton.

Richards, P., 'Participatory Rural Appraisal: a quick and dirty critique', *PLA Notes*, vol. 24, 1995, pp.13–16.

Scoones, I. and Thompson, J. (1994) *Beyond Farmer First: rural people's knowledge, agricultural research and extension practice*, ITDG Publishing, London.

Speight, M., Muthengi, K. and Kilalo, C., 'World neighbors' experience of going beyond PRA in Kenya', *IDS Working Paper* 132, 2001, IDS, Brighton.

Stirrat, R.L. (1996) 'The new orthodoxy and old truths: participation, empowerment and other buzz words,' in Bastien, S. and Bastien, N. (eds), *Assessing Participation: a debate from South Asia*, Konark Publishers, Delhi.

Thompson, J., 'Participatory approaches in government bureaucracies: facilitating the process of institutional change', *World Development*, vol. 23(9), 1995, pp.1521–54

Wright, S., and Nelson, N. (1995) 'Participation and power', in Nelson, N. and Wright, S., *Power and Participatory Development*, ITDG Publishing, London.

CHAPTER 1
John Kennedy Alumasa

Hanging on the edge of a cliff: my loud thoughts as I walk along the winding path of participatory development in Kenya

My pathway in the field of participatory development is short but winding. There are many small paths that coalesce into the main pathway. Some are smooth and others are rough – the bumps and potholes that litter the way have sometimes caused a lot of frustration.

While on my seat at the Participatory Methodologies Forum of Kenya (PAMFORK), which I consider to be the 'pillar of participation', I must admit that my reflections started shortly after I discovered things were not working as well in practice as on paper. For me, therefore, it has been quite a struggle to get things going. If PAMFORK, the purveyor of participation, is more vulnerable than its member organizations, what future does participation hold? I had never worked for a network before. But I keep wondering, if network members have pathways that are at cross purposes, how can we forge ahead as a united front for participation? In this brief encounter, I share with you my pathway to participation.

A winding path

My journey on the winding path of participatory development can be traced way back to the mid-1980s when, while studying for my A levels, I visualized myself as a community worker. As Participatory Rural Appraisal (PRA) was taking root in Kenya during the same period, I was being 'prepared' in class to work as its future advocate. I then enrolled as a student of anthropology in the Institute of African Studies, University of Nairobi.

When I graduated in 1990, I gravitated more towards community work as I felt I had acquired the right knowledge and skills to work in the community. I applied for employment in the public service and specified the positions that I felt suited me in order of priority, that is social development officer and cultural officer. But on the two occasions that I appeared before the interview panel, I was interviewed for the position of employment officer! Even then, I was not offered the position.

11

The early 1990s were difficult times for Kenya as a whole. Dictatorship had reached its peak and the economy was in a slump. Censorship was the order of the day and suspicions were growing. Feelings of insecurity increased with the rise of human rights abuse. As Kenyans looked for political space and agitated for a new system that embraced and allowed the participation of all, I found myself involved in many pro-democracy demonstrations. How else would a young man armed with a university degree and high ideals utilize them?

The prevailing socio-economic and political situation, it was argued, had made many donors withdraw their funding programmes from the country. Even with the first multi-party elections in 1992, things did not blossom immediately.

Engagement and survival

After giving up on employment in the public service, I trekked on paths of opportunity in the NGO sector. In 1992, I was employed as a programme development officer by the Christian Children's Fund Inc (CCF), an international NGO operating in Kenya. I was posted to the Nangina Family Helper Project. This was an affiliate of CCF based in western Kenya.

When I reported, the programme manager, a white lady whom I later learnt was from the Netherlands, addressed me at the reception. After I had explained my mission, she advised me to 'seek for greener pastures elsewhere', since I was a graduate. She never looked at my appointment letter nor was she willing to discuss the same with the authorities in CCF headquarters! Back at the headquarters, I found myself on a path that was closed. The senior staff at the headquarters could not help me as the Dutch lady threatened to disaffiliate if I was imposed on the project. This was the first time that CCF had employed graduates to work in the community in its affiliated programmes. I am still reflecting. Did this manager have her way because of her skin colour? Would a Kenyan manager have had her way too?

To save face I was then engaged on a part-time basis to evaluate some CCF-affiliated projects in Kenya. I later served on a primary healthcare programme in Nairobi and in the arid north. This is what I have come to consider as the pathlet of exposure. During this short period I studied the operations of all the affiliated projects I visited. I was way ahead of my colleagues who were already serving as project development officers (PDOs). I trace my involvement in participatory development to these enlightening engagements. As these engagements became untenable, I found myself on yet another pathlet, the pathlet of survival. Remember, I had to feed, clothe and house myself. Short-term engagements could not guarantee this.

When the first-ever Participatory Poverty Assessment (PPA) in Kenya, sponsored by the World Bank/UNICEF/ODA/AMREF, was done in 1994, I was offered an opportunity to work as a research assistant, thanks to the strong research networks I was part of. I first served as a research assistant in 1988, when I was a second-year student at the University. By 1994, I had acquired much-needed knowledge and skills in research after working as a research assistant for various organizations.

We were taken through a rigorous training in participatory research tools and methodologies by two experienced practitioners, Deepa Narayan and Charity Kabutha. Never before had I been involved in an exercise that appeared simple yet generated in-depth information that was easily triangulated. The enthusiasm I have for participatory development stems from my PPA pathlet. Fascinated by the PPA process, I decided to go for a refresher course in PRA in 1995. This was facilitated by a reputable Nairobi-based participatory development training organization. I was disappointed when this PRA training became an academic exercise!

Participation – for whom?

When I think about the critical events in my development experience which have influenced my growth, the PPA serves as the spur. Before going through the PPA, I had not understood participation and what it means in development. The PPA experience gave a new meaning to my future development work. I am still reading about participation and its many contexts.

During the 1994 PPA, communities fatigued by extractive academic researchers lamented: 'You people come and get information from us and disappear. You use our information to get degrees and publish books from which you earn money, and then you forget us! Why can't you talk to whoever talked to us last year?' This was a challenge by communities on the utilitarian value of information obtained from communities. It made me reflect on instances when participation becomes a manipulative process. The problem is sustained by the lack of a culture of documentation of PRA experiences by many practitioners in Kenya. This calls for the need to disseminate our experiences widely through interactive and community-friendly processes.

Sometimes, through participation, we collect tons of information whose end product is an abridged report that ignores most of the rich data collected from the field. Does our abridged report voice the people's aspirations and frustrations? In the name of participation, we need to let communities 'voice' their struggles and experiences of academic, socio-economic and political poverty. What I am increasingly seeing are processes where the poor participate in generating the information, which is then owned by scholars and researchers, with little credit going to those who generated the information.

Straight talk

I am still pursuing the PPA pathlet, as participation has become the rallying call of my work. Armed with participatory research tools and methodologies, I was engaged as a researcher in 1995 by the Kenya Association of Professional Counsellors. For nine months I investigated the feasibility of an adolescent newspaper, using participatory tools. I worked with adolescents through a process that created space for them to openly discuss their sexual and reproductive health concerns. I was happy to oversee the development of a tripartite communication between adolescents, teachers and parents.

With the launching of *Straight Talk*, a UNICEF-initiated health newspaper targeting young people, I steered the project to develop into a programme with several components. These are one-to-one and group counselling sessions, topical group discussions, a life skills training programme, Straight Talk Clubs and the monthly newspaper.

However, my experience, which was exciting at the beginning, turned sour. Empowered adolescents posed a great challenge to the organization. They promoted Straight Talk to an extent that the programme was widely known and more popular than the organization. Indeed, counselling and participatory processes could not go hand in hand for long. The space that adolescents had enjoyed and utilized to their advantage was withdrawn. They were accused of turning the organization's premises into a market-place. My spirit of nurturing participatory processes for adolescent development was further exorcised when the organization withdrew its moral and financial support for all the adolescent activities I organized. I turned into an office 'prisoner'. With all my movements curtailed and limited, I found myself in a 'well of still waters'. I jumped out moments before a lid was put on and landed at PAMFORK. In 1999, I applied, was interviewed and appointed to the position of network co-ordinator. My participation experience had been suffocated enough.

PAMFORK

PAMFORK has not been a bed of roses either. As the new network co-ordinator at PAMFORK, I am dealing with the 'sins' of the past that culminated in membership apathy. The nagging question I had was: has PAMFORK achieved its mission, or are the members unhappy with its vision and mission? Efforts have been made to address this. In the beginning, it was disturbing to note that the administrator was not well versed in participatory development despite his long tenure. I must admit he was very economical with the truth regarding the status of PAMFORK. In time I came to understand the true picture.

The first activity I organized, the annual general meeting (AGM), had no quorum. This was the first devastating event in my tenure. The second AGM also failed to take place. What was even more disturbing is that it had fewer members than the first one. In these two instances, the elected steering committee members failed to 'hand over the stick' of leadership. If only all the elected members turned up in both instances the day's business would have been concluded. A task force was appointed to investigate the growing apathy – things worked until the task force met the steering committee and then they suspended the exercise.

PAMFORK had increasingly been associated with a select ethnic group, who it was believed had turned the network into a closed shop. Some members started believing that PAMFORK was for a select few, whom it assisted to get consultancies. This stigma played a major role in alienating many members. Something had to be done and all the dissenting members had to be brought back into the fold. As a network, it also emerged that PAMFORK lacked a strong grassroots constituency in practice, although there was talk of regional focal points on paper.

In preparation for the Pathways to Participation process, I launched focal points in the Coast, Western and North Rift regions. During the sharing forums, people saw PAMFORK in a new light and renewed their commitment to the organization. It is no wonder that the Pathways to Participation process later generated unprecedented interest. The challenge that I now face is how to sustain this interest through increased grassroots activities at the focal points.

My little experience here leaves me 'hanging on the edge of a cliff'. This is the case when I reflect on sustainability. Though it promotes participatory approaches, PAMFORK still faces the same sustainability concerns that afflict many network members. When members are faced with choosing between the network activities and their own activities, the latter prevail. With northern organizations fundraising in the south, intense competition for limited funds poses a great danger, especially for networks such as PAMFORK. The situation is so grave that I would not shy away from saying that PAMFORK as a network is currently more vulnerable than its membership!

A pathway of hope

All is not lost, however. I am currently riding on a pathway of hope. With increasing interest in PAMFORK's activities, there is light at the end of the tunnel. My priority then is to redefine the vision, mission and mandate of PAMFORK so that it can accommodate shifting membership interests.

The challenges and questions arising out of my experiences provide a 'mirror' for all practitioners to stop and ponder over the challenges that the new millennium poses for participation. First, I fail to notice the culture and tradition of PRA. After a decade of experimenting and/or piloting community participation through a whole range of approaches, how come we are still struggling with the question of institutionalization? This makes participatory development seem like a donor-driven condition in Kenya, yet history abounds with examples of people-initiated development initiatives through *harambee*, the spirit of togetherness.

Participation has now been commercialized, with many NGO staff resigning to launch consultancies. Many programmes on participation, be it training or processes, have are now well beyond the reach of the common man. PAMFORK promotes participatory methodologies, the best known being PRA. There are other methodologies that are home grown and which are derived from PRA. However, out of these, I pose the following challenge. Are these home-grown approaches to participation building on the weaknesses of previous approaches? To empower or not to empower through participation is the question! But when middlemen control the process, who takes care of quality standards?

There is a shift in funding policies, at least for us in the Third World. Funding is now pegged on levels of democratization and participation. The key word that has to be marked is 'participation'. The politics of donor funding and support for the developing world is increasingly being associated with the concept of participation.

With the Participation Group at IDS increasingly consulting for the Bretton Woods institutions, is it not falling prey to donor manipulation in impoverishing the Third World? By serving the participation interests of multilateral organizations and assisting in policy development, which is pushed down the throats of Third World countries, are IDS and many other international organizations working in the Third World not then helping to create a conducive environment for neo-colonialism? These are concerns that cannot be parried. In fact it is feared that the Bretton Woods may already have used experts to develop country-specific Poverty Reduction Strategy Papers (PRSPs). And now what is the future of participation with multilateral organizations adopting it, and the Third World concern that it could be used to nurture modern neo-colonialism!

Closely following this is the issue of participatory practice in Kenya and whose interests are served and met. For those who may not know, there are two schools of PRA in Kenya, or so it is claimed: the British and the American versions. One of these versions is said to be theoretical while the other is practical. The truth of this is left for us to digest. It is claimed that the British version is imported and promoted through PAMFORK, while the American version is easily accessed through Egerton University. PAMFORK doesn't have a PRA training unit while Egerton University has. Egerton has had strong links with Clark University in the United States, while PAMFORK networks with IDS. The challenge this poses is: do the two versions bear the same fruit? If not, can they be harmonized?

My experience at PAMFORK has introduced me to the world of participation consultants who care less about standards, but are interested in participatory development in as much as it empowers them economically. One may ask: does it mean that satiated participatory development practitioners who 'wheel' from workshop to workshop in five-star hotels are the ones who empower communities? Whether hungry or not, these middlemen, who are increasingly being viewed as 'merchants of participation', ought to know that true community empowerment might mean, though painfully, no business or job for them.

There is need to ponder over whether PRA is a means or an end. Is it the panacea to participatory development? Has it empowered communities? Let it not skip our attention that the past decade has also seen institutionalized misuse of PRA by many organizations. If it is used in a region over a long time-span it becomes an end in itself, and not a means. Does it not disrupt social processes in a region when one organization withdraws and another takes over, thus institutionalizing dependency! If an organization takes a long time to 'pass the stick', participatory development becomes an extractive academic exercise. Perhaps when the Pathways to Participation project in Kenya develops a practitioners' code of conduct, things will be clearer.

CHAPTER 2
Eloy Anello

My pathway to work on participation in local governance

Making a start in participation and health

In this chapter, I will recount some of my personal experiences in participatory research, and share my reflections on recent work I have been involved in on participation in local governance. My first systematic venture in working with participatory methods was during the 1970s, when I worked as a public health adviser for a primary healthcare project in the tropical lowlands of north-eastern Bolivia for six years. I was responsible for the advising activities related to organizing and strengthening community health committees and for setting up the logistical support system for health services, from the community level up through the local, district and regional levels of the Ministry of Health. It became clear that the success of the primary healthcare system depended greatly on the effectiveness of community participation in the decision-making processes related to the selection and supervision of health promoters, the management of the local health posts, and the promotion and utilization of health services.

My colleagues and I developed methods for gathering information at the community level, and for processing and interpreting the information with the community. Our purpose was to raise critical consciousness about health issues, and about the need for community participation in addressing priority health issues. We applied a simple household questionnaire and interview menu that were used to assess and categorize the homes in terms of high-, medium- and low-risk indicators. The information was processed with the families and at community meetings, and was used to determine the frequency and activity focus of the household visits by the health promoters. Although it may now seem elementary in light of established participatory research practice, at that time the act of sharing the information gathered with the community and inviting the community to help interpret it was not conventional public health research practice. It could easily have been perceived as subversive by the military regime that ruled Bolivia during that period.

The nature of the primary healthcare project made it necessary to structure community participation through the election and organization of local health committees. Once elected, the members of the health committees needed training in order to carry out their responsibilities as defined in the 'agreement of shared responsibilities' that had been established between the project and the community. We discovered that it was not enough simply to train the members of the health committees in basic administrative practices for the management of the health posts and for supervising the health promoters. We found it was also necessary to train the members of the health committees and promoters in a leadership approach that was participatory in nature and tended to empower the community. It was necessary to assist the committee members to develop specific leadership capacities and attitudes for the application of methods that facilitated community participation.

The innovative work done at that time, by the Ministry of Education of Ecuador and the Center for International Education (CIE) of the University of Massachusetts in Amherst, in applying participatory methods in non-formal education was a source of inspiration for my work in Bolivia. During that period I became familiar with the work of Paulo Freire. I attempted to apply the little that I understood at the time of his discourse and methods for critical consciousness raising.

During 1979, after a brief democratic regime, there was another military coup in Bolivia, which undermined funding for our project and effectively dismantled the primary health system we had piloted. The 'Manual for Community Organization', which I had co-authored as a result of the project, was still circulating in the Ministry of Health, but my assessment was that Bolivia still had a long way to go before it could develop a primary healthcare system based on genuine community participation. Quite frankly, the setback caused by the military coup affected me for a time and provoked me into an existential crisis regarding the meaning of my work.

Exploring education for participatory development

In 1982, I was one of the co-founders of the Fundación para el Desarrollo Integral de Bolivia (FUNDESIB), which is an NGO that was the sponsoring agency for the establishment of Nur University in Santa Cruz, Bolivia. After assisting Nur University to launch its first academic year, I felt the need to learn more about the role of higher education in the field of development, and thus decided to enter the doctoral programme in education at CIE. While at CIE, I had a real opportunity to study the work of Paulo Freire and the field of participatory research in depth, under the tutelage of folks like David Kinsey, David Evans and Paulo Freire, when he visited CIE as a visiting scholar during 1986.

19

My studies at CIE had a great impact on my understanding of the process of development and the role that education and training can play in facilitating empowerment for community participation. During the 1990s, I devoted my efforts to help strengthen civil society organizations throughout Latin America by giving training workshops, and by developing a postgraduate course on NGO management offered in Colombia and Chile. During this same period, through a programme developed by Nur University, I participated in giving training workshops to over 150 NGOs in Bolivia. The workshops and postgraduate courses were an effective means for promoting the use of participatory methods in the internal processes of NGOs and in their work with rural communities.

Around 1994, a colleague at Nur University, Fernando Dick, participated in a course at Guelph University in Canada. During this course he was introduced to Participatory Rural Appraisal (PRA) methods. When he returned to Bolivia, he began to promote the work of Robert Chambers at Nur University and organized an international seminar on PRA, which was facilitated by experienced practitioners from Mexico. The Department of Research and Development Projects (DPID) at Nur University became the first centre of PRA promotion in Bolivia and in South America.

In 1995–96, I helped to establish a teacher training programme designed to train rural schoolteachers as community development facilitators. I co-authored 13 training modules for the programme. Two of the modules are entitled 'Community Participation' and 'Participatory Research'. The module on participatory research trains teachers in the use of PRA methods for the design of educational projects with community participation. Over 2500 teachers have taken this course in Bolivia, Ecuador and Argentina. In Ecuador, over 204 educational projects have been designed by rural and urban teachers using the PRA methods they learned by taking the course.

A National Working Group for promoting participation was formed a few years ago by DPID–Nur University and a network of Bolivian NGOs that are engaged in applying PRA and other participatory methods. Fernando Dick has been a key player in establishing collaborative inter-institutional ties between IDS and DPID–Nur University. I feel a great affinity between the work being done by IDS and Nur University. In 1999, I participated in a workshop at IDS on participatory governance, which has been very useful in our work with municipal governments within the context of the Law for Popular Participation currently being implemented in Bolivia.

Making the most of the Law for Popular Participation

The Law for Popular Participation (LPP) was passed in Bolivia in April 1994. Prior to the passing of this Law, citizen participation in the elaboration of municipal service projects and programmes was minimal. Now economic resources generated by taxes are distributed by the Central Government to the municipal governments for the purpose of designing and implementing service projects and programmes, the sum of which should constitute a municipality's Plan for Municipal Development (PDM) and its Annual Operating Plan (POA). According to the LPP, the PDM and the POAs should be prepared by each municipal government in participation with the Local Territorial Organizations (OTB) and Neighbourhood Councils (Junta Vecinales, JV). The OTBs and JVs are official representative organizations, authorized by the LPP, and recognized by the Government. We assert that popular participation is a complex, social dynamic, in which all the actors involved must be engaged in an ongoing learning process. In the context of the LPP, the immediate goal of collective learning should be to enhance citizen participation in the elaboration of local projects and programmes, and to improve the participatory planning process of the municipal governments when elaborating PDMs and POAs.

Unfortunately, the participation of the OTBs in the formulation of PDMs and POAs as contemplated in the Law has not been the norm. This situation is due to many conditioning factors. The lack of effective communication between the municipal governments and rural communities is a basic obstacle to the implementation of the Law, resulting in the formulation of PDMs and POAs that do not reflect the real needs of the rural communities they should serve. Another primary obstacle is the prevailing lack of capacity of the OTBs to facilitate a participatory assessment of community needs, and to formulate project profiles consistent with the priority needs of the community.

To address the situation, DPID–Nur University has recently implemented a project in which local community-based organizations, OTBs, were trained in the use of PRA methods for the design of local development projects. The projects were subsequently presented to municipal governments for incorporation into the PDMs and the POA. Training in community leadership was also provided for the members of the OTBs.

We had four specific goals for the project. We provided training to local leaders and organizations for the development of their capacity to facilitate the participatory formulation of community project profiles. We also assisted in the negotiations with the municipal governments for the implementation of the project profiles. We aimed to establish a system for the participatory follow-up, monitoring and evaluation of the projects and programmes. And finally, we worked to develop and promote a municipal management strategy that will improve the social investment of the resources provided by the LPP.

We divided the activities into three phases. The first phase included a training needs assessment and curriculum design, which led to the preparation of four training modules. The modules covered Leadership for Community Development, the Legal Framework for Popular Participation, Design of Project Profiles, and Community Management. We then proceeded with training and the formulation of project profiles. In the second phase, we undertook selection, negotiation and implementation of project profiles, and designed a participatory system of follow-up, monitoring and evaluation (SEP). In the third phase, we systematized and documented the project experience.

Lessons learned through the project

The training approach used by the project helped community leaders and local authorities to become conscious of their capacities to promote community development processes and their need to strengthen and develop capacities that they lacked. This allowed for collective capacities to be understood, developed and valued, as well.

The project developed within rural communities the capacity to propose and negotiate community development projects. In the past, the community role tended to be limited to the provision of labour for construction of roads and infrastructure, supervision and control, but not the proactive formulation of project profiles that propose priorities for the use of municipal resources. The training modules were relevant and effective in responding to the training needs of community leaders and local organizations in promoting participation. The focus on the participatory formulation of project profiles tended to have an empowering effect on the participants in the training events. The community views the project proposal as a product of community participation that is in itself a significant collective achievement. This sense of achievement has an empowering effect on all the active participants and the community at large.

The concepts of community leadership developed in the workshops helped to transform dysfunctional mental models of leadership that have tended to undermine participation. There has been a marked change of mentality among the Agents of the Syndicate of Village Affairs who participated in the training workshops, from a somewhat aggressive, confrontational posture, towards one that deals with project proposals for constructive social action based on community consultation and consensus. The workshops tended to generate a more accepting attitude among the Agents of the Syndicate towards other existing community leaders. Some participants in the workshops have gone on to stand as candidates in recent elections, and some are now members of the city councils of El Torno and Comarpa. However, authoritarian mental models of leadership still prevail among many Agents of the Syndicate. Also, more affirmative action and consciousness raising is required to promote and secure the genuine participation of women in the formulation project profiles. Traditional gender roles and 'machista' attitudes tend to preclude the participation of women in activities related to the Syndicate of Village Affairs.

The weakest point of the programme was the lack of receptivity on the part of some of the municipal governments to the participatory planning process. They tend to believe that it is faster and more efficient if they contract expert consultants to elaborate their PDM and POAs, and that the participation of OTBs, the Agents of the Syndicate of Village Affairs and other local actors is a waste of time. The officials of these municipal governments have prejudices regarding the capacities of community leadership and organizations to participate effectively in a planning process. The project helped the community to express its voice, but the municipal governments were not able to listen. Although the training and strengthening of the OTBs and community leadership in the participatory formulation of project profiles is essential, it is not enough. If the municipal governments do not appreciate the value of participation and are not adequately motivated and competent in the application of a participatory planning methodology, it is highly probable that the project profiles formulated by the OTBs will not be considered and incorporated in the PDMs and POAs. We need to design training workshops for the municipal governments to enhance their capacity to listen and to participate effectively in participatory planning processes. A lot of work needs to be done in this area.

Also in the future, reflection events and workshop seminars are needed for the sharing and systematization of experiences among Bolivian NGOs that are engaged in capacity building for participation at the grassroots and municipal levels. A systematization of experiences in this area of work is needed on an international level as well, to generate a body of knowledge that can serve as the basis for the design of integral training programmes for community leaders, grassroots organizations, NGOs and municipal governments. The decentralization of authority and resources to municipal governments is a trend that has been in operation during the past decade and continues to spread throughout Latin America. This trend represents a strategic opportunity for the promotion, establishment and consolidation of participatory governance.

Learning technologies and telecommunications systems need to be applied strategically to facilitate participatory learning processes on a massive scale. The training task is too colossal for traditional training approaches to make any significant dent. We need to rethink our training strategies to incorporate the Internet and satellite transmission to remote classrooms. Donor agencies need to assist in the democratization of these technologies for learning and capacity building. We must learn to use these technologies as a means for achieving our shared vision of social justice.

The piecemeal approach to funding projects also needs to change. The prevailing approach for North–South transference of resources is not effective in responding to the real magnitude and urgency of the challenge facing NGOs, community organizations and municipal governments. Serious consideration needs to be given by donor agencies to providing block funding for at least five years to proven NGO networks that are doing significant work in this critical area of research and action. A funding strategy of this type would facilitate the work of NGOs and allow them to demonstrate significant results over time. Obviously, such a strategy would require a mature partnership of equals between southern NGOs/universities and their northern counterparts. This is the direction we must move in if we hope to become more than an anecdote, and begin to write history.

CHAPTER 3

Qais Anwar

Six experiences with PRA

My first job – experiences of a faithful statistician

After doing my masters in statistics, I joined the government service in Pakistan in 1987 as a research investigator, mainly responsible for managing data on production. At the outset, it was a great surprise for me that instead of relying on the data provided by the field offices, we had to engineer data in the headquarters. Being a faithful statistician, initially I thought I could revolutionize the system by introducing new questionnaires and formats.

It took me two years to appreciate that it was impossible for the already overburdened field officers to meet our information demands. Whatever we received from them was 'safe' information showing enormous increases in production in the sector. We in the headquarters were supposed to fix it again to make it safer for our organization. I remember one day when we were working on the data provided by the field officers, the representative of the official agency responsible for publishing the data visited our office to collect the yearly information. The deadline had already passed and we had no option but to hurriedly apply, as usual, a projection formula. When the report was published, a senior told me that our manual calculation was wrong and the data did not match the past trends. Now, whenever I see someone giving arguments using the official data, I suddenly see in my mind's eye a researcher giving the explanation for the unusual production for the year when our calculation went wrong.

Some months later, I got a chance to lead a development project focusing on poor fishing households, where I could collect the 'correct' data. Here, I was more confident in applying my expertise; I developed an excellent questionnaire for a baseline needs assessment in early 1992. In January 1995, when the project had been completed and I was working on another project, I heard the news that the data had been analysed.

Around mid-1992, when I was working on the project (and waiting for the results of the needs assessment survey), I started practising Participatory Rural Appraisal (PRA) for the first time. These were the days when I first met (the now late) Dr Akhter Hameed, a veteran development practitioner in Pakistan. When I enthusiastically started telling him the stories of my achievements, he inquired about the expenditures on different components of the project. When he came to know that we were spending Rs200 000 on a needs assessment survey, half of the total community human resource development (HRD) cost, he said 'Son! Suppose you get less accurate data and expend the funds allocated for the baseline on the poor instead, what difference will it make?' This question led me re-examine what I was taught in the university and ultimately changed my whole way of thinking.

My team and I had already discovered the value of being low profile. In the government sector, we who were working with people were considered incapable of doing the prestigious technical jobs. The powerful technical people in the department always disowned us. Even the lowest grade person in the project area was not prepared to facilitate us. This powerlessness made us harmless in the eyes of the poor in the area and later helped us to win their friendship.

Fitting PRA into conventional frameworks

In December 1994, I joined a slum-upgrading project. I was monitoring and evaluation specialist there and I was supposed to collect data through PRA. It was an interesting combination of two groups, the donor wanting to reduce the construction and maintenance costs by using participatory techniques, and the implementation organizations most interested in physical targets. We had to fit the PRA results into logframes. Within a year, all of us realized that PRA is the least useful approach to serve logframes.

From Toyota to Sohrab[1]

It was as a manager for ActionAid Bahawalnagar that I discovered new dimensions of PRA by combining my experience of 'disempowering ourselves in the community' with the experience of participatory management by colleagues like Humera Malik.

I had realized from my early experiences that during a PRA initiated by outsiders, when many areas of local life are analysed, the community's expectations of some assistance based on a very genuine feeling – why are these outsiders here? – cannot be avoided. The level of these expectations corresponds with the profile and the attitude of the outsiders. Most of the time, the prioritization of problems using PRA tools presents a prioritized 'expectations list'.

In December 1995, when we started working in Bahawalnagar, the community took up some large-scale projects like water supply and road construction for discussion during the PRA. When the project team examined the issues later, one opinion that emerged was that we should improve our entry in the community by adopting a modest style. The team at this point also discussed its ethical aspects. The primary question was: when we enter into a community in a modest manner, do we deceive that community? In the office and at other places we use better facilities, but when we go to the communities we adopt the local style. Does this, in any way, indicate that we follow double standards? Similarly, advising the following of a simple style of life for the people who work in the community, while providing all kinds of facilities to those who work in the central offices, also gives rise to several questions. This duplicity creates disappointment among the workers who are directly involved in the community work and weakens their level of commitment. In addition, the community soon becomes aware of this duplicity.

Based on this analysis, the team changed its style of work. As a first step, they bought locally made air coolers instead of buying air conditioners, for which donors had provided the budget. They started going to the project areas on bicycles instead of in air-conditioned cars. In order to bridge the gap between theory and practice, some steps were taken within the Action-Aid set-up. The management team members started using public transport more often for travelling in the city and between the cities. To bring them closer to the field staff, one of the facilities allowed in the policy – air travel to other cities – was totally abandoned. An important development in this regard was that the female staff also refused to travel by air.

Now, quite contrary to the team's previous experiences, people's expectations from ActionAid Pakistan (AAPk) are very limited, which has helped the team to focus its work on empowerment-related issues. One of the interesting observations reported by a partner organization staff member, who has been using public transport for visiting the community, is about the community offering him a ride. Normally, community members demand rides from the project staff, as the community's transportation means are slow and uncomfortable. In such cases, the project staff of development organizations are advised that the practice of giving rides to the community should not be encouraged. However, in AAPk Bahawalnagar's work, the staff member reported that whenever he had to work until late and had to come back, the people of the community offered him a ride to the bus stand on their bicycles.

Initially, it looks very hard to disempower ourselves. By making humility a lifestyle, one loses all that respect which is generated by power. While it helps the disempowered to become empowered, those who are powerful may not listen to us and may even oppose us. The team thinks that the capacity to absorb the initial shocks, persistent behaviour, commitment and assertiveness before the powerful is a prerequisite for this style of work.

For the team in Bahawalnagar, this approach is pro-poor, as the rich have no interest in the powerless outsiders, whereas the poor, particularly the women, are attracted by it.

A shift towards REFLECT

In REFLECT, participants use diagrams, maps, songs and drama, etc., developed during PRA, as a code. A dialogue is initiated around this code and the participants analyse their condition, enhance their skills to communicate their analysis to others, and receive and relate outside knowledge with their own analysis. As a result, local political action is started. REFLECT stretches PRA beyond local analysis and relates it to global realities. Regular PRA by people in a closed place, street or field empowers people to deepen their knowledge and start sound action based on that knowledge.

In Bahawalnagar, I observed for the first time the strength of this political PRA when the housewives in a village staged a sit-in without the outsider's facilitation. The water supply scheme in this village had not been functional for many years. The men of the village had no interest in this issue as the women had to bear the burden of fetching water. Sometimes young boys used to damage the water supply line so that the young girls would have to come out of their homes, and then the boys could follow them. The water issue remained the topic of discussion for many days. The women analysed all dimensions of the issue, like who instals schemes, who is responsible for maintenance, who allocates funds, etc. And one day, the women decided to visit the public health engineering department, where they were told that the funds are allocated by the member of provincial assembly (MPA). Then 40 women decided to meet the MPA. When they reached his office, his secretary told them that he was not present. The women thought that he was cheating. They entered his office where they saw a water cooler. They brought the water cooler out of the office, saying that he himself drinks cold water whereas we do not even have access to street taps. When the MPA found out that the women voters from a village of 1200 households had gone against him, he visited the village a few days later and announced the allocation of funds for the scheme.

In another area, the Urdu service of the BBC and the newspaper are used as codes. The awareness level of this group ultimately led them to challenge the austerities of the local police. This group says that the police have become so powerless against the people's action that the department sends a police head to this area as a punishment.

Using PRA in all activities

In December 1998, when I was in a subgroup discussion of a workshop, I said that whatever we do in our project we should call it PRA. The result was loud laughter. Let me explain here why I made such a statement.

The first example is our saving and credit programme. Normally PRA is not used in such programmes due to financial risks, pressure to follow the accounting principles, and lack of innovation and flexibility. Although radical changes in favour of the poor have been introduced in the saving and credit sector, it is very difficult for many organizations to get rid of complex forms, pass books and lengthy procedures. The basic assumptions behind all these formalities are that the people forget, misuse loans and do not pay loans back. We found that when a poor person receives credit from relatives or local moneylenders, accountability to society provides the guarantee for repayment. Since both parties are insiders, most of the time it is the first priority of the borrower to pay the loan back, because this is the only way the people can survive in the local system.

Similarly, the team observed that the people always remember how much they have borrowed. It also identified, through the local analysis and the experiences of some other institutions, that the contents of the passbooks and the forms (something the illiterate majority cannot understand) make people hesitant to take credit from the formal system.

When we initiated the saving and credit programme in the community, it did not use any sort of application or form. The borrowers use a visual passbook, which is a pie chart divided into 12 parts (showing 12 months of the year). When a person pays an instalment, s/he fills in one part of this pie chart. The core of this programme is the belief that the people are the best users of their money. That is why the programme does not impose any conditions on the borrowers regarding the use of credit. The AAPk team says that when the borrowers pay loans back with interest, why should we bind them to use the credit in the areas identified by us?

The initial results of this saving and credit programme, which is based on verbal agreement, were astonishing. The repayment rate was 100%. This percentage decreased after some time, but it was due to other factors, such as frequent staff turnover.

My second example is RILA – the Research, Information, Learning and Advocacy approach. The RILA approach to information management is a methodological innovation in which the community leads the information-generation process. The monitoring and evaluation becomes an ongoing activity and occurs within the routine facilitation process. The basic assumptions of RILA are that different stakeholders may have different and independent information systems. One stakeholder, while making use of the information system of others, should not distort or lead the system of other stakeholders, particularly of the key stakeholder – the community.

In RILA, the information generated by the community is recorded in original order, i.e. diagrams/maps, process records and videos, etc. In the multiple accountability environment, in order to meet the taste and needs of other stakeholders who do not accept visuals, the original information is translated or rearranged. The translation cost is paid by the external stakeholder. In RILA, separate studies or meetings to serve the needs of the outsiders are not held. All information related to the project phases, defined by the outsiders, is expected to be generated during the routine community meetings in which multiple issues are discussed. In RILA, if it becomes necessary to use the outsiders' checklist, information collection against the checklist topics is not done as a separate activity. Instead, the field workers wait for the proper time when the community has some interest in the topic.

My third example is about using PRA for project management. In our work, sharing is used as a key project steering tool. The field team shares their work with their supervisors, specialists and outside visitors through process recording forms. The supervisors and specialists meet weekly to share and to plan. This frequent sharing minimizes the chances of errors, as corrective measures are taken as soon as a problem is encountered. This regular sharing results in continuous planning, implementation, monitoring and evaluation.

And now a general impact of PRA – we have changed our office timings. Our office hours for male staff in Bahwalangar start in the afternoon. The staff go to the villages and stay there for the night. When they hold meetings in the community, the agenda is set visually. All those who have an issue to discuss put something on the land to represent his/her agenda point. And then all the points are discussed in order. The staff members work on the partner's farm once a fortnight to gain practical experience the life of the poor.

I hope now you will support me when I say that whatever we do in our Bahwalnagar project is PRA.

Sharing hunger, sorrows and hot sun with people

The AAPk team members in Bahawalnagar sometimes quote that 'one cannot understand poverty until he encounters *dukh* (sorrows), *bhukh* (hunger) and *dhup* (hot sun)'. We learnt this from an old man of a remote village of Pakistan where we organized an Information and Skills Exchange Meeting (ISEM) of Pakistan Participatory Learning and Action Network (PakPLAN).

The ISEM is our alternative to training. In some ISEMs, people's organizations from different parts of Pakistan invite the PakPLAN members to their village, where they stay for two days to share their experiences of life with local people. On the first day, the participants of the ISEM are attached to a local family, with whom they dine and stay for the night. The household members and their neighbours share their knowledge and experience with the visitors, who apply PRA tools to enable them to express themselves freely. The next day the guests and the local people gather at a central place where they give feedback on the whole process. In a ten-day ISEM, the participants improve their skills. Instead of one or two resource persons, all the participants act as learners as well as teachers. Some teach PRA skills and the others teach how to live like the people. It is a cross-cutting experience – tensions, punishments and sufferings.

All the experiences above should not give the impression that most of the time PRA practitioners have a favourable organizational environment. Humera Malik's paper explains well what happens when you challenge the managers. Some have to leave and those who opt for upward advocacy face tensions and pressures. How can you expect powerful head office people or managers to come to you and use public transport? If they don't, how will you answer the questions raised by your field staff? And even sometimes a young volunteer asks you why you make us lose marketable skills? You yourself cannot work in a senior position because your communication in the colonial language is not good, and you cannot improve it because you live with people speaking local languages. You often organize meetings after consultation with all others and your boss asks to cancel it. And some days you are transferred to headquarters to give output on a form, something that you always rejected. And if you cannot, you receive reprimands. You need to go to advocacy meetings in big hotels.

Perhaps we will have to live with it, because we are the careerists who are not prepared to de-class ourselves. We need money and facilities for our families. But do we, the practitioners, give due respect to those who are doing real PRA? One of my fellow PRA practitioners, Irfan Ilahi, who has been working with tuberculosis (TB) patients by living with them, has contracted TB himself. He has transmitted it to his one-year-old son, who is also paying the cost of doing real PRA. How many like Irfan Ilahi are recognized in the PRA community as good practitioners?

Note

[1] Toyota double cabin vehicles, which are considered luxury cars, are used in most of INGO work in Pakistan. Sohrab is a locally manufactured bicycle.

CHAPTER 4

Karen Brock

Participation, policy, poverty: where now?

Context

My critical reflections emerge from several years of trying to do research in a participatory way in two related but distinct areas: poverty reduction and natural resources management. I came to participation from a background in natural resources management, through reading *Beyond Farmer First* (Scoones and Thompson 1994), having Participatory Rural Appraisal (PRA) training as part of a postgraduate degree course, and facilitating agro-ecosystems appraisals with farmers in southern Mexico. I have worked in both the NGO sector and in government agricultural research and extension services, mostly in Africa.

Most of my recent and current work in the Participation Group at IDS has been focused on poverty reduction, with particular emphasis on increasing participation in policy making. The questions this work raises concern the way that different voices and opinions are included or excluded from the processes by which policy gets made. What do we mean when we talk about participation in the context of policy making or policy influence?

I was involved with 'Consultations with the Poor', a World Bank 23-country study of poverty, which used participatory research methods and several participatory poverty research processes in Africa, including the Uganda Participatory Poverty Assessment Process and work with the Participatory Assessment Group in Zambia. All of these processes were about getting directly involved in ongoing attempts to do participatory work to influence policy. I am now working on a research project in Nigeria and Uganda, which is not about direct involvement – it aims to question and understand how poverty-reduction policy processes work. This involves asking how policy changes, and where the spaces are in policy processes for marginalized and excluded voices to have a greater influence.

In this short chapter, I raise four issues that have emerged from my direct involvement in participatory work to influence policy: they come from observations about my own practice and the processes I have been involved with.

Words and actions: what is participation?

Many of the issues that I have found difficult and confusing in trying to work in a participatory way arise from the diversity of meaning that is attached to terms like PRA, participation, participatory research – and especially how these relate to ethics. I think that diversity of definition is healthy, and inevitable, a route to the growth of good practice, a path to iterative, self-reflective movement forward. So what happens when the word 'participation' is used to suggest 'empowerment' of 'the marginalized', positive change and development, but the actions that go with it reveal that it's just another way for those with power to do exactly the same things that they would have done anyway? It seems that the people at the bottom get let down when words and actions get divorced.

If I believe in diversity, does it mean that I have to accept the version of participation where words and actions are divorced? Or does that come down to an individual ethical decision for each of us to make as practitioners – when is it right for me to impose my version or accept yours?

Who is participating and what kind of participation is it?

The gap between words and actions becomes particularly noticeable when the language of participation enters rigid, hierarchical bureaucracies. What is given the name 'participatory research' happens in such bureaucracies as part of a process, a series of episodes strung together. One of these episodes – usually not the first – involves non-local researchers visiting local people and facilitating a research process which can often be exemplary in terms of using participatory tools and methods, not raising people's expectations, seeking out vulnerable or marginalized groups within the community, feeding back results to community meetings… The participatory quality of this particular episode in the process is held up as the defining feature of the entire process. Yet it is often the shortest part, and the episodes that precede it and follow it are usually not exemplary in terms of including local people in setting priorities of any kind (local or non-local), sharing, learning, feeding back, bringing local people and decision makers together, or indeed ensuring any kind of positive action for change at the local level. The non-local episodes, which take place in the bureaucratic hierarchy, are embedded in a set of power relations where even the open sharing of information can be impossible.

What kind of participation is going on here, and who is benefiting from it?

Detached from history: hearing other voices

One of the outcomes of the kind of generic episodic participatory research process described above is that it often produces a snapshot of information, frozen in time, extracted and represented as truth. The importance of history in defining the content of the snapshot is usually ignored. The importance of history in defining the actors and institutions that use the snapshot is usually ignored. How did poor people get to be poor? How did powerful people get to be powerful?

What are local histories of participation and of decision making – do they give us any clues at all about the way we should work together? Why do we usually not take the time to find out what these are?

Aggregate participation: whose words are important?

The following is extracted from the 'Consultations with the Poor' Global Synthesis summary. It illustrates how findings from a research process that used participatory methods were presented, and a policy recommendation that arose from the findings.

> The problems of corruption, 'connections', and violation of basic human rights with impunity were voiced over and over again by the poor... Again and again, in country after country, and site after site, poor women and men spoke of corruption. It took many forms: corruption in the distribution of seeds, medicines and social assistance for the destitute and vulnerable; corruption in getting loans; corruption in getting teachers to teach; corruption in customs and border crossings; corruption in the construction of roads; corruption in getting permission to move in and out of cities or stay in certain areas; corruption in street and market trading; corruption in identity cards. In many places, the poor reported having to pay managers, hooligans and police 'protection' money to save themselves from the worst forms of harassment, theft and abuse...
>
> Societal norms about corruption being expected and tolerated must change ... societal norms about corruption must shift back to the expectation of honesty and justice.
>
> (Narayan et al. 1999)

Who defines corruption here? Did every poor person who described their problems in getting a loan, or crossing a border, or getting a teacher to teach, describe this problem in terms of corruption? If so, what did they mean when they said it? Did they all agree that changing societal norms about the toleration of corruption was the solution to this problem? Is there any historical evidence to suggest that 'societal norms' used to expect honesty and justice? Whose 'societal norms' are they? Do these questions bear

34

any relevance to the participatory nature of any part of the process that generated the findings?

Conclusions

Questions such as these are not asked; the powerful do not engage in such debates. There is no time to think of such things in the rush to transmit the 'voices of the poor, the true poverty experts' to the global policy makers, who may or may not be listening... Which way forward? Powerful people and global institutions will continue to make policy, and less powerful people in other places will continue to be affected by it.

One year after the 'Consultations', five of the teams involved in that process returned to the communities where they had worked to see if the research had resulted in any changes. In some communities, involvement in the process had no effect. In others, the findings of the research were successfully used by community leaders to advocate for change. In some countries, the study had an important impact in government, in others it was ignored.

As practitioners of participation, our place within participatory processes for policy influence is both a personal, ethical decision and a strategic one. There are trade-offs involved – particularly the distortion of 'participation' versus the opportunity to advocate for change among the powerful. My learning over the past few years suggests to me that if I don't understand how policy is made, I will not be able to influence it effectively, as an individual, a practitioner or as an advocate.

My future pathway will therefore lead towards engaging with people from countries in the South to share and develop our understandings of policy processes, to understand better how they change, and to create spaces within them in which the agency of excluded and less powerful people can be exercised – rather than their 'voices' simply being 'heard'.

References

Narayan, D., Chambers, R., Shah, M.K. and Petesch, P., 'Global Synthesis', prepared for the Global Synthesis Workshop: Consultations with the Poor, World Bank, Washington, DC, 1999.

Scoones, I. and Thompson, J. (eds) (1994) *Beyond Farmer First: rural people's knowledge, agricultural research and extension practice*, ITDG Publishing, London.

CHAPTER 5

Robert Chambers

Reflections on PRA experience

Icome to this having been a participant-observer of some of the evolution of Participatory Rural Appraisal (PRA). I had the incredible privilege of being around when others were innovating in some of its early days. More recently, from a base in the Institute for Development Studies (IDS), I have been trying with others to keep up with developments and to support net-working and good practice. This has been an amazing experience. I have to pinch myself to be sure it is for real and not some fantasy. Few people have been so lucky.

But...

I am tied in four knots. For me the PRA experience, if I can call it that, has been quite extraordinary and wonderful. I want to share that with others. I would like them to be able to choose to have similar experiences. But I have a deep horror of evangelism, and that makes me hold back. I have an ingrained male, middle-class English reticence about talking about feelings. But feelings of anxiety, thrill, fun, wonderment and fulfilment have been central in my PRA-related experience, and they keep on coming. I dislike hypocrisy (English art form though it may be). I think personal behaviour and attitudes are central to good PRA. But the more I talk about behaviour and attitudes, the more of a hypocrite I know myself to be. And you can't win this one, because repeated confessions of hypocrisy without changing behaviour compound themselves into a complacent habit. And last, I think it is terrifically important not to take oneself too seriously. But any writing about personal experience risks just that.

Notwithstanding these inhibitions

Two personal discoveries stand out for me. Both turn things on their heads. Both can be captured in slogans. The first is 'others can do it', meaning that other people, especially those who are 'lowers' in a context, can usually do much more and much better than 'uppers' believe. The second is 'enjoy and learn', meaning that there is fulfilment, fun and learning to be found in experiences otherwise felt as threatening because what will happen is hard to predict or control.

Others can do it

Probably many of us have had mind-blowing experiences in PRA contexts. It has come as a revelation to me writing this, that most of mine have been discovering that other people could do things I did not believe they could: farmers in Ethiopia who understood a histogram; women in West Bengal who drew a seasonal labour diagram; a farmer in Tanzania who drew a map of agro-ecological zones; villagers in Karnataka who made a 3-D coloured model of their watershed on the ground; farmers in Gujarat who kept and updated their own map of underground aquifers.

Then there were people doing things 'the wrong way'. The first time I saw matrix scoring I only knew about ranking, and nearly intervened to say 'that's not the way to do it'. Sometimes my incompetence made space for other people's creativity. So it was with a group of women in Tanzania. My limited Swahili prevented my telling them fully how to matrix score out of 5 or 10, so they did it their own way, with free scoring. This was new to me and, as I came to understand, has its own special strengths. I began to learn not to give instructions in detail. At one time I would take half an hour to 'teach' matrix scoring, with lots of dos and don'ts. I came to realize that two to three minutes could be enough,[1] that there was no single right way, and that people could learn and invent for themselves.

Then there has been the wonderment when others have an experience that changes how they see things. A soil and water conservation officer in India, after a transect to observe farmers' own soil and water conservation measures, said it had been one of the most remarkable days of his life. And no one who was on the first PRA South–South in India will ever forget the late Saiti ('Ambassador') Makuku's immense and inspiring enthusiasm after a similar experience.

Then there has been slowly learning how changing one's behaviour can empower others to speak up and give feedback. In Iran, it was only after I had sat silent on the floor for a minute that someone told me that I had started off the workshop in a culturally insensitive way. Had I not sat silent, I might never have learnt that.

And the last part of this learning has been the revelation that others, especially those who in context are 'lowers' to me, can often, even usually, do things better than I can. This has been startling, sobering and humbling, but easily converted into delight at what they find and show they can do. Peers are better at facilitating peers: villagers, for example, can be much better facilitators of other villagers than I could ever be. Making space for others to take over one's roles brings its own fulfilment.

Enjoy and learn

What I want to say here is that more and more, in our turbulently changing world, we need new ways of learning and being. I hesitate over 'new', because little is new under the sun: but so much is changing so fast that we are driven to innovate and to discover things for ourselves, and to learn better how to learn. We seem to need some way of combining continuous creativity, innovation and adaptation. We do not have time always to search and see whether what we do is new or a rediscovery. And that is how it should be. That we are finding what works for us is enough.

Is it like white water canoeing?[2] Faced with rapids, you do not know what you are in for. You commit. The white water boils up around you. It is all unpredictable, risky, unstable, exhilarating. It demands intense alertness, instant adaptation and learning, learning, learning on the run. No one else can learn for you. There are ideas in books, but you can only really learn by doing, by messing up and trying again. And an early (and nearly late) lesson for me was that the moment you think you are through a rapid, the moment your attention wanders, that is when you tip up. The moment any of us thinks we have got it about participation, that we have somehow arrived, that we have learnt what we need to know – is that the moment we lose the plot? Is that the very moment when we tip up and go under?

Faced with chaotic uncertainties, it is natural to be tense, taut and uptight. But that does not work. Are the keys then a relaxed alertness, coming to love uncertainty and to embrace anxiety? As stimuli and opportunities for learning? I have always been nervous about uncontrollable public situations. PRA processes are unpredictable. So much of PRA is launching out and taking risks. Have any of us not known that pit-of-the-stomach butterflies feeling before a workshop, a training or part of a PRA process in the field? What will happen? Will it work out this time? Will I make a fool of myself? But trying to minimize anxiety through control, through routinization, can blunt, even brutalize the process. The paradox I have had to learn is that things work out better with less control. The challenge is to move towards being happy hosting the visceral butterflies, exulting in optimal unpreparedness, and revelling in the fun of flexibility and improvisation.

Then there is excitement. For me personally, and I know for many others, this PRA thing has been extraordinarily exciting. But how widely can this excitement be part of PRA for others in the future?

In exploratory rock climbing, those who do a new route name it, record the first ascent and write up the details for a guidebook. Later climbers gain pleasure from repeating the routes, but they never have quite the same thrill of exploration. The quality of that first experience, of that uncertainty, that sense of achievement, can never be repeated. Can PRA be different? We have source books. Some of them are described as manuals. Most of them describe methods and how to facilitate them. Some of them lay down sequences. They all have their uses. But is the big challenge to see how the freshness, the exhilaration, the eternal novelty, the interactive creativity of PRA can be continuous discoveries and rediscoveries for practitioners? And if so, what should we as practitioners and trainers be doing now so that others are not denied the privileged experiences we have had?

Can excitement and exhilaration somehow be a permanent part of PRA? Can the thrill of exploration be generic, embedded in good practice, an assured and recurring feature? Every situation and every experience is new. So can PRA processes always, everywhere, have the potential to startle, amaze, excite, inspire? And to show that things one did not dream of can be done, by people one did not believe could do them?

With anything new, there is a danger of settling down. In other fields, an era of innovation passes and practice settles into ruts. Much PRA too has been routinized; and some things done in the name of PRA abuse poor people. But could bad practice be made simply a phase, a misfit in early adoption and an opportunity to learn? Could there be less and less PRA by rote in the future? Could it increasingly be different each time, more and more empowering lowers, more and more an exploration, a new experience, unique, creative and leading to unknowns which become personal discoveries, ever fresh?

Ways of living, being and learning?

Whether we call it PRA or something else (and long live pluralism and sharing without boundaries), are we groping for an evolving way of living? Is there a convergence here between traditions? Do we have in common a search for ways of being and learning which fit us better for a fulfilling life in a world of accelerating change? And if so, where should PRA go now? Is there more it can contribute?

Perhaps we should all seek our own answers on our own new pathways. Some may want to slough off the label, others to change what it stands for, yet others to describe what they do in some other way. We can celebrate and share our diversity. Above all, we should not get stuck. Anyone doing the same as two years ago has lost the plot. Something may be terribly wrong. There are sayings associated with PRA, like 'Don't rush', 'Embrace error',

'Use your own best judgement at all times', 'Hand over the stick', and 'Ask them'. To these should we now add:

- 'Do something different'
- 'Learn'
- 'Change'
- 'Enjoy'?

Notes

[1] I am not suggesting that this is always right. People complain that they need more instructions. Other trainer/facilitators take longer and get good results. Still, brief instructions fit the pattern that 'lowers' can discover and invent for themselves much more than 'uppers' normally suppose.

[2] See Peter Vaill, *Learning as a Way of Being: strategies for survival in a world of permanent white water*, (1996) Jossey-Bass, San Francisco. (The book costs, alas, £24.95 in the UK.)

CHAPTER 6

Rene D. Clemente

From participatory appraisal to participation in governance in the Philippines

My personal involvement with Participatory Rural Appraisal (PRA) began in mid-1993. I was working then for a national secretariat of a network promoting sustainable agriculture and appropriate technology in the Philippine countryside. Our co-ordinator and a colleague had just undergone PRA training and wanted to try giving a training course to see if it would 'click'. We knew other PRA practitioners and tapped them for the training. It went very well and we had such positive feedback that PRA became a part of our regular training. More and more I began to focus on giving PRA training. However, after working for seven years in that organization, I decided to move on. From 1994 to 1995, I was a freelance PRA trainer, but by early 1996 I had joined KAISAHAN, a Manila-based non-governmental organization (NGO), to help develop their programme on using PRA for local development planning.

In 1997, eight national NGOs formed an alliance to promote democratic participation in governance. We playfully called it the BATMAN (or the Barangay[1] Administrator's Trainings on Management) Consortium. It has a more formal name today – the Barangay-Bayan[2] Governance Consortium (BBGC) – but somehow, the 'BATMAN' nickname stuck. The BBGC has five main training modules, and PRA for local development planning is one of the most popularly requested. From the original eight NGOs, the network now has 40 members scattered all over the Philippine archipelago, helping to spread the approach.

This chapter is a reflection on three of the major challenges we face regarding PRA and local governance in the Philippines. I have organized a list of my reflections under three broad issues. First, not all practice makes perfect; I reflect on some of the less commonly acknowledged features of PRA exercises and their implications for how we understand people's participation. Second, I have some reflections to share on the need to check our attitudes and behaviour in facilitation. And third, I want to share some issues with regard to scaling up participatory planning approaches.

Dilemmas of participation

Women often volunteer to do the kitchen work for the PRA teams. We often have a small budget to offer to the kitchen team so that the PRA team can focus on the job at hand, rather than on going to the market, cooking, finding or borrowing kitchen utensils, etc. Are we not further marginalizing them instead of enhancing their involvement? Sometimes we need to ask members of the kitchen crew to stop what they are doing and join in the data gathering, as some of them are key people.

In some far-flung areas, we prepare lunch and snacks for the five days or so of the actual PRA and planning activity so that we will not be an additional burden to the community. But sometimes, the food itself becomes the major motivation for people to participate. In a PRA we held in South Cotabato, the mothers would come in with all their children, adding to the festive (and sometimes chaotic) atmosphere. Participants numbers would increase near lunchtime and dwindle by around 2 or 3 pm.

Some people jump at the chance to be able to 'get back against' the current officials (especially if they are of a different political party). They give out all sorts of negative comments but cannot back them up with concrete examples. We try to balance the situation as best as we can. We point out that the main reason for gathering people's perspectives is to find out areas for improvement of village management.

We usually work with organized groups, since it is easier to do the social preparations and mobilize the people for the PRA and planning process. But working with a particular group (NGO, people's organization (PO) or Local Government Unit (LGU)) may mean that other groups may already be excluded from the process – women, indigenous peoples, people with other religious or political affiliations, etc. In one PRA we were doing in Pampanga in Central Luzon, we held the community orientation at the house of a certain barangay official. Walking around the community later, we learned that there was strong factionalism present in the community and because we held the orientation in that particular house, other people were no longer willing to participate in the process. How do we get people to participate in a common activity despite political differences? Explanations do not seem to make a difference.

In cases where we work with the municipal people such as the mayor or municipal planning and development co-ordinator, a lot of the barangay officials (especially the more traditional ones) resent being 'forced' to undergo this approach. Some just 'go through the motions' without really imbibing the attitudes and principles.

Maximizing people's participation in communities that are urbanizing presents different challenges. People from urban communities have different concerns and priorities from rural people and are generally harder to involve in the participatory local development process. Most of them will say that they have better use for their time. This was the experience of our partner NGO in doing PRA in Kaypian, San Jose del Monte, which is peripherally located to the Greater Manila Area. At one point, people even asked how much they would be paid to participate.

Checking our attitudes and behaviour in facilitation

With the rapid spread of PRA as a tool for local development planning, we are interested now in checking the quality of our work. After all, tools are mere tools and even PRA tools can be abused and used manipulatively and extractively. As we are trying to keep up with the huge amount of requests for this approach, how do we maintain good quality facilitation? We are in the process now of strengthening our Participatory Monitoring and Evaluation (PM&E) systems. But this is still very much in a formative stage.

Should we influence the people at the community level towards our orientation? This has been the dilemma of many an NGO worker facilitating PRAs at the community level. We want the communities to take a progressive stance on issues such as gender fairness, ecological nurturance, equity, etc. When we did a PRA activity in an indigenous people's community in Surigao del Sur, it was a highly patriarchal society. The village chief had the first and last say and the people readily agreed to whatever he was saying. Should we accept this as being part of their cultural identity or should we advocate for changes? But who decides which culture is right, better or 'more progressive'? How do we know when the community is ready to undergo a more participatory process?

How do we keep the facilitators inspired and motivated? At the start, they may be highly motivated, but it becomes a different story if they have to facilitate the process in three villages per month for the next two or three years. After some time, facilitation becomes mechanical. We tap their help in organizing conferences and cross visits or study tours. Soon, we will conduct refresher courses for facilitators for them to review once again their processes and attitudes, and hopefully to refresh their commitment.

The challenges of scaling up

Scaling up participatory approaches raises a lot of challenges. Government officials and workers may feel threatened by participatory processes. In the municipality of Banaybanay, Davao del Norte, for example, the mayor was open to working with a participatory approach. However, the local Department of Interior and Local Government (DILG) was not. They questioned our authority and credibility to teach barangay officials about local development planning. Traditionally, the DILG is the agency involved in giving this sort of training to newly elected officials. Some officials feel threatened by sharing power (especially decision-making power over how the barangay funds should be allocated). Their resistance can effectively slow down the process. This is the reason why a lot of NGOs prefer to facilitate participatory planning unhampered by the inefficiency and bureaucracy of some LGU staff.

Changes in the administration can be disruptive to institutionalizing the participatory approach. In the case of Naujan, Mindoro Oriental, we were working with the former mayor. Unfortunately, it was his last term and the next elected mayor did not approve of this approach. The change in administration gravely affected the programme for the municipality.

Situations of conflict present further challenges. How is it possible to do participatory governance in a conflict situation? In some provinces in the southern island of Mindanao, there is a strong military presence as well as a strong resistance movement. A lot of our local NGO partners have no choice but to meet with the leftist groups to discuss what they are doing in the interior communities. But as a matter of protocol, clearance from military and government officials is also needed. At the same time, people from the community cannot value and prioritize this sort of work if there is military conflict.

Issues of scale present further dilemmas. How do we adopt the participatory local development planning process in very big communities? On average, a barangay in the Philippines can have 2000 people or around 350–400 registered voters. A current challenge right now is doing participatory planning for Davao City, a city in Mindanao that has expressed interest in this approach. It has 181 barangays. The largest barangay, Barangay Bucana, already has 102 puroks[3] and about 35 000 registered voters. Our partner NGO based there is training trainers purok by purok, plus they have asked for the assistance of an interested university, but clearly, this will still take a long time to complete.

What can help to address the challenges of scaling up? Networking with open-minded and progressive LGU officials (barangay, municipal, city, provincial or even national) and like-minded organizations is very important. The LGU can be an effective 'enabler', but this does not mean that we cannot do anything without their support. In the municipality of Toboso, Negros Occidental, we worked with the vice-mayor and municipal planning officer. After finishing all the barangay development plans, they also came up with a municipal development plan using the same participatory approach. Together with a local NGO, we facilitated participatory barangay development planning initially in three barangays, and gradually spread the approach. Later, as the mayor was replaced, their advocacy paid off. They have been asked, in fact, by the provincial governor to help spread the participatory approach to all the barangays in the entire province of Agusan del Sur.

Enabling laws are very important. As facilitators, we try to keep abreast of new issuances, particularly those that affect barangay governance. Many issues in the Local Government Code directly affect barangay management. The ongoing review of this Code includes the need for passage of an enabling law for local sectoral representatives at local legislative bodies, constraints on the use of the barangay budget, clear guidelines for NGO–PO accreditation into local special bodies, and a review of the barangay justice system.

The passage of a National Land and Water Use Act is also an important issue. We are presently pushing for this since it affects land use plans down to the barangay level. Without this legislation there is rampant land conversion, which affects land use planning (and its negative effects, including destruction of forest, watersheds and ecologically sensitive areas). The draft Act that the NGOs are pushing for takes into consideration a participatory approach to identification, maintenance, and monitoring of agricultural and ecologically sensitive areas.

Increasing resources available to LGUs is another important challenge. We are advocating for an increase in Internal Revenue Allottment (IRA) to LGUs. Presently, 60% of the IRA goes to the national government, all the LGUs at provincial, municipal, city and barangay level share only 40%. More IRA for the LGUs, especially the barangay LGUs, would mean more funds for their development projects.

Lastly, we need to improve the quality and extent of effective and efficient partnership between the LGUs, NGOs and POs in local governance. Although the NGOs and POs acted as vigilant guardians to monitor the performance of local officials in the past, they can also act (if the LGUs are open to working with them) as effective partners in development. Today, we are encouraging the Barangay Development Commmittee (BDC) to have more PO representatives.

The long journey

The road from participatory appraisal to participation in governance has been a long one, fraught with a lot of limitations and frustrations, but at the same time sprinkled with some victories as well.

Significant inroads have been made with the passage of the Local Government Code, which seeks democratization. But the Code does not provide the methodologies with which to achieve democratization. With PRA and its participatory, visual tools, some answers were found. But, as was said, not all practice makes perfect, not all attitudes and behaviour are imbibed in facilitation, and scaling up presents more problems.

Despite the difficulties, we persist. We learn new things as we go along. We learn the value of getting together to discuss problems we have encountered and sharing them with facilitators from other areas and NGOs. We learn the value of pushing for candidates who will espouse the same ideas as we are pursuing. We learn the importance of engaging with government and sticking to our positions as advocates.

The journey may be a long one, with the end still not in sight. But as we proceed, interesting insights, discoveries and small victories present themselves, making the getting there worthwhile.

Notes

[1] The equivalent of a village. It is the basic political unit in the Philippines.
[2] The next higher local government unit from the barangay.
[3] Puroks are sub-villages of the barangay, formed to deal with clusters of housing within a barangay. They do not have a formal status in the governance system of the Philippines, but generally councillors elected from the barangay as a whole take responsibility for specific puroks.

CHAPTER 7

Andrea Cornwall

Winding paths, broken journeys: travels with PRA

Beginnings

I first encountered participatory research by accident. Working as a volunteer teacher in a remote Zimbabwean rural area, I became concerned about the stories I was hearing of girls downing handfuls of pills or drinking washing soda in attempts to deal with one of the consequences of unprotected sex. Classroom role-plays revealed further dilemmas. My attempt to provide information met a brick wall when some of the girls rounded on me and accused me of encouraging them to have sex. So, to find a better way of reaching them, I visited their mothers to ask them what I could do. And I found myself being asked for advice about a medicine that made many of them sick: the pill. A participatory research project, on women's bodily knowledge and reproductive rights, was born.

In my desire to do something to improve the possibilities for an informed choice I realized that simply giving women information wasn't enough. Rummaging around in Harare for books on what to do, I came across the *Training for Transformation* manuals (Hope and Timmel 1984). To the techniques I picked up from there – skits, problem analysis, story telling – I added a Rapid Rural Appraisal (RRA) technique, pair-wise ranking, which I'd watched a fellow researcher use. As I struggled to understand what women told me about their bodies, I asked them to draw pictures[1]. Often they'd ask me to draw mine too. I was convinced that if it hadn't been for these pictures, we'd have found it really hard to talk. When women came together to share their body maps, their experiences and their knowledge, there was a buzz of energy as they learnt from each other.

At the time, it seemed to me that these visual methods were really useful. I saw them as tools – a great way to get people talking, to overcome the problem of assuming shared meanings for words, and to engage people in reflecting about their bodies and their lives. I remember coming across early *RRA Notes* issues around that time. For quite a while, I thought what RRA was all about was the visual methods that seemed to so excite contributors to *RRA Notes* and which I had found so useful in my work. I found out more when I returned to the UK with the intention of learning how to do what I'd been doing 'properly' – by studying anthropology. And, exposed to the critique of RRA as a short cut, superficial, pseudo-social science, I became an RRA-basher. Things like lists of 'intriguing beliefs and practices' that were recorded like quaint rituals and then discarded made me weep. But my anthropological training did more than rubbish RRA. It quickly put paid to all that creative fun I'd had doing action research *with* people. Anthropologists, after all, were supposed to observe and analyse but not get involved in trying to change anything: participate but not really join in.

(Re)discovering PRA

I remained an ambivalent anthropologist. For what anthropology didn't iron out was the activist in me. And it was this, coupled with irritation at the arrogance of anthropology, that brought me back into engaging with what was, by then, becoming PRA – *Participatory* Rural Appraisal. My discomfort with RRA had been with the claims that were made based on brief incursions into poor people's lives, which were often so charged with expectations that the 'findings' that emerged often told their own story. As I began to hear more about these methods being used to engage people in doing their own analysis and in longer-term processes of change, I started to change my tune. In 1991, I had my first experience as a trainer. At a time at which initial enthralment with PRA had begun to take off, it seemed there were never enough trainers to meet the growing demand. So there I was, only marginally less sceptical than I'd been before, now a trainer. And I was terrified. I did, however, have one thing I was sure of: whatever I did, I would try to move those I worked with beyond versions that claimed to speak about and for 'the community' and to provoke more reflection on context, power and process.

Two powerful memories of my first training experience remain. One was the look on a middle-aged extension worker's face. His eyes shone as he told me with astonishment of how a farmer had told him about things he'd never known, and never believed illiterate farmers were capable of knowing. The other was the shrill, excitable, voices of children making such an extensive map of their area that even those men who had elbowed them out of their way in the first place took a sharp intake of breath as the children presented it. I remember the team member assigned to working with them. At first, he sulked. He lurked around them, trying to catch a glimpse of what the men were doing nearby. He looked as if he'd really drawn the short straw. But at the end, he was more amazed than anyone. His face glowed with pride: 'They know so much! We'd never think of asking children, but look!'

These were 'classic' conversion experiences. In the flush of excitement, I found it easier to switch off the anthropologist in me who would otherwise have questioned the ways in which what the team came up with from these encounters were represented as if they were facts. Or the dangers of taking what people said at face value. This mattered less, at that time, than the spaces PRA opened to listen to people routinely denied a voice and excluded from development processes – and the expressions on those development workers' faces. I remained (and remain) deeply sceptical about the claims to know, let alone to 'empower', that are made about consultative exercises that consist of a few short days in complex communities with a team of outsiders running around getting people to participate. But what hooked me then, and what excites me now, is the transformative possibilities of the interaction between people trained not to listen and people used to being ignored and excluded. And despite all that has been done with PRA that has served the development business, its potential for building bridges, challenging prejudices and abuses of power, and, more than anything else, for recognizing our shared humanity remains as vivid and as real.

Hypocrisy or pragmatism? 'PRA' in my own back yard

Fast forward five years. I'm living on a housing estate in London, trying to co-ordinate a participatory well-being assessment. I'm dealing with busy managers, who say they simply can't attend a long training course and can spare only a couple of afternoons for fieldwork. I'm spending time with community members who have, they say, been 'consulted to death' and have no interest in getting worked up about things, only to be disregarded again. Replay the tape. There I am, sceptical about the use of PRA in short-run consultation exercises. And here I am running a process that no one has much time for, shepherd to a large group of service providers, managers and community workers.

Four months down the line, I'm once again feeling that buzz. Surrounded by a vivid display of what residents want to see change, groups of professionals and residents huddle together to work through what can be done. Three years later and some of the things that people had been complaining about for years have been addressed. Again, my memories are of people. Of residents like John holding up the report to a top government official who was visiting the estate, saying 'It's all here in our book. You can't ignore us now!' And Ken, who stood in front of a packed audience at a public health conference to attention so rapt that you could have heard a pin drop. Of arriving at the estate and finding a senior manager deeply wrapped up in conversation with a group of residents, watching them laughing and chatting. Of being told by another senior manager at a local health alliance meeting to stop, once residents started raising politically sensitive issues about quality of care. And realizing, as I looked around the room, that virtually everyone there was on the team. I didn't need to say a word; one by one they spoke, with passion and indignation, pointing out that he couldn't carry on ignoring residents' complaints, not now.

Working in my own 'back yard' taught me more about PRA than any of the experiences I'd had in other countries. And, funnily enough, it made me appreciate my anthropological training. For my experience in London brought the two together. I lived on the estate, doing 'behind-the-scenes' facilitation and learning a lot through informal participant observation. Each team member spent the equivalent of less than three whole days on the estate, the same amount of time as those rapid PRAs I'd been so sceptical about. Nothing we unearthed was particularly new to anyone who lived there. Nothing that came out of the PRA work went beyond what I'd found out in my first few days as a virtual resident, armed only with curiosity and an ability to strike up conversations with people at any opportunity. I could have written a report based on participant observation, but I am convinced that it would have had scarcely any impact. It became ever more evident to me in the process that *who* knows and *how* they come to know matters much more in bringing about change.

What *was* new to people on the estate was not information about their well-being but a space to voice concerns that had rumbled for years and to use this process as a lever to press for action to now be taken. The visibility created by making public space for people to air their views placed an onus on authorities to be seen to respond. And the emphasis on not simply producing information but co-creating knowledge made a huge difference, as the 'owners' of that knowledge were not only the residents but also those in the authorities with responsibilities to listen and act. Through public space events and experiential learning, officials and bureaucrats were coming to confront issues that couldn't simply be swept aside.

Participation, policy, politics

This experience made me reflect more on the politics of knowledge production and use. As used for community learning and planning, PRA has the potential to amplify people's voices and enable them to build alliances with each other and with service providers, to seize spaces made available 'from above' for their own projects. But one very present concern remains: whose voices and whose solutions do participatory processes include or serve to mobilize? And what happens if, when space is made for voice, 'local people' come up with needs or actions that further entrench dominant values or beliefs? What, for example, if white estate dwellers decided that one 'need' they had was to get rid of the mainly black asylum seekers whose presence so many complained about? And how would the health authorities respond to calls for more curative care, when there is a marked lack of response to preventive efforts to deal with the very conditions that additional doctors would end up treating? Where is the line drawn between 'the community know what's best for them' and a recognition that actually sometimes 'the community' can make exclusionary choices – whether on the grounds of race, gender, sexualities, age or ethnicity, etc. – and that sometimes they don't necessarily 'know what's best for them' at all? Who has the right to decide? Clearly, the politics of priority setting at the local level is more complex than simply 'handing over the stick'.

When it comes to the use of participatory methodologies in policy research, further concerns arise. As discussions in PRA circles shifted towards the use of PRA in policy research, I found it increasingly hard to shut off the sceptical anthropologist/activist. In 1998, I read for the first time the entire contents of a Participatory Poverty Assessment (PPA) report. In it, I found currents of colonial policy and representations of 'women' and 'the poor' that echoed rather than challenged mainstream development narratives. I found it a deeply depressing read. It seemed to me little different in what it seemed to have sought to do from the 'extractive' research PPA advocates were so quick to criticize; and the quality of the data and analysis showed significant weaknesses, made all the more serious for being touted as the 'voices' and choices of poor people.

I've since seen versions of 'poor people's voices' that so closely mimic the very policy lines that supra-national institutions have been so bent on pushing, that it is hard not to begin to ask questions about how these 'voices' come to be mediated, filtered and packaged into acceptable narratives. For all the talk about mutual learning, there seems to be scant opportunity for poor people to do their own participatory research on the institutions and policies that affect their lives – turning tables to use PPA teams as informants rather than interlocutors.

If *who* knows and *how* they come to know is as important as the information that is produced, this involves more than getting the methods right. More attention needs to be given to ways of opening up deliberation and reflection on taken-for-granted assumptions, making space for the kind of mutual learning that can challenge and change the root causes of poverty rather than amass 'voices' talking about its symptoms. Rather than fall into rendering technical the politics of inequity, inspiration might be drawn from bringing 'older' participatory practices into new generation PPA-style initiatives: from Participatory Action Research (PAR), Training for Transformation, the Theatre of the Oppressed.

Current preoccupations and excitements

Three issues currently preoccupy me. One is the need to go beyond vague rhetoric about 'participation' and 'empowerment' to critically examine what is claimed, what is done and what can be done. This captures the reason for initiating the Pathways project: to take stock neither by inflating nor detracting from success, to move towards a better understanding of what works in different contexts. The second is the issue of 'quality', which has been on the agenda in PRA circles for years. What are we talking about when we talk of 'quality'? Of information? Of knowledge? Of learning? Of change? Who defines 'quality' – and for whom? Clearly, there cannot be any single version: what is deemed 'right' or 'good' depends on purpose, context, politics, strategy. What debates about quality do offer is an opportunity to bring buried differences into the open and create space for constructive dialogue. I think this is a very exciting step, as it allows us – at last! – to break free of the compulsion to advocate and defend participation in all shapes and forms, for any purpose. By opening up debate and deliberation, raising some of the concerns that have been virtually unspeakable during the era of promotion and spread, we can develop new ways of working that bring a greater congruence and integrity to what we do as participation practitioners. Central to this must be making the principle of critical self-reflection real and embedding it in our practice.

The last is the challenge of inclusion and with it the possibility of a shift towards a focus on rights. As well as extending our definitions of poverty to embrace exclusion and discrimination, talking in terms of rights focuses on what we *all* need to be fully human. It gives us a set of referents and a series of entry points for work towards social justice and a focus that goes beyond alleviating misery, often symptomatically, to addressing issues of inequity more directly. It is this move, from seeking out and meeting needs to enabling people to make demands on those who are obliged to respect their rights, that restores in me the wellspring of commitment that keeps me in this participation business. It also throws into sharp relief the double-speak of institutions that profess participation while perpetuating the violations of social and economic rights that we are now witnessing on a global scale.

The future may not present the opportunities for broad-based consensus that brought participation into the mainstream in the 1990s. But these moves open up the possibilities of recovering the ideals that became submerged in struggles for legitimacy and putting social justice and equity firmly back on the participation agenda. Gone is the era of uncritical, defensive promotion. What's needed now is greater clarity of politics and of purpose, and the reflexivity and honesty with which to reclaim participation's radical promise.

Note

[1]Influenced by Carol MacCormack's 1985 pioneering work with Jamaican women, I went on to use these 'body maps' more extensively to explore women's reproductive knowledge and explanations of contraception (see Cornwall 2002).

References

Cornwall, A. (2002) 'Body mapping: bridging the gap between biomedical messages, popular knowledge and lived experience', in Cornwall, A. and Welbourn, A. (eds) *Realizing Rights: Transforming approaches to sexual and reproductive wellbeing*, Zed Books, London.
Hope, A. and Timmel, S. (1984) *Training for Transformation: A handbook for community workers*, vols 1–3, ITDG Publishing, London.
MacCormack, C. (1985) 'Lay perceptions affecting utilisation of family planning services in Jamaica', *Journal of Tropical Medicine and Hygiene*, 88:281-5.

CHAPTER 8

Chandan Datta

Participation of the people

My first job took me to Orissa to collect data for block-level planning. With the aim of collecting village-level information, we used questionnaire surveys with hundreds of families to assess needs and understand employment, income, expenditure and consumption patterns. Some years later, I was involved in a study of pollution control practices in the electroplating industry. The World Bank consultant to the Central Pollution Control Board (CPCB) had suggested a series of methods for pollution control to be adopted by the electroplating industry, which were demonstrated to the electroplaters. Our study sought to find out why they were not following the suggested processes. I interacted with the small entrepreneurs at their workplace for 12 weeks. This produced some new operational ideas, which led to partial acceptance of the new methods. These experiences led me to think about why development programmes do not really provide benefits to the people. Basically, it was because of the top-down approach followed, i.e. planning done by a few people without consulting the people for whom it is being planned.

Encountering participatory research

Around mid-1986, I came in contact with the Society for Participatory Research in Asia (PRIA) and read about participatory research. At that particular time PRIA was involved in practising participatory philosophy in research and training. It was very interesting. Conceptually it was a people-centred, people-controlled, people-managed process – be it in research or in training. Participatory research attempts to present people as researchers themselves in pursuit of awareness about the questions of their daily struggle and survival. The participatory philosophy also links with the social, economic reality and focuses on change. This philosophy draws on oral traditions and the use of art and culture in its various forms and manifestations as the major way of sharing and understanding the knowledge of illiterate people. As I read more about this approach, I tried in my own way to follow it in some of my own field-based studies.

In February 1991, I attended the Training of Trainers (TOT) programme of PRIA. In this training, I understood the concept of participant-centred training and how to facilitate this. Then I became involved as a facilitator in a participatory study, People and Forest. A series of dialogues with villagers and forest dwellers, and interactions among the forest dwellers and the forest officials, led to articulation by rural people of their own reality. They expressed the need for this study. We sat with local people and their representatives to prepare the framework. They collected the information, explained to others, convinced others, organized meetings among themselves and government officials, and analysed the data from their point of view. They then started dialogue with the administration. Ultimately, they convinced the administration to change the policy. Even after this, the local people were involved in follow-up initiatives in some places and initiated people-centred resource management in a cluster of villages. The same process has also been followed in some other areas.

After all these experiences, my feeling was that participation means involvement, commitment and pride. It also means poor and marginalized people's involvement in the process of their development.

PRA and participation

During the early 1990s, I read about Participatory Rural Appraisal (PRA). At that time, PRA had come to be extensively used in India in planning with government staff involved in rural development, who normally are detached from the people and their realities. This rapid approach seemed appropriate for government, who could go to villages, interact with people and collect information in a very short space of time, which would help them prepare more appropriate plans. What was most important was the attitude of these officials in their interactions with local people.

For me, it seemed that PRA was closely linked with participation, which is a philosophy and not a tool or methodology, one that respects people, their experience, their views, suggestions and involvement in the entire process. To many people, however, PRA is a combination of tools and methods for information gathering (social mapping, wealth ranking, resource mapping, transect, seasonal analysis, time line, etc). Interest in using PRA has developed primarily because many international funding agencies suggested to – perhaps also imposed on – their partners a requirement that PRA should be followed. As a result, many organizations started using it without understanding the real meaning of participation.

The core principles of the PRA approach are to learn from the local people and to get beyond standard answers, i.e. raising questions like 'Why?', 'What?' and 'How?'. At the same time, some people agree that the PRA approach should be quick, flexible and adequate. This has led to further problems with interpretation of what 'participation' involves. Most of the PRA exercises were useful for government staff for agricultural planning (like choice of seasonal crops – through mapping and seasonal rainfall charts) or for generating data quickly for health-related planning (such as the incidence of disease during various seasons). The PRA approach by and large did not seem to involve local people in analysis and follow up of the decisions taken. To me, PRA should mean participation of the people, particularly those whom development is supposed to concern (which is mainly marginalized, poor, women, dalit, tribals) to change their situation. The component of learning and knowledge building throughout the entire process is essential. This learning should be utilized in other places. In this way, PRA can contribute towards development and also change people's attitude, behaviour and mindset.

From the expansion and scaling up point of view, PRA seems to be still in the conceptual stage. Many people have vague and wrong ideas about it. How to really practise participation through PRA remains a challenge. PRA says that people are participants. But the point is not simply to participate. They should have the control in the process, decision and follow-up. The challenge, then, is how can this be operationalized? In the South, Voluntary Development Organizations (VDOs) are adopting the slogan of people's participation. Most of these VDOs are not directly working with the poor at the village level. They are acting as a third party. They promote local organizations to practise their concept. In this way, an 'us' and 'them' situation is created. Many times knowingly 'we' impose our thoughts and ideas on 'them'.

Principles and practice of participation

Participatory philosophy says that people have the knowledge base. This knowledge comes from their experience. In my childhood, I learnt the names of various stars from my aunt, she explained to me about the different types of clouds. She was not a 'well-educated' lady. In my working situation, I have tried to learn many things from practitioners.

One of the things I have tried to practise is the idea that to promote participation it is better to stand back and let others take over, rather than to participate directly oneself. In many situations, however, I play an active role. The question is, how long should I play this role? How can I integrate others to play the same role? Unless I move away and provide space to others, how can others participate effectively? In my personal experience, I have noticed contradictions. Leaders of organizations continue to play a leadership role for years. Organizations say they believe in participatory philosophy, but they also promote individual leadership and not a participatory process of management. At times I feel sorry that my values, beliefs and practice are not being recognized, not noticed in the 'speed of development'. People look at me as a soft person, so when I push something strongly, they say I am not reasonable.

Putting participation into practice

These days, the participatory philosophy is effectively practised in other sectors, like industries and the corporate sector. Profit-oriented organizations nowadays are more concerned about their customers. Customer satisfaction is their goal. In many ways they are more articulate and practical than development organizations. For example, many companies believe that 'there are no workers, no managers, there are only team members and facilitators'. They are steadily coming out from the old belief in 'participation because it is convenient for bargaining' to emphasize that involvement means participation plus commitment plus pride.

Looking at the practice of participation in development organizations, it seems the corporate sector is one step ahead. Recently a senior person in the VDO sector narrated one of his experiences. One of his friends, a well-known PRA practitioner, was invited by a VDO to do a PRA. The VDO is working for socio-economic development of the village. Before starting the job, the PRA practitioner said, 'I will do a quick PRA on villagers' perceptions of the organization (VDO)'. He asked the question 'What is this organization doing in this village?' to many people in different places around the village. The reply was, 'They come in a car occasionally, meet the people, we don't know what they do…'. This clearly shows that this VDO is not working in a transparent way, that they do not involve or inform villagers in general about what they do, and are only concerned with a chosen few. This story may be exaggerated, but this is the reality.

This is happening because practice of PRA has been carried on mainly within the context of 'development projects' funded by external agencies. Much confusion has resulted from their understandings of participation. Participation has implied the involvement of all the people for the achievement of some implicit end in the interests of all. Unfortunately at the time of discussion, planning and conduct of PRA, the concept of social change is completely buried by tools and techniques. Through local people's participation, project authorities collect relevant, appropriate data and information. But major decisions continue to be taken by 'outside experts'. Similarly, external agencies usually decide the parameters of participation. For example, World Bank policy documents have detailed guidelines. Many

Northern consultants are going to Southern countries with these guidelines and without trying to understand the local people and their experience base, they try to gather information from them and organize the information collected through a participatory process. Northern consultants are coming to Southern countries, urban educated people are going to rural areas (south in the South) and both exploit and misutilize the participatory philosophy.

Going beyond the already converted

PRA is being debated, discussed and practised in a controlled climate with like-minded groups and individuals. We try to work with the non-converted. For example, I was involved in a series of training programmes on participatory development for the district-level government officials who are implementing a UNICEF-supported water, sanitation, education and health project. Similarly, I was involved in training European Union-supported watershed development project personnel. Through a series of interventions, the project staff's attitude towards the villagers changed and their intervention with them became more cordial. Through our facilitation, we were able to establish a bridge between the project personnel and the villagers. The project personnel realized that villagers' involvement will help them to plan and implement the project. I feel our success was due to our forceful argument and to our example of working with people, bringing the two groups together and, through facilitation, bringing out villagers' knowledge base in the area, their experiments and successful introduction of various crops, and their strong arguments on certain issues. The government staff who, until recently, believed that only they know everything, have realized that this is not the case. This brought me great satisfaction.

During the past three years, I have been involved in the promotion of participatory micro-planning. The initial planning process was facilitated by a group of trained village-level youth. A series of meetings were organized, which were followed by the use of PRA methods. Through these meetings, villagers' problems, solutions and priority problems to be addressed were identified. Out of 11 hamlets, eight identified infrastructure like link roads, culverts (small bridges) and drinking water connections as their priority needs, while health, education and sanitation were not the priority. Many government officials argued with us, why did we put so much emphasis on infrastructure needs? Our answer was that it comes out through dialogue with local women and men. Initially, the government was not interested in supporting this plan. Villagers agreed to contribute one-third of the cost in cash as well as in kind. We tried to convince the government officials and politicians at various levels. After a series of dialogues and discussions with the administration at block, district and state levels, the State Cabinet accepted the 'participatory micro-planning' as the basis of local planning, and government agreed to support this plan. The intervening period of one-and-a-half years was a period of frustration. Now the challenge before us is how to develop/facilitate the participatory planning process in over 4000 Gram Panchayats.[1] It requires a large number of committed practitioners/facilitators. It requires positive support from the government to provide support in the implementation of the plan. The success and challenge stimulates me to move ahead to overcome criticism and problems.

Note

[1]The local unit of the elected body in the state.

CHAPTER 9

Michael Drinkwater

Reflections on participation and empowerment

Formation

My first really formative experiences with working with peasant farmers was in Zimbabwe during the mid-1980s, when I spent an agricultural season conducting research with farmers in two rural communities. I remember approaching this work with several emotions. Relief, on the one hand, at having sorted out the endless work permit problems and finally to be starting the 'real' work, and also a great deal of trepidation – will things work out? They did. The experience ended up much richer than I could possibly have imagined.

For me, this fieldwork probably had three important long-term consequences. One was the huge respect I developed for most of those with whom I was working. During the season I made regular visits to a group of around 30 farmers. I used to arrange prior appointments at specific times and tried to be there on time, to accompany the women and men during their agricultural and other work. In a clockless society, people were virtually always where they said they would be at the agreed time. Since then, on endless occasions, I have had field staff tell me that they arrange meeting times an hour or so before they intend to be there, 'because people are always late'. They aren't. They are late because the field staff are late. The point is one of respect. Good, productive relationships are built on a foundation of mutual respect, which evolves and deepens over time. Respect is a recognition of the other as a person of equal worth and dignity, who makes the most of their life, whatever circumstances, skills, resources and trials they have received in the lottery of fate.

The second was an appreciation for the contexts of poverty in which people struggle. I have worked throughout rural and urban environments especially in Southern, but also in other parts of, Africa. Scrubby, dusty rural landscapes, or crowded, discordant and unsanitary urban informal settlements may not have much to recommend them in the ordinary scheme of things. But they provide people with an opportunity to organize and control their own lives, and glimpses of elegance and beauty can be found everywhere. Lastly, conducting extended fieldwork taught me important lessons about the limits of what we take as truths, based either on our own convictions or on existing knowledge. Most of what I had previously taken for granted was disproved in my fieldwork. To understand this in participatory work is very helpful. It helps us not to get too carried away, and to focus a little more thoroughly on the rigour of the process.

Experimentation

At the end of 1989, I moved to Zambia to work in farming systems research as a rural sociologist. With a group of fellow novices we began to experiment with Participatory Rural Appraisal (PRA) methods. Armed with copies of *RRA Notes*, I introduced methods and processes none of us had tried before. I remember the first map that we asked a group of people to draw with local materials on the ground, and all of us being both amazed and exhilarated that people actually did it. We evolved a process of conducting 12-day PRA exercises, camping out in areas and working through a two- or three-stage iterative process: information collection, analysis/synthesis and potential strategy generation. Now, these 12-day camping trips in Zambia seem a luxury compared with the Participatory Learning and Action (PLA) exercises we now undertake, no more than five and sometimes as few as two days long. It is clear, on the positive side, that interactive methods that focus actively on developing trust and relationships do hasten the ability to learn about the lives and contexts of those one is working with. But it is critical to remember too that such learning is a rushed job, and therefore inevitably incomplete. The dilemma of such partial understanding is how much and what part of it we can rely on; and how much is of value to other participants. In both cases, the answers to such questions come to depend on what happens subsequently.

Critical concerns

These experiences raise three main critical concerns that I have regarding the use of participatory, or, to use the more accurate term, interactive methodologies:

- the need to deepen our understanding of participation as a process of empowerment
- issues of quality control, which relate to the degree to which practitioners have a theoretical grounding for what they do and how they understand

the principles of participatory practice, and how they label these practices

- the intrinsic skills of being participatory, and the means of coming to learn and understand them.

My discussion of these concerns includes the use of participatory methodologies at scale, in large programmes that work with many thousands of people. In this context, participation is about the transformation of personalized approaches into methodologies and processes that can be broadly replicated. This is not to say that I am talking about losing the primacy of the personal, since this remains the linchpin of any interactive experience. But if participatory approaches are to replace more conventional ones, they must be amenable to being used at scale.

Participation as a process of empowerment

By and large, most people accept that when talking about participation we mean not just a one-off exercise, but a process that unfolds over time. This is not to say that a great deal of participatory work is not fundamentally concerned with single occasions. But if this is the case, then the grounding and context of such exercises should be clear. I work with CARE International and, in conjunction with an array of other partners, we implement projects. Given this, it is easier for us than for many others to say that we will undertake a participatory exercise with a given community only if we believe there is a reasonable certainty of some form of follow-up occurring.

I do not believe this is absolutely essential. Previously I have used participatory methodologies purely for research purposes. Well, that was *my* aim. What I came to understand over time with the people I/we were working with, was that if they, like you, are improving their own understanding through the process, they will continue to interact with you for the benefit of learning more about their own circumstances. This means that for a participatory process to be worthwhile, as many of those participating as possible should be gaining personal growth and learning from the process.

A few years back, when an evaluator was visiting village management groups with a food security project in Livingstone, Zambia, he asked a village group what were the most important things they had benefited from in their work with CARE. The mixed group of men and women agreed first on drought-tolerant varieties of seed, since the programme had begun with drought mitigation objectives. Second, though, the group rated the ability to organize themselves. Men made comments along the lines of 'we have been able to learn from each other in ways that were not possible before' and

'I have lived with these women for 30 years, but this is the first time I have been able to learn from them'. Women remarked on their liberation from the confines of lineage leadership. Interestingly, this project has sparked off whole debates about the roles of women and youth in what has been a very traditional male elder-dominated society. It also led me to become much more interested in the principles and circumstances under which participatory processes are most likely to be empowering.

Juxtaposed against this notion of participatory action is the critique of development practice as being ignorantly interventionist in people's lives. It is easy enough to say that the aim of development work should be to hand control of change processes over to the 'participants', but we all know that life is not this uncomplicated. If we are to interact with people in ways that are truly empowering, the process has to take account of the layers of social, political and economic realities pertaining to and affecting the local level. *This means that we are not neutral in the way we intervene, a factor that raises a whole host of issues that much participatory practice does not deal with very well.*

Many of these issues boil down to the fact that well-intentioned but ignorant interventions may have negative (dependency-increasing) effects rather than positive (empowering) for many of those involved. To what extent is it feasible for us to outline the principles of facilitating change processes most effectively in this regard?

Theoretical grounding and quality assurance of participatory practice

These days it has become *de rigeur* to use participatory methodologies in the development field. But while the rhetoric of participatory practice abounds, laudatory practice is a great deal thinner. This abuse of the term 'participation' is understandable but highly dangerous.

There are a few inherent problems here. One is that I am sure that many of us have become increasingly suspicious about the type of information that is reproduced from a so-called 'participatory' process. Often the truth claims made are either poorly backed up or incredibly vague. 'People said that water was their priority', or even, 'People ranked water as their number one priority in a needs assessment exercise'. Which people?, who do they represent?, and how was the methodological process grounded? Was it not merely an arbitrary exercise in shopping-list manipulation dominated by the loudest or most powerful voice(s)? Often these types of question are scantily addressed. The second problem is that the lack of theoretical grounding for quantitative and qualitative methodological rigour in participatory practice makes the latter easy prey for those anxious to defend the realm of (formal) academic research as the proper repository of good social science practice.

There are two issues here: theory and method. On the theoretical side, the above critique of participatory methods is somewhat ironic if we set it in the context of contemporary science. Seen through this lens, participatory practice actually has everything going for it, and formal (social) scientific method, little. Even a modicum of quantum physics grounds what most of us know intuitively: that the world is as we see it and as we construct it through interaction with others. In short, there is not a detached world that exists out there independent of any specific viewer or participant. This means that any notion of scientific method that presupposes an objective or value-free observer is invalid. Among the implications of this (and notions such as Heisenberg's Uncertainty Principle[1]) are:

- The questions we ask in any situation determine the answers we get.
- Any structure results in outcomes that preclude other outcomes.
- When we interfere with a quantum system we change it (from Zohar 1997, pp.59–64).

In short, the way we interact with the world changes it, and determines the options for change.

Methodologically, this is why I prefer the term 'interactive' to 'participatory', since the use of the term 'interactive' perforce means that we have to have regard for the roles of all parties in the interactive process – 'us' as well as 'them'. People will respond to you the way you project yourself. And since this works reciprocally you, in turn, respond to people the way they project themselves.

A practical example of this comes from a rural livelihoods assessment exercise I was recently involved in with CARE Zimbabwe. Instead of concluding by prioritizing needs, we spent an additional day on opportunity analysis and visioning. The whole experience was intriguing, not least because of the huge sea change in mood as well as results between the two days. Both days were conducted with groups self-selecting on the basis of livelihood categories identified earlier. With the much larger poorer group, the day spent on problem analysis was utterly depressing and not particularly productive. People's focus was on handouts. The appreciative enquiry day had a wholly different atmosphere to it. People were engaged and productive. Two or three of the poorer groups showed themselves as wonderful graphic artists. And they took to the challenge of outlining future visions, and then mapping the path to achieving these, in very practical ways. They looked to their own skills, resources and opportunities first, outlining ideas that were considerably more progressive and achievable than the dire analyses of the previous day (we have no food and money, which leads to malnutrition and death, and hence we need to be given handouts).

Participatory skills

As noted above, working participatively is arguably much more difficult and challenging than working 'normally', largely because to interact well with others, and yet not to lose the plot, requires strong intuitive, lateral thinking and adaptive skills. We are all aware that it is wrong to assume that we can learn (or teach) participatory methods by rote, and that the simple application of a step-by-step process will result in a truly participatory practice. It won't. It will tend only to result in the stilted reproduction of set methods, with largely unenlightening consequences for all involved. People need to be encouraged to think while doing, and in my experience, people's skills at achieving this do not at all correlate with formal education. While this is in part an indictment of training systems, it is also to say that it is a particular way of thinking that makes one more or less disposed to using participatory methods well. This parallels the distinction between applying rule-based logic and being guided by the emergent product of interactive processes, and letting that shape what is learnt.

Future: the notion of participatory governance

Like most other users of participatory methods, when I first started I just wanted to see if and how such methods worked. In Zambia, we took delight in the mere fact that if one was open and showed a genuine interest, people were tremendously responsive. They were able to provide us with a depth of understanding about their lives, expressed especially through visual and focus group methods, which previously could be attained only through extensive field research. Soon though, our ambitions moved on and we began to experiment with methods and processes of conducting participatory research. We encouraged the formation of farmer research groups in the Central and Copperbelt Province communities we were working in, and assisted the groups in learning how they could plan, manage and evaluate their own adaptive research programmes.

In this way, my own understanding of participation shifted from taking delight in its occurrence in particular events, to exploring its potential for achieving far-reaching change when facilitated as a process. Since then, in working with CARE, my work has embraced the encouragement of even longer-term participatory processes of social, economic and institutional change – or, as we label it, of livelihood improvement. Most recently, CARE has moved towards incorporating a stronger rights emphasis in its organizational use of a livelihoods approach, and one of the core principles of this emerging framework is the concept of participatory governance.

As a principle, participatory governance expresses the right that all people should be able to participate in, and have access to, information relating to the decision-making processes that affect their lives. This principle is based on the assumption that people, given the opportunity and capacity for achieving greater control over their lives, will accept greater responsibility for the realization of this potential. A key feature of this is the acceptance that principles such as participatory governance must be embraced and exemplified in the way we work ourselves, before we can expect others to do the same. In livelihoods-based programmes, participatory governance is thus being developed as a way of improving vastly the representation and voice of the poor in development processes. To expand such processes at scale, mechanisms that genuinely represent the interests and aspirations of the poor, vulnerable and other marginalized groups need to become an accepted and feasible lowest level of governance structures.

This shift towards incorporating participation in governance shows just how much, in little over a decade, our collective concern with participation has achieved and evolved as a concept. Still, as a rights emphasis in our programming now leads us to a greater concern with examining root causes, and to tackle the larger issue of dealing more effectively with the power relations that constrain access to resources and opportunities, it is also clear how incipient our achievements to date remain. One key question I have, as we as practitioners seek to consolidate and build on the promising start of the previous decade, is the extent to which it is possible for all of us to learn to work participatively (rather than didactically), if encouraged in appropriate ways. And if so, what are the inherent practical and intellectual attributes that are required and need to be explored and stimulated? This of course echoes back to the whole knowledge, attitudes and practices issue and entails overcoming many of the biases of much conventional technical training of both professionals and field extension workers. It also relates back to issues of power relations.

As Sen suggests, even the most collaborative of relations incorporate elements of 'co-operative conflict', since few processes benefit all equally. In accepting this, it is always necessary to recognize but move beyond the particularistic in negotiation processes that seek to broaden perceptions and understandings of longer-term benefits of potential social change. This is particularly important when the effort is to persuade the more powerful to yield control over assets and resources in the short term. This makes even more challenging the question as to what extent can 'being participative' (open, unprejudiced and thoughtful in interactive situations) become a way of life for all?

Note

[1]This principle states that, 'We can focus on the position or on the momentum of a particle, but never on both.'

Reference

Zohar, D. (1997) *Rewiring the Corporate Brain: using the new science to rethink how we structure and lead organisations*, Berrett-Koehler, San Francisco.

CHAPTER 10

Marc Fiedrich

Maps turning to minefields: local knowledge of PRA in a Ugandan village

For the past 18 months I have had the opportunity to regularly observe an adult literacy class in a central Ugandan village.[1] I joined the group only a couple of months after the facilitator had completed a two-week training in REFLECT, an approach to learning how to read and write on the basis of Participatory Rural Appraisal (PRA) graphics and debates. My interest lay in finding out how people make use of PRA when it is used for learning purposes and not primarily for facilitating relationships between poor people and external agents.

I wanted to understand what REFLECT participants make of PRA. How (if at all) did they adapt it to suit their circumstances? Do the fundamental premises of PRA, such as equity, respect for others and their opinions, and an interest in analysing and validating local knowledge, match the expectations with which participants came to the classes? These are some of the questions I want to address in this chapter, not least because they reflect my own anxiety about how much value to attach to participation in and by itself.

Kilemba: another case of 'poor PRA'?

Susan, the facilitator in Kilemba's circle, is a dynamic, middle-aged former schoolteacher who moved to the village three years ago. Being the facilitator in the REFLECT circle is a considerable source of pride to her.

What fills her with pride is that the participants are attending regularly, that they dress well for the occasion, are attentive and take the recommendations seriously. During her training, Susan was exposed to various PRA tools and she now prepares each session using a facilitator's guide. Her main 'adaptation' of these guidelines consists of dispensing with the construction of graphics on the ground. Instead she herself swiftly draws up the tool's framework on a flip chart and then fills it in by probing individual participants on what she should put where. She doesn't hand over the stick; rather she prompts participants to give her answers, which she then fills in. 'Incorrect' answers are either 'corrected' by her directly or are thrown back to the audience for reconsideration. Done in this fashion, a graphic can be completed in less than 15 minutes. Susan derives considerable satisfaction from being efficient with time and will often remind participants to speed up and 'keep time', seemingly convinced that this adds to the urgency of the message conveyed.

When asked what she wants to achieve with her teaching, Susan does mention participation as one of her priorities, though only in third place to 'them putting into practice what I have taught them' and 'for the lessons to be clear'. Her valuing participation shines through though, as she explains '...that is why we people of Kilemba are a bit ahead, because sometimes I put myself down a bit and ask them what they want to do'. Participation, then, is a privilege to be granted or withdrawn at the discretion of the facilitator.

Establishing who decided how to construct the graphics proves difficult. At one point Susan told participants: 'You are old enough to use blackboard and papers, not sand.' At other times she reports that the participants pressurized her: 'You have a box of chalk, you use it!' In any event, it is clear that interests colluded on this matter: '[The trainers] told me to always listen to my participants so I have no alternative (broad smile).' Constructing graphics in another way would seriously rupture the debating culture that has been established in this circle. The guidelines that Susan has received from ActionAid offer questions which facilitators can use to structure debate around the graphics constructed. Susan sticks to these questions religiously. She writes one on a flip chart and starts collecting 'points' (using the English word). 'Come on, you participate, everyone give me at least two points, Nalongo you start.' In this fashion long lists are created with speed and Susan frames them with discourses she delivers. Such discourses are invigorated by frequently prompting participants to supply the continuation of what she was going to say ('...and then we are going to plant potatoes. Then we are going to plant the what?'; chorus: 'the potatoes') Often the response will come in unison. At other times participants break into laughter as answers differ. Susan will then either repeat the question or will elaborate through further questioning or soliciting of comments before regaining her rhythm.

Susan has a way of showing quite clearly which solutions she prefers, by asking suggestive questions, listening to answers selectively, asking carefully chosen participants to comment on other participants' contributions and, most effectively, by stopping the debate when she sees fit and retaining from it what she deems appropriate. Throughout debates, Susan always retains her position as master of ceremonies. She gives and takes parole, interrupts, uses strong body language to show approval or disapproval, speaks loudest, stands up while all others sit on the ground, occasionally mocks participants, illustrates points by gesticulating wildly, and so on.

Both Susan and the participants profess to having come a long way since the first lesson, stating that they are now free to express themselves and no longer fear to talk in public.

What is the appeal of Susan's approach? First, that it is entertaining; both Susan and the participants enjoy it. There are, however, other good reasons that Susan and the participants have for doing it in this way, rather than in a more approved participatory style. It is linear and progressive in a way that is visible and comprehensible to everyone involved. The snippets supplied by participants not only allow Susan to check for everyone's attention, they also affirm what has been said and allow the group to move further along with her. Many participants associate uneducated people with being 'unstructured' and 'having no plan', while educated people 'know how to think and plan', 'they have an intention, they don't just go saying this or that'. Highly structured talk is therefore an important status marker, allowing participants to disassociate themselves from their 'uneducated past'. Making 'points', drawing up long lists, keeping a close watch on time, and lavishly using flip charts and markers are all attractive means of making the transition to be an educated, modern person.

Second, the use of this procedure implies that the creation of unity is an important function; everyone publicly subscribes to a given point of view and thus a common body of knowledge is suggested, contributing to the bond that participants are seeking to create among each other.

Susan will sometimes encourage women to contribute from their own experience during sessions, although such interventions are delicately managed, by both her and the participants, so as not to impose practical consequences, let alone collective action. While a gender-sensitive researcher could easily come to the conclusion that women in Kilemba would have many good reasons for uniting, the reality is that individual women build social capital by carefully dosing (non-) co-operation with other women (and men). It is then much safer to remain with broad pledges such as 'we must stop fighting with each other'. Sticking to a generalized discourse on unity also conveniently ties in with the messages received from other important institutions such as the church or the government. This not only helps to situate the circle in a prestigious context; it also signals to everyone that eminent words do not require imminent action.

Third, and closely related to my previous point, the procedure allows for a controlled managing of controversy. The main speaker sets the scene and decides at which points other people's contributions come in. More often than not, the contributions are defined as factual in nature, requiring

70

participants to affirm something mentioned before, to make true/false assertions, or to supply a brief piece of information. When controversy does arise, intended or unintended, it is up to the main speaker to decide how much space to grant individuals' contributions. This is made easier by the fact that any participant's contribution that is longer than a short sentence is an interruption to the rhythm of the procedure and the main speaker can therefore dismiss it as a deterrent to linear progression quite easily if she so chooses. Such 'closed' debate is then an extremely valuable tool in situations where no one deems that 'open' debate is a risk worth taking.

To sum up, this way of talking in public is very popular in Uganda; it produces a momentary sense of unity, minimizes public dissent, delineates the speaker as an educated person and invites listeners to align behind her. It is a style that visiting dignitaries, such as political leaders, clergy or development workers, often use. But it also sits uneasily with the way REFLECT and PRA envisage knowledge as being relative and not absolute. Contradictions and controversy are desired outcomes of a PRA analysis, and linear progression would be frowned upon almost as much as the insistence on one objective truth.

We could easily (de-)classify this account of Susan's and the participants' efforts as yet another example to be added to the long list of 'poor PRA'. We could justify this by finding that training was insufficient or of poor quality, that support and genuine exchange was lacking, that the context of literacy training gives the wrong connotations from the start, and so on. Suitably misguided development professionals could be found to take the blame for this 'abuse' of PRA, and a call for 'quality PRA' would end the case. The validity of some such criticisms couldn't be denied, but reality has a tendency to be messy, and by discounting it in this way we deny ourselves the opportunity to gain a more grounded understanding of the practice of PRA as opposed to its ideals.

No longer village rats: analysing PRA

I have illustrated that participants in Kilemba are displaying a glaring disregard for some of the ideals that we PRA practitioners hold dear. They do so for good reason. The hierarchical structure they have adopted for their meetings, seemingly without much prior reflection, can be narrowly interpreted as a deterrent to 'meaningful' participation. But that doesn't say much about the actual practice of participation, which differs markedly from the way participants would act outside the circle.

Being part of an official discourse is a new experience for many participants. This experience is elevated in significance by making it as official as possible. During the first few months, for example, the participants in this circle were wearing name tags, presumably to emphasize the 'conference character' of their proceedings, since they all knew each other by name. Women, who make up the majority of regular participants, have little occasion to experiment with new roles and contexts. Familiarizing oneself with the tedium of post-colonial bureaucratic orders might not be the first thing that comes to our minds when musing about rural African women's empowerment, but to the women participants in Kilemba that is the code of power to which they have no access. A more rigorous application of participatory ideals would have to find ways to cater for such desires.

Conversely, local knowledge is something that the participants prefer to negate, or rather, have negated for them, in the circle sessions; though they obviously know of its practical value in their day-to-day lives. Without dwelling much on the content of the classes, it can be said that there is a pattern of 'confessionals', which participants slip into when the facilitator interrogates them on their practices of daily life. This doesn't take the form of indiscretions whispered in a hushed voice to gain absolution. Instead the facilitator might ask them what they usually do when there is food in plenty, and the participants, knowing full well where this question will lead, will report how it all goes to waste in feasting and generous giving away. Much laughter about one's own and other participants' 'backward ways' is then followed by the solemn resolution to stop wasting food and to work harder. To call such analysis superficial is to put it mildly, but that is beside the point. Again, what participants enjoy about this is the opportunity to make a public pledge to 'better their ways', to show that one is a person who acts rationally and 'has a plan', who is no longer 'just a village rat'.

The other important point we often miss about local knowledge is that it is dangerous. When we talk of local knowledge we often mean it to be the extensive body of knowledge about their own environment that poor people possess and manipulate with great skill. We marvel at the huge amount of names and classifications that exist for local plants or the elaborate techniques for forecasting the weather. It is indeed tragic that such knowledge is rarely brought into the open, although, on a side note, it has to be said that our own marvel at its existence precariously edges on the patronizing. The issue here is that this is a very narrow and romanticized perspective on local knowledge. There is that other, more nasty local knowledge where everybody carries about a few open wounds that others may or may not want to poke into. In practice, this latter type of knowledge is impossible to separate from the more factual and cherished kind of local knowledge.

The ever-popular household map, indicating the number of adults and children in each household, seems a harmless enough tool in which one would perhaps not expect to find 'nasty' local knowledge. Unless, of course, there are a few men around whose wives have just run away, or a married couple without children, or a single woman whom everyone suspects of having nightly 'visitors'. We won't even start to mention the complications of how to cater for polygamous relationships without offending anyone. An external facilitator may still be excused for clumsily traipsing about in people's privacy in such a way. S/he is unlikely to notice the embarrassment caused, and participants are likely to forgive it; but it is obvious that the map turns into a minefield for a local facilitator who is aware, and is known to be aware, of the status of each household. Here, a good dose of superficiality is strongly recommended.

As outsiders, we are often astonished by the level of seemingly intimate and controversial debate that can emerge on the basis of PRA graphics. I have often thought that it is a particular merit of graphics that they allow people to keep things at an abstract level; wherever participants deem it necessary. Perhaps so, but individual participants will have varying degrees of control over what is done with the graphic and we rarely get to know what is left out from the debate or why what is debated has come to the fore in the first place. If anything, I have noticed people in Kilemba taking seemingly abstract statements to have a hidden, personal agenda.

All of this is to say that there are serious limitations to what we would consider 'open debate' in Kilemba. In a place where talking is far too dangerous an activity to be done casually, mincing one's words is essential. Keeping things vague is helpful to keep one's options open, and careful lying represents a useful and necessary strategy to keep others at bay. There have been situations in the circle where blatant lies have been told and listened to so elegantly that one could have thought that the people present didn't know each other. On other occasions, people fervently accused each other of lying and relished in the offence caused.

Conclusion

No one is, should be, or can be in a position to ensure that a participatory process doesn't cause offence. Here, I have chosen to focus mainly on those practices of the REFLECT circle in Kilemba which contradict participatory ideals. I have done so because I feel that the kind of populist idealization we so often engage in when talking of both 'the poor' and PRA blinds us to aspirations poor people hold which are not in line with the aspirations we hold for them. In situations where powerful outsiders are present, PRA participants may be inclined to dispense with the kind of officialdom and formalism that PRA sets itself against. Perhaps the mere association with such an outsider is sign enough of the 'seriousness' of the situation so that 'anything goes'. However, in Kilemba, where PRA is used 'by themselves', legitimacy needs to be struggled for, and here an atmosphere of casual informality would be detrimental to the intentions of those who come to the sessions.

Though we have rightly placed a great deal of emphasis on issues of process in PRA, it is startling to see how much of this debate centres narrowly on the expression of power relations during PRA sessions. We rarely seek to find out what people actually think about PRA and how PRA sessions fit in with the broader dynamics of power relations in the given context. My account of some features of the use of PRA in Kilemba is not aimed at exposing 'poor PRA', but at illustrating tensions in the practice of PRA which, I feel, need to be addressed to retain the momentum that, no doubt, has been created through its widespread use.

Note

[1] In the context of an ActionAid study entitled 'Literacy, Gender and Social Agency' funded by DFID.

CHAPTER 11

Bara Gueye

Pathways to participation in French-speaking Africa: a learner's itinerary

Participatory methods were first introduced in Francophone Africa at the end of the 1980s, and were to develop quite rapidly. However, it seems that the circumstances of that first contact with participatory methods vary from one individual to the next. This chapter is an attempt to trace a simplified personal itinerary by describing the main phases of a learning process I have been part of in Francophone Africa.

Phase 1 – Between curiosity and scepticism: the first contact, 1989–90

In 1989, I was introduced first to Rapid Rural Appraisal (RRA), and then to Participatory Rural Appraisal (PRA).[1] It is important to stress that an external impetus led to the first training in RRA in West Africa. The first workshop was an initiative of the International Research and Development Centre (IRDC), with the International Institute for Environment and Development (IIED) supplying training facilitation support. Therefore our introduction to RRA did not stem from a direct, field-based process, but rather from a traditional training one. It should also be noted that participants in that first workshop were selected based on their individual capability and the aptitude of their institutions to go beyond the lessons learned on to broader thinking about and practical use of the tools. As for my own involvement, I was a member of a research and training organization already notorious for promoting methods for approaching local development issues. The organization therefore offered a fertile environment for thought on any new methodological approach.

Paradoxically though, my institution was rather sceptical at first regarding this new debate on *'rapid method'*, as it disturbed a well-established methodological order. Personally, this institutional resistance only raised my motivation as I finally drew the conclusion that such resistance was one consequence of the lack of deep understanding of this new paradigm and its tools. I then decided that the best way to go about overcoming the resistance would be to gather as many persuasive arguments as possible, both through methodological expertise and a process of information diffusion. Being in charge of applied research within my organization, I was able to make proposals for the strengthening of methodological skills. One of the first 'scapegoats', I also had greater interest in pursuing the search towards a more systematic understanding of those methods.

During the introductory phase, the role of the training facilitator is central, because people's will to keep the experience going is greatly influenced by the capacity of the facilitator to 'sell' the idea. In the case of West Africa, the first workshop was mainly facilitated by a staff member from IIED, Jules Pretty, which indeed gave value to the training due to the fame of both the facilitator and his institution in relation to the methods. Curiosity was thus teased and it became each learner's responsibility to keep the fire burning.

Phase 2 – From curiosity to interest expression: 1990–92

At the time RRA emerged in Francophone Africa, the region lacked qualified resource persons and adequate literature in French. The few documents that existed were published in English. Since the introductory phase had stimulated interest in deepening the RRA knowledge base, efforts were channelled into producing literature and to translating some key didactic aids. Our efforts were fostered by several factors:

- Similarity between the RRA principles and the approaches and methods of our home institutions had already developed.
- Natural complementarities existed between RRA and the then current approaches to local development, especially as RRA could eventually fill the gap in tools and techniques that would facilitate the participation of populations in development discussions. This lack of tools and techniques for enabling participation had always been viewed as one of the limitations of the methods we were using then.
- The somewhat exotic nature of the debate on rapid-labelled surveys and their tools led to the formation of two opposite positions. The first was mere rejection by some researchers and development practitioners under the assumption that the pragmatic and quick application of those methods was bound to undermine strict scientific criteria. Others took the second position, one of curiosity and interest, supported by the principle that one has to find out about things prior to taking a stand for or against them. I belonged in the latter category.

This phase was actually one of exploring the RRA promise. It should be acknowledged that the naive aspect of the debate on those methods at the time has greatly contributed to shaping various people's views with strong populist and idealistic tendencies. To some extent, this has led to the entrenchment of countering radical and critical positions, mostly among academics.

Phase 3 – Learning to acquire technical know-how: 1992–94/5

Many of the pioneers who had exposure to the rapid-labelled methods in French-speaking Africa did not continue beyond the interest-raising phase to further develop their skills. There are several reasons behind that situation. First, for one reason or another, some people felt that the methods did not comply with their own methodological practices. Moreover, many among the pioneers were in positions or institutional environments that did not allow them to deepen the methodology, either because the culture of their home institutions did not match this new paradigm, or because they had no time to pursue the learning process.

As for myself, my institutional environment was particularly favourable to furthering thinking. Despite the resistance I noticed earlier in some of my colleagues, the nature of the institution provided opportunities for discussion and experimentation, at least at a personal level. However, there was also a personal challenge behind my commitment since I was part of the very first group of RRA trainees in West Africa and some of us had pledged to share the experience on a wider scale. During that phase, extensive efforts were made to develop documentation. Those efforts peaked when, faced with the vacuum in French-written literature on the subject, I decided with my colleague Karen Schoonmaker Freuedenberger to produce a first RRA manual in French. The document had great impact in the development arena.

In the beginning, it was our wish to have a better grasp of the way the methods operated in order to make our research process more pragmatic, which drove our efforts to develop our skills. That is why in most cases in Francophone Africa the main motives were to improve the efficiency of data collection procedures rather than to empower populations. That latter concern appeared later on, when methods and tools were demystified. Concerns about ensuring quality were quite marginal in our discussions and in the few training sessions that were held, the main objective was to master the instrumental process. This was essentially due to the fact that the region did not boast a satisfactory number of resource persons experienced enough with the methods to be in a position to share feedback on their strengths and weaknesses, as well as the deviations from good practice that people commonly fall into. Looking back, one can now better comprehend the impact of the idealistic and naive vision of the previous phase. As a matter of fact, the seeds that yielded the deviations noticed later were actually sown right then. Pre-eminence of automatic application over critical thinking led to several misuses, such as the routine and standard character stamped on the process, the overwhelming power of tools and techniques, the extractive nature of applications and the 'merchandising turn' direction the process was taking due to high demand for training.

Phase 4 – Exhilaration and the quality challenge: 1995–97

The adaptation phase of RRA in Francophone Africa took about three years, after which the rapid methods developed at a phenomenal rate, especially between 1994 and 1997. Non-governmental organizations (NGOs) and national resource management (NRM) projects had just been introduced to RRA, mainly thanks to the efforts of IIED. This development was mostly underlain by operational concerns (due to the widespread NRM approach in the region) and these new methods were an opportunity to palliate the lack so far of tools and techniques specific to NRM. By the end of that period, the first serious questions started to arise. As a matter of fact, the elating first stages were curbed by the fact that those methods, wrongly perceived as a panacea, did not induce noticeable change in many programmes that had used them. Personally, I had many observations and questions.

- Organizations using the methods tried to change other people's practices while keeping their own unchanged.
- The high demand for support exceeded the capacity of the few well-trained persons available to respond.
- The scale of the movement was such that quality and critical thinking was almost impossible.
- Bad practices emerged for various reasons, such as poorly trained facilitators, donor pressure, etc.

However, despite the hardships, several stimulating signs came to light during that period and were powerful incentives to continue.

A few successes were noticed here and there to prove that good practices could indeed induce change. In Senegal, we experimented with training of community facilitators, which raised considerable enthusiasm and helped to build self-analysis skills in villages. On the other hand, that experience convinced us that weaknesses were not inherent in the methods themselves and that moreover, replicating and disseminating successes would substantially palliate the scepticism and criticism that originated from experiences of failure.

The debate over quality was particularly important by the end of that period, notwithstanding the fact that no one could really define in a pragmatic manner how to ensure and monitor quality. Several questions related to the process of quality control had remained unanswered. Who had the authority to define quality? What quality standard was aimed at? Who were those actors upon whom the quality of the participatory process depended? How does one assess quality? In the face of the difficulty of answering such complex questions, organizations in Francophone Africa finally chose to go for an individual strategy.

During that phase, greater attention was paid to the meaning of words, since their interpretation, which was often contentious, raised all kinds of arguments about the pros and cons of participatory methods. The use and understanding of words such as 'rapid', 'methods', 'tools', 'research', 'appraisal', 'rural', etc., became suddenly quite intricate in the Sahelian context. The emerging debate on quality was to be supplemented with yet another important one on semantics. It was right then that in Francophone Africa, we went from the label Rapid Rural Appraisal to Active and Participatory Research and Planning (while still keeping the same French acronym of 'MARP') in order to be in line with the new paradigm of Participatory Rural Appraisal. This phase was eventually to play a significant role in the next stages of the debate on, and practice of, participatory methods in Francophone Africa. The debate at the time highlighted a fundamental lesson: impact is not an exclusive function of the application of methods. Impact depends much more on conditions and circumstances under which those tools and methods are used.

Phase 5 – Institutionalization and the impact challenge: 1997–2000

By the beginning of 1997, a new, more realistic and more pragmatic debate emerged, thus discarding the naive and populist one. One had to put forward convincing arguments that participatory methods are not a panacea, and even less so a miracle recipe. Rather, they are components of a whole set of factors that are vital in providing the impulse for sustainable change within the organization. In fact, the scarce results from the elating earlier period eventually demonstrated that the most influential elements in organizational change are not to be found in the tools and techniques used alone. The key elements are found more within the culture of the organization itself, the attitudes and behaviour of its staff, and the overall environment. At a personal level, this translated into radical change in my programme implementation. I replaced scattered research and training activities to build technical capacities among the staff of NGOs and community-based organizations (CBOs) with a more integrated action-research approach that focused on sustainable and gradual change within the organizations. Such an option substantially modified the nature of my questioning, away from stressing the 'capacity' of the organization, but rather to questioning its 'desire to be'. Naturally, such an approach is more complex and it did call for a new personal commitment to acquiring new skills, well beyond the mechanical application of tools. This new orientation is now shaping up in Francophone Africa, and, interestingly enough, it is selective. This new approach gradually stops influencing the dynamics of organizations that do not show genuine interest in undertaking internal change.

The more we move forward in the institutionalization process, the more we witness the development of a new perception of participatory methods. In fact, we unendingly realize that tools and techniques have for too long served as a shield that prevented us from seeing and understanding the realities behind participation. From a personal viewpoint, institutionalization is undoubtedly the most fascinating of all the challenges we have gone through so far, because it implies a much more complex process and requires for its implementation consistent commitment and diverse skills that go far beyond the sheer application of tools and techniques. But the complexity of this process unveils our methodological vulnerability in addressing certain issues, a dilemma that inevitably leads us into a new phase of questioning.

Phase 6 – New uncertainties and new questions are arising: 2000+

In many regards, the current phase seems to evoke the very beginning of our learning process, simply because today, as then, we have many question marks lurking. One of them stems from our firm belief that the challenge of achieving impact will not be overcome easily unless we adequately put across practices and policies, as well as the understanding and stimulation of their mutual influence. However, it seems that institutions and individuals who preach participatory methods are not equipped to address the current challenge. It is already crystal clear that the current challenge is much more complex than the former ones because it is at the same time institutional, methodological and political. So far, participatory methods have been applied from the perspective of 'thinking locally and acting locally'. In fact, the articulations between global phenomena and local realities have seldom been taken into account, whereas today, even in the most remote areas, communities are directly impacted by, and more aware of, the stakes of globalization. The globalization of markets, the phenomenal development of information and communication technologies, climate change, etc., call imperatively for a new vision to be integrated in the development of participatory approaches.

How are we going to redirect our thinking on participation within the context of globalization? What new methodological tools are we to come up with in order to be in line with that context?

Note

[1] In French-speaking Africa, only one acronym, namely 'MARP', is used to talk about RRA and PRA. But the meaning behind the French MARP acronym translates differently when cross-referencing the Anglo-American acronyms. The first translation of MARP, i.e. Rapid and Participatory Research Method, relates more to RRA, whereas the most current wording in use today, i.e. Active Method for Participatory Research and Planning, refers much more to the concept of Participatory Rural Appraisal.

CHAPTER 12
Irene Guijt

Intrigued and frustrated, enthusiastic and critical: reflections on PRA

Early days

Knowing where someone has started helps, I feel, to place their words, feelings and actions. My own history with Participatory Rural Appraisal (PRA) started in 1988, when, as a young land use planner holding an article on agroecosystem analysis and Rapid Rural Appraisal (RRA) I wandered in a rather confused state through the squatter settlement in Brazil where I had to 'use it'. Conflict and lack of social cohesion emerged clearly as the main obstacles to local development in that context, yet the method did not provide me with ideas about collective debate on desired futures and community actions. Methodologically immature and raised in a technological tradition, social engagement techniques were certainly not my forte. Frustrated, I had no interest in 'doing' RRA again unless there was a way to involve people more.

In 1990, the emergence of the first versions of PRA, particularly from India with the Aga Khan Rural Support Programme India (AKRSP-India), seemed to start filling that hole. The early 1990s, coinciding with my arrival at the International Institute for Environment and Development (IIED), became the P(R?)RA period. We[1] knew it wasn't yet as 'participatory' as we wanted and hoped for. On the other hand, what we were doing was no longer RRA – actors' roles were shifting away from outsider dominance (in some ways). Clumsily worded, the 'participatory rapid' appraisals gave way over time, to more use of PRA. Intense discussions with colleagues did not resolve what we called what we did – personal preferences and norms of what 'participatory' constituted shaped the nomenclature as much as any formal definitions that were in circulation.

Tugs-of-war between the purists and the pragmatists marked most of the early IIED–IDS (Institute of Development Studies) PRA meetings. If local people did not *plan*, then it was not PRA – the purists said. The pragmatists countered with arguments that surely being more participatory was already a step forward. Early debates also focused on methods. The fixation with matrix ranking and scoring in all its versions, the 'oohhing' and 'aahhing' over maps and calendars marked the scramble in those early years for ever more diverse and spectacular examples of methods. The trading of slides, like baseball cards, were the hallmark of our fieldwork and of our training. 'Empowerment' was little discussed – either as an aim or as process. Our implicit assumptions about how people were 'empowered' by, for example, making a map or a Venn diagram, remained undebated. Why was that? I believe it was certainly, in part, a result of our disciplinary limitations.

We were not pursuing 'the truth' or seeking to substitute social research methods. Working mainly with natural scientists, we were simply very enthusiastic about finding what we felt seemed to be an extremely useful way to open up discussion with people who needed to be involved in decisions about agricultural research, about land use plans, about collective action. As natural scientists, we did not (in general) understand social change processes nor know enough to look at local governance, politics and conflict. Unintentionally, the image of PRA as a substitute for in-depth social research grew. With it, though, as we learned and as critique grew, we started seeing the relevance of these overarching questions of social context and the need to draw in social scientists. I personally owe much to discussions with anthropologists, our fiercest critics, to wake me up in this respect.

We were sometimes able to undertake field-based training together. On several occasions, after returning from such workshops with a colleague, I was struck by our different portrayals of 'its success'. My colleague would explain what had gone well – the shifts in attitudes of workshop participants – while my version would be more muted – I hadn't seen many women engaging, I hadn't seen much critical debate or careful documentation, I hadn't seen organisational commitment to next steps, I had seen too many researchers scoffing at farmers' views. My point is not to judge whose version was correct – I simply concluded that we seemed to be approaching PRA with different expectations and with different and usually unclear norms of 'performance'. Noting divergences in quality, some early attempts between IIED and IDS to set quality standards were stranded. It would, we felt, inhibit the diversity and experimentation that was so needed. Above all, who were we to decide what was 'correct practice'?

Emerging quality questions

The overwhelming experience of that early wave of enthusiasm did not preclude my growing concerns about quality. I will name a few that I remember causing me sleepless nights and leading to my moving out of the PRA field.

Critical analysis, not simple lists

The high points of fieldwork notwithstanding, I inevitably landed with a thud on the ground when it came to analysis and documentation. Why was it that the richness of debates were summarized in generalized statements, such as 'people grow maize and sorghum and most have some livestock' or 'the methods went fairly well though it was difficult to get everyone to participate'. Where did diversity and divergence go? What did such generalized statements mean? Why weren't workshop participants asking themselves 'so what?' after returning with arms full of diagrams and heads full of discussions? How could critical reflection and analysis of the discussions be fostered? How can the learning process be made explicit? Many questions, from long ago, still remain poorly discussed and answered in PRA circles. Suggested formats for documentation, introducing workshop exercises on 'analysis' and on note taking are no guarantee. Many people seem to find critical reflection difficult, and the question is whether this can be trained or fostered, and to what extent registering of the process and outputs can be tackled more creatively than via the written word. Critics of participatory development often point out the superficial and descriptive nature of documentation, asking how conclusions were reached and whose conclusions they are. Facilitators can get carried away with visual methods while forgetting their main purpose – critical reflection. Furthermore, the very concept of external, written documentation of such analyses was not being questioned. We still have far to go in this respect.

Equity and gender (yes, still)

In 1992, I starting feeling frustrated about the lack of women under the heading 'people'. If it was all meant to be 'participatory', then who was participating and who wasn't? Alice Welbourn's early work (1991) with separate groups of women and men came as a breath of fresh air and inspired my work that followed on gender and PRA, also stimulating others. Particularly powerful for me was collaboration with Redd Barna Uganda, which clearly made a footnote of the PRA methods and put an end to my simplistic thinking on how social change occurs, as conflict and analysis across social groups were so obviously central. What emerged strikingly was the inevitability of longer, painful processes of understanding social difference and negotiating for social space to pursue interests that were not shared by all in the community, yet were extremely critical to subgroups. PRA became an 18-month process, with the visual methods appearing as one small catalytic event in the form of what we called a field immersion (of five to seven days), though providing a reference point throughout the longer cycle of change.

However, even in this work, women's involvement and engagement, besides still being complex and not well understood, did not mean that gender issues were discussed sufficiently. The step from women and gender, and indeed the link between the two, is still poorly understood and practised. Now, frustrated by the stagnation of gender debates, I am more interested in the broader issue of 'power'. Power as a concept and area of theoretical understanding still does not, it seems to me, inform the practice of PRA to the extent necessary to allow meaningful discussion of discrimination, oppression and difference.

Stakeholder burnout and raising expectations

I remember starting to ask myself in about 1993, 'What do local people think of all this?' It became a standard part of my discussions in the field – had the debate, the visualization of discussions been of any use to local people? One incident in Burkina Faso is burned in my mind. After elaborating a map of soil erosion critical spots and prioritizing them for local action, one man explained the relevance to him. He liked the map, he said, because now he said he saw that making a permanent model of the village would be useful when more outsider development workers came in and asked questions about the village. PRA as useful locally for triggering collective action? I think not. Inflating this incident excessively would be inappropriate, as just as often using PRA raised inflated expectations for local change. By working on a new vision for the future, which lies at the core of participatory development, local people's expectations are raised that this can be achieved. Yet much stands in the way of success, risking what I call 'stakeholder burnout'.

These contrasting phenomena have made me think more critically of what was in it for 'them' and to reduce my expectations in that direction – and increase efforts to understand and avoid 'stakeholder burnout'. Participation 'fatigue' and cynicism is increasing (though I say this without empirical evidence!) and is an issue that requires more attention.

High investment of local people's time and emotions with little result, in the face of urgent survival priorities, seems a recipe for disillusionment and drop-off. What understanding do we have of how stakeholder burnout occurs? What implications does the high risk of local burnout have for what we do? I have been toying around with a 'formula' to describe stakeholder burnout, equally applicable to participation in planning and monitoring[2]:

$$EC + (ITE)*f(PP) > PB - UP = SB.$$

(If Expectation of Change + Invested Time and Effort, as a function of Pressing Problems, is greater than the Perceived Benefits – Unexpected Problems, Stakeholder Burnout occurs.)

Raised expectations also affect implementing organizations, who can also experience burnout. For example, work with PRA in Brazil did not lead to the magnificent results reported from places like India and Kenya, and did lead to some organizational depression and doubt. This in turn led colleagues and myself to question the assumptions of social landscapes that are implicit in many examples of participatory planning (Sidersky and Guijt 1999). In northeast Brazil, we did not have the scale or type of social organization prevalent in parts of India, for example, that had driven the early PRA work and given the world its images of what PRA could be and could achieve. We all know that social conditions, political histories and culturally determined communication shape methodology and outcomes, yet somehow still expect (and are certainly expected to deliver to donors) quick and widespread results.

From planning (shoddy) one-offs to continual learning and quality assurance

While the diversity of context has led to much diversity of practice, two features are worrying. First, the standardization of method and outcome continues, and with it the assumptions we hold about how social change occurs as a result. My main concern in this is the ongoing focus on appraisal with some increased interest in planning, to the detriment of adequate experience with ongoing appraisals and updating planning and deepening learning. Working more recently on participatory monitoring as a way to force people to think more systemically about avoiding one-off community plans has led me to conclude that 'PRA' in all its diversity is intensely weak at looking at long-term processes of learning. What theories of learning do we carry with us implicitly? How do we think it occurs, with whom and when? How do people update their insights and how is social consensus recreated? These questions continue to intrigue me.

The second feature of practice that concerns me is the ongoing absence of quality standards – around which all that I have written above is focused. It is no longer, for me, a matter of 'if' it should happen. PRA and the organizations holding it up as a symbol of good, democratic, sustainable practice must be as subject to critical scrutiny as the working methods of the World Bank or multinational companies, our so-called democracies, etc, that are ripped into with glee. When will the world of PRA start setting standards? And who should do it and how should this happen? These are complex questions – establishing norms will inevitably lead to a clashing of social and organizational practices as new, commonly shared ones are forged.

PRA now for me?

My experiences of PRA makes me view it as an extremely diverse set of practices and principles, making it impossible to use the PRA label – and thus PRA is something that I no longer claim to do. I am interested in questions of citizen engagement and citizen apathy, of interactive policy making and inter-organizational and inter-stakeholder learning. All these are clearly related to questions of participation. Depending on the task at hand, I use some principles and some methods – when I feel they will make a critical difference. But I no longer 'do' PRA, I am not a 'PRA' trainer.

For me, 'it' is not about a set of methods or a certain workshop format or a specific output or outcome. I guide myself with the 'Five Cs':

- Clarity of objective – to ensure the purpose and intention of engaging people in new ways is clear.
- Communication – to maintain the focus on sharing and avoid reducing the process of data or information.
- Commitment – to seeing the process through.
- Creativity – to find ways to express, communicate, analyse.
- Critical reflection – to ensure that the validity and 'so what?' factor of information is questioned and personal intentions are continually scrutinized.

Notes

[1] I appreciate the problems of speaking in the 'we' form. I use this to describe my personal memory of our collective discussions.
[2] With thanks to Annemarie Groot for some critical comments.

References

Sidersky, P. and Guijt, I. (1999) 'Matching participatory agricultural development with the social landscape of northeast Brazil', in Hinchcliffe, F., Thompson, J., Pretty, J.N., Guijt, I. and Shah, P. (eds), *Fertile Ground: the impacts of participatory watershed management*, ITDG Publishing, London.

Welbourn, A. (1991) 'RRA and the analysis of difference', in *RRA Notes*, 14:14–23.

CHAPTER 13

Regis M. Gwaba

Reflecting on PRA, participation and gender

My path into PRA

It was like learning about a new fashion trend. A friend of mine who had been in agricultural research for a long time told me about the new research method that did not involve preparation of 'predetermined, rigid question-naires'. He offered to let me join a research team that was preparing for an assessment of 'agricultural supply response under structural adjustment in a gender perspective'. Having been involved in financing agricultural production, it was an interesting opportunity for me to experience the new research method and to understand the perception of the community of agricultural market-ing under structural adjustment. Thus began my association with Participa-tory Rural Appraisal (PRA) and my interest in gender and participation.

What did PRA mean to me? I had the advantage of observing the use of tools and techniques before reading the literature. To me, it meant getting all the people present to take an active part. Before I explore my reflection on this issue, I think it is important for me to look at what I later came to understand as the meaning of participation from the perspective of most of the community members that I have interacted with.

Understanding participation from a community perspective

In one of the Zambian languages, participation is translated as 'to be a part of or to give oneself to what is going on'. With this definition, participation means that all community members are part of or give themselves to what is going on in the community. Building on the community definition of 'participation', PRA practitioners solicit and encourage the participation of all the people they interact with during PRA. However, for all community members to be 'part of or give themselves to what is going on' requires skill on the part of the facilitator to promote this participation. It also requires certain levels of understanding of the people one is working with.

The 'community' in PRA

My experience has been that when one talks about a community, there is an implication that this is one group. Hidden within this 'one group belief' is the notion that the community is homogeneous. Indeed, it is a lot easier to treat the community in this way. The reality, however, is that there are such significant differences within any given community that these need to be taken into account when using PRA methods and tools.

In an urban setting, people come from various backgrounds with different interests and values. They become 'a community' only by virtue of proximity within a neighbourhood. This does not imply that there are no areas of commonality within these communities. However, because of the diverse backgrounds of its members there are significant differences, more significant than those in rural areas, where there may be greater homogeneity as a result of kinship, language and culture. In both rural and urban settings, the community is a heterogeneous group, comprising men, women, youths and children. Communities themselves may differentiate between their members in terms of levels of wealth and well-being, marital status and many other criteria.

Making room for difference

One of my experiences with the treatment of a community as a homogeneous group was during a research exercise using PRA tools in the Northern Province of Zambia. The idea was to find out community perceptions about the impact of agricultural market liberalization on the livelihood of a community that had hitherto been dependent on a more centrally controlled marketing system for agricultural produce. Our strategy was to conduct focus group discussions and use other visualization tools with small mixed-sex groups. Throughout the discussion the men would be the first to make their point. The women would confirm it. Much as we tried, we were unable to get the women to take the lead on any topic that we introduced. For example, the men insisted that their main problem was the lack of a market for their crops. The women confirmed this, but did not volunteer any problems other than those already suggested by the men. The problem of marketing was ranked as number one for the community.

In another case, we had conducted all the exercises in mixed groups when we realized that there were underlying issues and perceptions within the community that seemed to be hindering free exchange. We debated whether we should separate women and men or continue the discussion and try to draw out participation from the women. Our dilemma was time. This was a research exercise. Eventually we decided to work with three groups separately and hold a report-back session with a large group, during which we would allow each group to present what they perceived to be the community problems and to rank these problems. During this session, we also aimed to establish whether there was a link between the problems identified by different groups.

The discussion in the plenary session did not yield a high level of participation from the women either. The first barrier was the seating arrangement. The women came to join the men, who were already in a semicircle. Even though this was broken, the women were a bit far away from the facilitator. Talking to the women meant half turning in order for all the women to see the facilitator. The next barrier was that women were in the minority, about half the number of men. A third was time. The plenary session took place at 2pm and the meeting had been going on since 10am.

We tried to get the women to participate by focusing first on the issues they'd raised in their group. One of these issues was the lack of female health workers at the clinic. Women had said that they felt it was embarrassing to be attended to by a male nurse during child labour. By focusing on the consequences of this problem, we hoped that women would begin to open up and develop confidence to discuss other community-wide issues. However, because of time constraints we were not able to achieve this. Much as we had some input from women in the identification of problems, more time would have allowed us to have a more fruitful interaction.

Learning from experience

Learning from these experiences of the difficulties of getting everyone to participate when we worked with single groups composed of men and women, we tried a different method of working with the community. This was through dividing the community according to a criterion that they decided and agreed upon. In one community, the following criteria for the establishment of groups were agreed upon:

1 First according to sex (two groups of male and female).
2 Second according to age. (This separated the youths from the adults and within the adult group a distinction was made between the elderly and the relatively young adults.)
3 The third criterion was for the separation of the youths according to marital status. (This gave us four groups of youths: single female youths, single male youths, married female youths and married male youths.)

It was interesting to discover that when these criteria were applied to group formation, the level of participation by individual group members was very high. As one of the youths put it, 'It is difficult to talk in front of those old men as some of them are mischievous and can work on you at night.' This was with reference to the perception among the youths that some of the adult men practise witchcraft. Among their own peers, the discussions with the youths were lively with a lot of humour. The level of participation among the women was also very high. However, for the adult women, the initial level of participation was slow. This increased only after a few women had been participating for some time and the other women started to develop confidence to speak.

The community with which we worked for this exercise was only a few kilometres away from the one we had worked with earlier – the community that had highlighted marketing of agricultural produce as the biggest problem they were facing. In contrast, in the groups decided according to community criteria, different perceptions emerged. Among the male youth, the highest-ranking problem was the problem of improving soil fertility. The issue of agricultural marketing was secondary. For the women, the issue of being 'suppressed' by men was their major problem and one that affects their day-to-day existence, as they cannot take any decisions without the consent of a man.

According to the women, all the best parts of the food are given to the husband, irrespective of food availability within a household. Women and children eat the remainder. As one woman said, 'If your husband is good, then he will offer you and the children part of the best food. But he should not reveal this information as he will be considered weak and his friends will advise him that his wife has not been brought up properly.' Women pointed out that the issue of sharing food is the main problem that causes their children to have inadequate quantities of good, healthy food. In the plenary session, the men confirmed this, but argued that it was according to tradition and in any case the men are the ones who have to do heavy manual labour and therefore require better food.

It was evident from this that the perceptions of the community can be different if the groups are not separated. It also makes it easy to encourage the participation of all in a group with which they are comfortable or share the same characteristics.

Challenges of working with different groups

While working with the different groups, the women and youth specifically requested that some of the issues that they raised should not be presented during plenary sessions with the large group. They were afraid of being identified as the source of some of the controversial issues and feared possible repercussions in the absence of the PRA team. This points to the need to separate the different groups of people within each community in order to find out some of these views which would not normally come out. Some of the points that they did not wish to be brought out were crucial in the long-term development of the community. For example, the youths were particularly uncomfortable with the issue of youth participation in the community-based organization (CBO) being discussed in plenary sessions. The youths felt that they had the zeal and energy to carry out some tasks that could not be done by the elderly in their society. However, they feared that they would be seen as rebellious and therefore undesirables.

During plenary sessions, we had a chance to plan a strategy on how to comply with such requests and at the same time seek community consensus on the issues raised. An interesting discussion ensued during one of the report-back sessions, which centred on family planning. According to the adult men's group, the problem of lack of child spacing was caused by the women's failure to follow traditional teaching on family planning. We were able to solicit and get the response of women on this issue. According to the women, the problem lay with men who expected the women to take care of family planning needs alone. This was an avenue for sharing a rather sensitive 'women's issue'. Throughout this discussion, the men kept on interjecting and disputing what the women said. At the end of the day we were able to get the men and women to share their perceptions and acknowledge the need for working together on issues of family planning.

The crucial point is that, partially as a result of the participation momentum created during group discussions, women and youth participation was noticeably more than if we had worked with one mixed group, as was the case in the North Western Province example. The challenge in this case is facilitating the discussion on the differences and creating harmony while maintaining the momentum of participation.

Setting the pace for participation

One of my other experiences has been the power of participatory tools in building confidence and in providing an avenue for women to air their views on issues that affect them. In both the cases I have highlighted above, I have observed that in a single-sex group, women generally start very cautiously, with a few developing confidence early, and the majority of them taking time to fully participate and express their views. When the women are in a mixed group with men, some of them tended to merely confirm what the men said without really expressing themselves on issues.

The pace at which people participate is different. Some will be quick to say what they think, while others will be slow. From my experience, this is caused by various factors. In one community in the Northern Province, the community leaders (of various positions from village head to leaders of groups), the rich, men and the wives of leaders tend to open up quite quickly compared to the rest of the people. I am going to describe this as the 'pace-setting phenomenon'. This pace setting is crucial in view of the limited time a PRA facilitator spends within the community.

In the North Western Province case, it was difficult to get all the community members to participate. The leaders and the prominent people set the pace of the discussion in that society and it became difficult to change this pace, as time was also a major constraint. We more or less ended up with the views of a few members of the community. In both the cases described above, one of our major problems was how to manage our time to facilitate participation by all the community members we interacted with.

Ensuring that gender is addressed

Gender is a crucial aspect to consider during PRA. Information on gender issues can provide in-depth understanding of a community. To fully incorporate gender, we need to revisit how we plan for and conduct PRAs. From my experiences some important questions need to be answered. Among these are the following:

- Do the tools and techniques that we use do justice to gender?
- Do we allow enough time to explore gender issues in view of the different paces at which people are able to relax and participate?
- Is the time during feedback sessions adequate to promote triangulation and further exploration of gender issues by different groups?

With a lot of focus on gender in the past few years, it becomes crucial that as PRA practitioners we focus more on the incorporation of gender in PRA through sharing of techniques that have been successful in bringing out gender issues.

Looking back

Reflecting on my experiences since the first PRA exercise I conducted in the Northern Province, I have found that my journey has involved a lot of learning, reflection and trying to improve on how I integrate gender and participation while learning from the community I interact with. The difficulties I have faced have regenerated my interest in participation, and this reinforces my belief that through participation everyone can exercise their 'right and power to decide'.

CHAPTER 14
Katja Jassey

PRA from an end-user's perspective

These reflections come from someone who has had to experience the wealth of Participatory Rural Appraisal (PRA) from behind desks in offices on the sixth and seventh floors in two big cities. I am the real end user, I would say, as the reports were probably read and used with much greater enthusiasm by me than by people back in the communities from which they came.

The setting for the first story is eastern and southern Africa, from 1994 to 1997. I was working as a socio-economist at a regional FAO programme that had a number of aims, one being participatory technology development. We were all engaged in trying to develop more appropriate technologies. The engineers working with the programme had been exposed to training in PRA and on-farm trials by my predecessor, so I was by no means treading on virgin ground when it came to advocacy for bringing farmers' perspectives into the research (although it should be stated here that our approach was purely instrumental and had nothing to do with the empowerment of people).

'Commanding' the troops

After the first year, we learnt that we were going to be merged into an even more encompassing regional programme, working with participatory methods around everything that happens at farm level. We were supposed to work in two field sites in every country. In order to do things right (I had read all the textbooks and thought I knew what was required of me...), we started off with something that we decided to call a participatory baseline in two places: one in Zimbabwe, the other in Tanzania. We were going to map the situation, get an idea of priorities, get to know the people and they would get to know us. A team of two was sent off to each site: one social scientist with PRA experience, and one agricultural engineer. These were identified in competition (not hand-picked from a friendship or long-standing relationship with the programme) and carefully prepared by myself (the junior anthropologist with a wealth of experience).

94

I was convinced that staying with the community was paramount, so the researchers were not allowed to lodge at the hotel in the nearest town, nor were they allowed to do a quick in-and-out job. My minimum requirement was four weeks, even though I felt that this was bordering on the quick and dirty. My white face, complete lack of any local language skills and four-year-old daughter made me feel that I should stay behind in Harare and not get in the way of their work. I had realized that I had few skills to offer that weren't already in abundance in the country. I'd be lying if I said that they were happy troopers going out, with their complete camping equipment, run-down old cars (our car fleet was in complete disarray due to what could be termed 'ownership' problems) and with the prospect of getting stuck in the mud where the rain had washed the road away. Naturally we opted for the poor, remote areas, off the tarmac road, since we had read that this is what you're supposed to do in one of Chambers' books. In retrospect I suppose it made for good stories, and plenty of film was used on pictures portraying their heroism.

Pleased at first

The reports they brought back were perfect. They'd done all the required exercises: mapping, seasonal charts, transect walks, focus group discussions, informal interviews, etc. Some information was even clear-cut policy messages – for example, in Zimbabwe not a single farm implement had been purchased since the abolishment of subsidies many years ago, implements of which they were in desperate need. In Tanzania, they had managed to identify excellent crop processing practices related to indigenous knowledge (brownie points from the anthropologist). Women, men and the youths had been allowed to voice their opinions separately. The researchers' reflections over the method were wise.

They had, as so many before them, encountered the difficulty of getting an open discussion around the different groups' findings. During community presentation the standard practice was to let the youths present first, then women, finally men and afterwards the chief did a summing up of what he felt should go into the report or what the community should make their priority. How to handle that I still don't know (but maybe it doesn't need handling, maybe it's just my Western way of seeing democracy that's blurring my vision). They also felt that the most interesting information was usually to be found during the informal sessions when you were in somebody's field, not during the more formal exercises (no matter how relaxed you try to be). This of course warmed my heart, as one who still believed in participant observation as the superior method. In short, I was very pleased and felt we had good material at our disposal.

Blueprint?

But this was only the beginning. Our programme continued with a number of PRAs in all the places that were going to become future field sites for experimentation. And it was as these reports started to come in that my colleagues and I began to realize that they were almost identical! Water was almost always the top priority, usually followed closely by farm power in terms of animal draught power. So why bother to do these PRA exercises? Differences in priorities could usually be related to researchers' priorities. When a team member had a history, for example in water harvesting, then usually that could be seen in the communities' list of priorities.

I don't think this was done on purpose in any way. The whole point of PRA is that you engage as a person (at least to some extent) and even if you're 'handing over the stick', you are still much more 'present' (and possibly influential) than during a questionnaire type of survey. It was also striking how similar the 'solutions' were. Sometimes I felt as if all of Africa had been turned into a gigantic development blueprint project, and the worst part of it was that it was the minds of people that we had processed through our Xerox machine; even people in the remotest villages. Or were these the obvious, natural and 'authentic' answers? But how could 'Let's have a micro-credit project' be the only answer in all cases at all times?

Not that we let any of this stop us. But it did make me think. What was so bad about, for example, Rapid Rural Appraisal (RRA) that we had to drop it from programmes like the one I was involved in? PRA takes a lot of valuable time from hard-working people. How can I ask for that if all the answers are the same anyway? Would I ever be able to trust the outcomes of a PRA exercise again (that I hadn't been involved in personally) knowing how easy it is to influence the results? Why did the solutions as prescribed by people leave me feeling hollow and disappointed? Was it because I was naive enough to expect something more dramatic, original and indigenous, or because they were in fact nothing but fading echoes of former projects?

New learning from stories and video techniques

Personally I have never felt entirely comfortable doing ranking exercises or drawing diagrams. I literally shrink with discomfort when the obligatory workshop cards are dealt out: write down your expectation, wish or question in three words and we'll let it not only guide our workshop but also use it for evaluation at the end. I understand why; it is definitely appealing to have a sense of order, but to me most of these exercises are as comfortable as a straitjacket. I prefer stories, telling them and listening to them, which is why I chose to go out into the field on my own 'empowerment' crusade with the aim of opening up communication between the powerless and those in power, aided by a video camera.

My mission was to team up with United Nations Volunteers (UNVs) and train a group of landless farm labourers and tenants in video techniques in a poor area in southern Zimbabwe. This area had a history of being the leisure area for gamblers and those looking for prostitutes. The residents were mainly young men, single mothers, children and grandparents. It was not a small-scale farming area, but one of poorer middle-sized farms without mechanization or irrigation. We teamed up with a group of both women and men of different ages and with different access to material wealth (I will refrain from dwelling on the complexities of that aspect here). And I did learn a few things that no PRA exercise had taught me.

At first I was a bit disheartened at the fact that the only story they wanted to tell was the one about the hardship that they experienced. We asked them countless times about good activities or kind and brave people in their society, thinking that anyone who could make a life under those conditions must be a fantastic and strong person. But they were very reluctant to admit to anything like that. Things were horrible, full stop. And the solutions they could see to their problem were pretty much the same as I had heard so many times before – we should start a savings scheme or have some sort of income-generating project making mats or knitting sweaters.

The difference was that doing this through a conventional video training exercise opened up questions that I normally wouldn't ask, questions such as 'What audience do you want to reach and why?' These are fundamental issues if you want to make a video. To get a message through you have to be very clear about why you want to say something, what your message is and who you are targeting, and this is something that I had never experienced in a PRA exercise. This community said that they had absolutely no interest in reaching other communities or even policy makers. The people they wanted to reach were donors. Why? Because donors are compassionate people and it's their mandate to help us. So clear, so distinct and so very revealing. After all, the very basic fundament behind all communication, no matter how we dress up our interactions, is that we always say a specific thing in a certain way depending on what we want to accomplish and who we want to reach. Obviously our statement is subsequently interpreted differently depending on how we are viewed and the given context. I think it was their hope that we, the donors, would look upon them as needy people deserving our help.

Another lesson that I learnt during a completely different video exercise, making a film about Tanzanian women farmers on a study trip to Vietnam, was that for some people the idea of who 'we' are (white development people born and bred in the North) is somewhat vague. One of my co-travellers expressed in our film her amazement when she said, 'Before coming here I always saw white people as somebody coming and going, but now I've seen for myself that they also have farms, husbands and children and that they work the same like us!' What that does for any possible exchange of views during a PRA exercise leaves much to the imagination...

What was 'participatory' about the exercises?

With all of this boiling in my head, I returned to a different post back home in Europe. Participation was once again one of my key areas, although this time from an even longer distance. I was faced with a situation where I was supposed to advocate the use of participatory methods, preferably on a large scale, as according to our policies, poor people should inform our work as much as possible. To my surprise, agencies like the World Bank were steaming ahead and seemingly spearheading participation in development. My surprise came partly from the fact that I had noted little of this interest during my time in the 'field'. I found myself sitting on two chairs. On the one hand, I honestly felt that the Participatory Poverty Assessments (PPAs) were a step in the right direction. But on the other hand, I had a feeling of compromising myself when arranging seminars and handing out publications with such pretentious titles as 'Voices of the Poor' – especially when many of my co-workers were quite enthusiastic about these voices.

I think that what I had learnt and what bothered me the most was that we seemed to label these exercises 'participatory' when in fact many times the only thing 'participatory' about them was that primary stakeholders had been allowed to produce information about themselves through various participatory techniques (such as PRA). The control over what to do with this information is seldom handed over. One of the reasons for this is that national issues can't be handled at local level. This may be true, but it seems to me that so often we are completely oblivious to the context in which this information was produced, not to mention the fact that we may under no circumstances purport to speak with the 'voices of the poor' as if these were unmediated, authentic voices. I now knew that whatever was said during a PRA exercise was said in a specific situation, by one person to another, and the person who made the statement had a reason for saying so at that time. Whatever was said had usually been somewhat translated or transformed by a mediating researcher or development worker. It was therefore neither the direct voice of a poor person or even necessarily something they would like us to quote in a completely different situation. At the same time, I do realize and understand that these narratives strike a chord with many development actors. Maybe they bring a feeling of blood, sweat and tears, a motivation to go on working?

The poor are no experts – but they have the right to choice and self-determination

I think that what I wish today was that I didn't have to go along with ideas like 'the poor are the true poverty experts' in order to let them have a say. I really don't think that they are poverty experts at all. They are experts at surviving under their specific circumstances, as we all are, but they know as little about all the mechanisms surrounding the production and re-production of poverty as the next person. In a way, we make it simple for ourselves by focusing so many of our poverty definitions and measurements on poor people, or on what it is to be poor, as it leads our attention away from other more fundamental structural issues, like who has something to gain from poverty.

What I would like to see is a situation where people would have a say, and where PRA could be used, not because they are experts, but because they should have the right to decide about their own life, and to make stupid or clever decisions as they choose.[1] If they choose to reproduce dominant ideas in forms of projects that they have seen before then that is their prerogative. It is not for me to say no. Besides, I would probably do the same myself if the tables were turned and someone showed up on my doorstep asking for solutions for a better life. We mustn't fool ourselves into believing that a simple technique like PRA can change decades-old – sometimes centuries-old – discourses on social and economic structures and realities.

Where we must go

Whether the right to have a say regardless of status or expert knowledge will come in the wake of all the talk about 'rights' and 'citizenship' that seems to be the latest development fad remains to be seen; and what we will do if people are granted that right only for it to be taken over by some groups within the community, region or nation to improve their positions at the cost of others. Participatory development is difficult, and if on top of that we attempt to render a form of aid that has been technical for ages into something political, then we are really skating on thin ice. But is that not the place where must take our business if we really want to make a change?

Note

[1] Obviously the whole notion of 'community' or 'them' is absurd, as in any given social situation there will be a number of interlinked and superimposed categories of richer, poorer, women, men, old, young, etc. But that is beyond the scope of these reflections.

CHAPTER 15

Barbara Kaim

Personal reflections – on petrol queue time

I am writing this chapter while sitting in a petrol queue. I've spent the past three hours here, biding my time reflecting on what the shortage of foreign currency and fuel in Zimbabwe, and the build-up to an election which just may topple an increasingly unpopular leadership, has to do with my personal/professional/political experiences in using participatory approaches in Zimbabwe – the topic of this chapter. I've concluded that the one has a lot to do with the other and I certainly have some time – petrol queue time – to explore this further.

I begin with a fantasy. I imagine what it would be like to mobilize everyone in this queue, in all queues in Harare, or better still in Zimbabwe, to undertake a few flow diagrams on the causes and effects of the present fuel shortages, then do an institutional analysis of the organizations responsible for the shortages, triangulate this information by possibly doing a matrix ranking and then move towards developing an action plan...

Beginnings

My personal, political and professional aspirations merge. I think about the first time I went to a Participatory Rural Appraisal (PRA) Network of Zimbabwe meeting, sometime in the mid-1990s. Everyone in that meeting was using participatory approaches in either agriculture or resource management. I was the only non-agriculture person there, with experience in using popular education techniques in HIV/AIDS work, but aware of its limitations, searching for additional approaches/tools/techniques to address issues of gender and power inequity, and ways of supporting people in changing their personal attitudes and sexual behaviour.

Those first few years in the Network were exciting, energizing, sometimes lonely, as I grappled with how to integrate PRA into the health/education sector. I was in the early stages of developing a programme on adolescent reproductive health and incorporated many of the PRA principles and tools into my work. I got involved in training and, inevitably, began to work closely with my colleagues in the HIV/AIDS/reproductive health community in sharing skills and experiences in participatory approaches. The Network membership shifted and became more inter-sectoral. Sharing of experiences became – and continues to be – an essential ingredient in my work.

The Adolescent Reproductive Health Project

Throughout this time, I was co-ordinating a programme on adolescent reproductive health education, working through a local non-governmental organization (NGO), the Training and Research Support Centre (TARSC). I have learnt a lot about the use of participatory approaches through this programme. It has been both exhilarating and sobering – sometimes both at the same time. Mostly exhilarating when working at community level; more restrained when dealing with issues of 'scaling up' or 'institutionalizing' of lessons learnt, especially when working with government. It is worth spending some time exploring this further.

The Adolescent Reproductive Health Project (ARHEP) was formed in response to the growing crisis of HIV/AIDS and other reproductive health issues in Zimbabwe, and their impact on young people. It is currently estimated that 23% of sexually active adults, or about 10% of the total population, are HIV-positive, with about 1600 deaths and 2000 new infections every week. With youth constituting about 40% of the population, figures show that 30% of girls aged 15–19 years are sexually active, with this percentage rising to 50% by age 18.8 years. Only 7.5% of girls and 11.4% of boys in the 15–19 year age group are using a modern contraceptive method. The vulnerability of these young people puts them at risk of contracting sexually transmitted diseases (STDs) or HIV/AIDS, or facing unwanted pregnancies, illegal abortions, infanticide and other reproductive health problems.

In this context, in early 1997 ARHEP began PRA research in a number of rural secondary schools in which we aimed to explore students' reproductive health needs and concerns, where they go for information and support, and to identify ways of strengthening existing information to adolescents. We also consciously tried to build the capacity of, and provide technical support to, a wide range of civic groups and government departments, especially in the Ministries of Education and Health.

Our initial research resulted in the production of a classroom-based activity pack for secondary school students called 'Auntie Stella'. Based on the question-and-answer format of letters to an 'agony aunt', the pack focuses on a range of issues, including normal reproductive development, social and economic pressures to have sex, gender roles, forced sex, communication in relationships and with parents, pregnancy, infertility, cervical cancer, HIV/AIDS and STDs. Both the content and the design of the pack came out of an intensive PRA process with students and teachers in four secondary schools over a period of four months.

The outcome of pilot testing 'Auntie Stella' in an additional eight schools was very encouraging. Students and their teachers noted an increase in communication with parents, community members and peers, a greater confidence and ability to make informed decisions and take initiative, and an enhanced ability to advise peers and younger siblings on a range of reproductive health issues. The overall consensus – reinforced by a participatory evaluation of the ARHEP programme – was that 'Auntie Stella' was an important contribution to ARH education and was ready for wider distribution.

Securing institutional ownership

The Ministry of Education was key to this process. This had already been acknowledged in our discussions with the Ministry two years earlier, when we signed a working agreement with them and placed a reproductive health education officer at head office to work with TARSC in pilot-testing 'Auntie Stella'. However, two years down the road and still no institution actually 'owned' 'Auntie Stella'. TARSC had neither the infrastructure nor the mandate to disseminate the pack on a wider scale. The Ministry, although keen to implement a policy developed in the early 1990s to introduce AIDS education in all primary and secondary schools in the country, was dragging its feet. 'Auntie Stella', they said, despite its evident successes, 'had not gone through the correct channels', the material had not been 'vetted'. In talking openly about sex, in mentioning sensitive issues such as the use of condoms or masturbation, the education pack was in danger of threatening the Ministry's stakeholders and, in particular, the church leadership (a strong lobby group with conservative views on reproductive health education).

There was clearly a conflict of views between various key players: what the youths themselves had said so eloquently about their reproductive health needs and concerns, and what policy makers were saying was acceptable in terms of reproductive health education policy.

To deal with this tension, in early 2000, TARSC entered into high-level discussions with the Ministries of Education and Health, focusing on positive approaches to ARH education (including, but not exclusively, 'Auntie Stella'), institutional roles and capacities, and co-ordination between the different agencies. Our hope was that these inter-ministerial meetings would, among other things, clarify ARHEP's future medium- and long-term work with them and help move the debate on the content of ARH education towards some conclusion.

This is, however, a difficult time in which to be working with government. As elections draw near, government officials are lying low, wary of addressing any new or sensitive issue for fear of rocking an already water-logged boat. Add to this the usual bureaucratic, top-down culture of this government, the antithesis of the ABCs of PRA, and it is clear that the way forward will be ponderously slow.

Lessons for 'scaling up'

There are many lessons ARHEP can draw from this experience. While local initiatives are useful in building approaches and ideas, given the scale of the adolescent reproductive health problem in Zimbabwe, government and civic groups have given inadequate attention to how these initiatives can be scaled up to national level. ARHEP now recognizes that we got into the Ministry of Education through the back door and that we were fortunate to have proven the credibility of 'Auntie Stella' before it was scrutinized by their Curriculum Development Unit. However, the very success of the pack – thanks to the participatory nature of the work we did with the youth – is a threat to policy makers.

Even though we placed an education officer in the Ministry to assist in the implementation of the programme, we didn't start early enough in building alliances with key Ministry officials and advocating our approach. We were also not sufficiently proactive in exploring and exploiting opportunities for strategic co-operation with other players in the field of ARH education. As a result, even though the concept of the 'Auntie Stella' pack has been praised by many, there is no clear strategy for how it can be distributed on a larger scale.

There is, however, a twist to this tale, an irony of sorts. 'Auntie Stella' may have been designed with and for school-going youth, but increasingly it is being used by young people in out-of-school contact points throughout the country – at youth-friendly clinics, in family planning centres, AIDS support groups, sex abuse clinics and with street childrens' associations. The feedback from these groups is that the pack is equally relevant in their contexts. Irrespective of the outcome of ARHEP's discussions with government, 'Auntie Stella' is already going national.

Making a difference

These experiences with ARHEP have influenced my personal journey with PRA. I remain solidly committed to using participatory approaches in my work and in my life. But I still have concerns. About the meaning of 'participation' and how often I've seen it abused, even unintentionally. About the value of PRA training and the motivation of PRA practitioners (as Pauline Hobane, a colleague and friend, once said to me – she, in turn, inspired by Shakespeare – 'some people are born PRA practitioners, some people acquire PRA skills and some people have PRA thrust upon them'). I also think we have a long way to go in addressing gender and power inequities at all levels. This is not only of concern to me in the work I do in sexual and reproductive health; it also poses the question of how successful participatory approaches have been in challenging the status quo. These are important issues and ones that I/we need to continue thinking about and acting upon.

I am home now, having got to the front of the petrol queue. I wish I could say that they filled my tank to the brim, but they didn't. Restricted to only Z$400 (a little over US$10), my tank is now half full. It's a good metaphor for the ARHEP programme. We are moving forward, sometimes in unpredictable ways, sometimes in ways that are slow and tedious and restricted by the political and economic climate, the bureaucratic nature of government and our own personal limitations. But we are participating in a process of change and that's what matters. Our programmatic tank is also half full. Better than half empty.

CHAPTER 16
Humera Malik

Sharing my dilemmas: mixed messages on PRA and participation

As part of a process of reflection, learning and sharing, I have documented in this chapter my personal experiences and observations of Participatory Rural Appraisal (PRA) work and development initiatives undertaken by various stakeholders. These stakeholders include government, international and national donors, and non-governmental organizations (NGOs)/community-based organizations (CBOs) (nowadays also known as civil society organizations or CSOs) working at national or local level. I have put individuals working in all these organizations at various levels as a separate category of stakeholders of development.

First, I would like to explain how I became involved with PRA. In 1992, I got involved with the approach through a training course organized by the Pakistan–Swiss Potato Development Project, facilitated by representatives from the Institute for Environment and Development (IIED), Jules Pretty and Irene Guijt. At that time I worked with a national NGO which was working for rural development and on policy issues, advocating to bring up front the concerns of common people.

After this training course I joined an international organization, Action-Aid, and started working in one of the very poor rural areas for development. Practical application of PRA facilitated community mobilization and an empowerment process in the area. It was very challenging and thrilling for me. Seeing the poorest and most vulnerable people, including women, challenge power structures was so encouraging. I was so confident that change is possible and that PRA is an approach that can facilitate this process.

The PRA approach not only brought about changes at the community level, but also within the organization, leading to a major practical change in organizational culture. Two basic principles of PRA – innovation and flexibility – work as magic for me in my personal life also. Testing, exploring and experimenting by myself for more learning and reflection were key factors of my involvement with this approach.

105

In this chapter, I focus more on my last two years of involvement and activities. One major reason for this is that there have been so many absorbing (sad and happy) things happening in Pakistan in the development sector. For example, there has been large-scale mushrooming of CSOs/NGOs, efforts by the government to suppress the CSO/NGO movement through legal restrictions, conflicts between CSOs/NGOs, conflicts within CSOs/NGOs, army takeover and prominent CSO/NGO representatives joining government.

Along with all these astonishing developments, there has been a clear shift of emphasis. Many donors, government organizations, NGOs, and in many cases private profit-oriented consulting firms, are now requesting, requiring and sometimes pushing that participatory approaches, specifically PRA, be used in their programmes and projects for sustainable development processes. This brings a lot of opportunities as well as dangers. Opportunities are related to initiating the process of change, empowerment of disadvantaged people, etc. Whereas dangers include misusing this term, pushing for PRA in a top-down mode, and using it without understanding its philosophy and its implications. The rapid growth or rather spread of PRA in various fields of life has also raised many questions for development practitioners.

My reflections cover three levels:

1 On personal and professional values, norms, attitude, behaviour and ethics.
2 Communities, raising questions at that level about: Whose empowerment? What would be the consequence of communities' empowerment? Are we ready to manage that empowerment? Or are we still thinking of controlling empowerment? Are we ready to disempower ourselves?
3 On organizational culture, structures, styles and practices of management in the context of claims to be 'learning organizations' or 'transforming organizations'.

Different personal opinions and feelings: some views to consider

Definitions of terms such as 'development', 'empowerment' and also 'PRA' have become very complicated over the past two years. Everyone has his or her own interpretation of these terms and keeps changing it with the passage of time, with different people and in different situations. It is essential to understand these complexities if someone has to work for development or for sustainable processes of change.

What follows are a few issues and messages conveyed to me during the past two years by friends, colleagues and development professionals (directly or indirectly). These are very important to deliberate on, especially in the context of participation and PRA.

- Compromise on principles, values and sometimes on participatory process is not wrong. Keep balance, we should not take a hard line. Professionalism requires compromise and without compromise it is emotionalism. Hard reality is to keep a balance between professionalism and emotionalism. (Still after ten years of work experience, I don't know what is professionalism and emotionalism in development, and what is the difference between the two.)
- If you will not do it, someone else will, and in that case it would be worse, so you had better do it and try to do it in a better way. For example, doing PRA training in two days, doing PRA with communities in two days, two days training is better than no training, etc.
- Participatory process, empowerment and development within the organization and for communities all depend on one position – the top manager. If he or she is willing, fine – if not, forget about it and adopt his or her interpretation of participation, empowerment, etc. If you resist or show any resentment, people will challenge your attitude and will label you as non-participatory, or a person challenging the authority of seniors, and it is against work ethics.
- Your definition of the right attitude and behaviour may not always be right for others. Who are you to judge what is right and what is wrong?
- Your definition of the right work ethics may not be right for others. Who are you to judge what is right and what is wrong?
- Organizational issues are like domestic (internal) issues. No one has the right to interfere in domestic issues. For example, if an organization is threatening its staff for raising their voice against non-participatory policies, structures, etc., the solution is not in shouting or complaining. If you are not comfortable, leave that organization. Don't ask for transparent or public accountability. (Thus a person who is responsible for the livelihood of six to eight people has no right to raise their voice.) Accountability is for global (external) issues. Do whatever you want to do about global or external issues, such as organize workshops or seminars, develop indicators or publish reports/books.
- PRA is only for communities. Go and have fun with them. It is not for organizations and no one has the right to question organizations because it is a domestic or internal issue.

Given below are a few personal experiences or reflections on my work in different circumstances, which highlight issues related to some of the above-mentioned messages. To find out what is right, what is wrong and why, is for the readers of this chapter to think, analyse and discuss.

Unfavourable and favourable environments

I want to share an experience of work in an environmental rehabilitation project funded by an international donor. There are many stakeholders of the project such as the government, NGO, community and a private consulting firm. Every one has an independent role to play, but they are also dependent on each other. No partner or stakeholder can work without each other's support. The goal of the project is rehabilitation of natural resources on a sustainable basis through community participation.

It was important to develop a common understanding at the beginning of the project about: What is participation? What is PRA? What is empowerment of communities? However, it was a very difficult and time-consuming task. All the stakeholders have different understandings about their work and have also had different training. Like many projects, it is also a time-bound project, seven years in length. Guiding documents or reference documents for the implementation of this project are different for different stakeholders, such as the government PC1,[1] the National Conservation Strategy[2] and Village Development Plans.[3]

It was very difficult for me to adjust within that environment. It was an environment where stakeholders have only one common objective, that is to implement the project within the given time frame, but each stakeholder had their own way or style of work and their own principles of work. They were not willing to develop a common understanding about work approach, principles, various terms, etc. What was right for one was not necessarily right for others. Although I knew this, I was not sure what to do. Everything was different from my understanding of the participatory development process, which I had learned over the past ten years of my work experience.

For instance, I was asked by my seniors and colleagues to conduct or organize PRA training for staff within two days, to do PRA with communities for data collection, and to develop formats and manuals for PRA. I was also asked to organize the participation of communities for labour work, to ask communities to organize and then the project would give incentives for environmental rehabilitation.

This frustrated me so much that I wanted to leave the project. I shared my feelings with many friends. However, I continued my efforts to bring change, sometimes more vigorously and sometimes at a very slow pace.

Sharing my dilemmas

One day one of my friends, famous nationally as well as internationally for participatory work, with whom I always share my experiences and frustrations, attended a workshop organized by this project. The objective of the workshop was to 'explore options for working in collaboration and partnership with stakeholders'. In this workshop, people involved in the project shared their work experiences and talked about the participatory process they had followed. They also requested all the donors and representatives of government departments present in the workshop to come forward and to help communities with whom the project was working. They were asked to establish partnership with communities. In front of approximately 40 to 50 people, this friend of mine stood up and said that s/he knew that everything is wrong, and that s/he was disappointed by the process this project was following, etc. After five minutes my friend had left the workshop, probably thinking that it was a waste of time.

That moment I was stunned – not sure what was right and what was wrong. I was saying to myself perhaps:

- my friend was right because s/he fulfilled his/her duty by pinpointing and highlighting the real issues
- my friend was wrong because s/he was given the opportunity to facilitate those who at least, with all their weakness and strengths, asked for assistance and support, but then left them alone once again
- my friend was right because s/he was thinking that it is a waste of time to try to change the attitude and behaviour of these people who are working in an environment where all these terms such as participation, empowerment, etc., have no meaning. And that they are perhaps doing this because of donor pressure or because it is written in their workplans, etc. It is better to spend time with those who are willing and have the attitude and behaviour for bringing about positive change
- my friend was wrong because maybe this time they genuinely asked for assistance and support and my friend's time was much more needed by them, although at present their attitude and behaviour does not fit with a participatory process
- I am wrong. I am wasting my time with all these people. I should also leave and work with those who are willing to work for participatory development the way I want
- I am right because at least I am able to bring them to a stage where they have openly shared their process and are asking for help.

I am wondering, what is needed more – work within a favourable or an unfavourable environment?[4]

What is a compromise in development?

This is an experience of an organization (NGO) working at national level, where all who work are like-minded people with different experience and different expertise, some as management, some as employees and some as board members. I am a founding member of this organization. It is a very favourable environment to work for a participatory process for change. All concerned have jointly developed organizational objectives, values and principles. The whole team has developed structure and policies together. There are differences of opinion; however, there is a consensus on values and principles. This organization is established with resources pooled by the founding members and contributions from our friends.

The organization started on a very small scale and is now gradually expanding its work. Most of the work is for the promotion of participatory development and PRA (training, networking, workshops, PRA mapping). Gradually, various donors have also started funding our small initiatives for the promotion of PRA work.

Recently, the organization has started a project funded by an international donor. The objective of the project is to ensure 100% enrolment of both boys and girls in primary education. No participatory process is involved, there is no analysis of community needs and there is no discussion with the community about the project.

We (staff, board members and management) had a long meeting to discuss the rationale for accepting the project, something we usually do before any project. We jointly agreed to accept the offer. Thus a project which is non-participatory in its nature was accepted in a participatory manner. I was reflecting on the overall process and asked myself the following questions but could not find the right answers. *Perhaps:*

- it was wrong to accept such a project, which would be implemented without a participatory process
- it was a right decision, because although we accepted that project on the donor's conditions, our rationale was: (a) that we will be able to generate resources and other donors, knowing that this organization is working with an international donor, most probably will fund our organization in future. We will then use those funds for participatory work (today's compromise on one thing for a better tomorrow); (b) if we do not accept this project someone else will accept it as a target-oriented project only. Then there would be no further hope for participatory work in the area. Our organization would at least consciously try to bring in a participatory process and we would facilitate the communities to organize themselves to generate local

and external resources for development work in the area; (c) other activities in the area can be initiated based on the community's priority needs

- it was a wrong decision based on the wrong approach. Currently there are no resources, so by initiating such a process we may be able to facilitate the communities for self-analysis, but in the end we may create frustrations by raising their expectations. Other donors may pose other conditions and then there is no end to it. Today's compromise on one thing may become a habit for tomorrow
- it was wrong to accept such a project because this is our first compromise and then for every new compromise we will give various attractive justifications to ourselves and then there will be no end
- it was a right decision because participatory work also requires resources and so doing one bad project with good intention, in a good way, and for future good work, is justifiable. And after all, communities need education.

Institutionalization versus individuals: a third experience

This third experience is from working with an international organization with a most favourable environment. The objective of the organization is poverty alleviation through the empowerment of communities. Every possible facility was available to work for the achievement of this objective, such as resources (human and financial), a supportive manager, a participatory organizational structure/style and policies, and open and participatory accountability systems. There were many stakeholders involved, such as government, other international donors, etc., but every one was supportive. (One of the major reasons for it was the organization's access and control over financial resources.) There were differences of opinion within the organization, but there was also a culture of discussion, negotiation and dialogue.

There were problems related to community work because the organizational approach was to empower the communities. The process was not very easy. There was resentment from those who were to be disempowered and from those also who were to be empowered. One challenge for us was to develop skills among ourselves for managing the empowerment process instead of controlling the empowerment process. We followed basic principles such as open accountability, transparency at all levels, mutual respect and above all the belief that the empowerment of communities cannot be achieved without empowering our own staff. The second challenge was to develop skills to manage the empowered staff. Skills were developed to manage them instead of controlling them – the organization was managed by teams instead of one person, and it was applicable at all levels.

Then there was a change in the top manager's position. With the new manager there was a change in organizational policies, structure, style and practice of management. The new person had a different interpretation of terms such as participation, empowerment, development, different personal and professional values, norms and behaviour.

Change was brought in within three months. The majority of the staff, who were following a pattern they had established themselves in an organization over five years, were disappointed by such a sudden change. They resented it because they had been empowered earlier to fight for their rights. For five years they had been empowering communities so that they can also fight for their rights and raise their voices against violations of human rights. This empowering process took a long period and it was done through capacity building, training and through providing such organizational culture. However, when they showed their resentment, a few were forced to leave the organization and another few staff members also decided to leave.

Why did this happen in an organization where participation was institutionalized? *Perhaps:*

- institutionalization of participatory culture within an organization is a myth and it depends on only one person, the manager
- it is wrong to expect organizations to develop all their policies following a participatory approach, because there are many dimensions to it and organizations cannot be participatory for all things. Thus discussions and efforts for institutionalization of participation in an organization are not worth pursuing
- everyone has their own interpretation of participation so one cannot force everyone else to think and interpret participation in his or her own way
- it was wrong on the part of all those empowered staff to expect the same understanding of participation from that new person
- it was the right expectation because induction provides all the information and the previous manager also tried to explain the situation, including the participatory nature of the organization.

Can participation be taught? Or can participation only be understood? Telling someone that you should behave in a certain way – is it participatory? Or is it participatory to let the other person feel what is right or wrong?

Notes

[1]PC1 is an official document approved by the Planning and Development Department. This document is an official document to be followed by each officer responsible to execute the project. The target for each activity is always given with funds, etc.

[2]National Conservation Strategy is a government document prepared by various stakeholders of development working in Pakistan, such as NGOs, the private sector, communities, etc.

[3]Village Development Plans are developed by communities with the facilitation of project staff.

[4]Favourable environment in terms of resources available for participatory development, support of management and availability of skill required for participatory development.

CHAPTER 17

Mwajuma Saiddy Masaiganah

Reflecting on the past: my journey to participation[1]

My journey takes me back to 1985, when for the first time I involved myself in Participatory Action Research (PAR) with fisherfolk communities in Tanzania, focusing specifically on women. Back then I used to do things the way I was told by higher authorities, taking directions or sending messages to communities, be they right or wrong, no questioning! Using PAR, and using video as a way of communicating, changed my way of looking at and doing things. It created in me a special interest for women and community issues, developed my respect for communities and totally changed my entire life.

A story to tell: '*hili li mama*' meaning 'this mama…'

I will give just part of my life history that tells of working with bureaucrats and within bureaucratic systems, the hurdles I encountered and how they helped shape my life. During my work with the communities in Mtwara and Lindi regions as a rural development adviser and then as facilitator with the fisherfolk communities, we managed to learn from one another, create awareness in communities and create allies (even with politicians). This helped us to integrate with higher government authorities and lobby for policy changes. Our aim was to stop dynamite and other illegal fishing methods that claimed lives, left people maimed and threatened people's livelihoods. Nobody thought that we were doing the right thing, because to some people, banning dynamite fishing and taking measures to stop it was interfering with their trade. The dynamite traders and illegal fishermen could lose money by stopping illegal deals.

I will narrate my story starting in December 1993, when I facilitated a five-day evaluation workshop with a group of fishermen in Sudi, Lindi district, as part of the Rural Integrated Project Support (RIPS) Marine Environment Project. Our first meeting was in Sudi village, where the Sudi Declaration was made by fishermen and women from 12 coastal villages of

114

Mtwara, Lindi and Kilwa districts. During this meeting it was agreed that a committee be formed, called the Sudi Committee, to oversee the whole issue of marine environment protection in the area and to raise awareness in all people in the area and at regional and national levels. This was to be done through mass meetings and leaders' (villagers') meetings, but using video as a medium of communication. This idea of using a video was just to start filming when we started the meeting, and to play back the video of the day's workshop proceedings every evening. This seemed to work, as people/villagers came forward and volunteered to talk freely in front of the camera, and expressed their concerns on the issue of dynamite fishing. This was because first, it was new in these areas so it was a source of pride for them to see themselves talking on film. Second, people had built up trust in us and believed that we would help to show their leaders what 'they', the people, had to say. Earlier they had fears that this would not happen, as many researchers had talked to them during many meetings in their villages but all the reports had been put on the shelf and nothing was done. They were tired because these meetings benefited researchers and their bosses and left them with nothing.

So, using this kind of media, we assured them that their leaders would see exactly what they said without filtering the information. We agreed that the Sudi Committee would use the video in their organized tours to create awareness. When we went back to the office, I happened to come across a personal note written by my chief technical adviser, Lars Johanson. It read '…I have never seen in my life such great facilitation skills as displayed by Mwajuma in this exercise…'. You can imagine how unbelievable it was for me and at the same time how good I felt. I developed and grew even stronger. But it was less than four years before this strength landed me in problems and friction with the regional authorities.

Things turn sour

In January 1997, things started to turn really sour. After the evaluation workshop, the Sudi Committee – the group formed from the strengthened fisherfolk who had been at the workshop – agreed to meet and draft a constitution to start an NGO called Shirikisho, so that they could be independent to do the things that concern their lives. In that meeting one member reported that the situation in the neighbouring region of Kilwa was so bad that illegal fishermen had raised a flag on one of the islands stating, *'Kilwa Hakuna Serikali'* meaning, 'There is no government in Kilwa'.

As we were also using the media to put pressure on the Government to change their policy, I told this story to one Father Reverend, who was giving news to Radio One. The next morning it was like a hot cake, repeated on the headline news for about a day and a half. After looking for me the whole morning, the Kilwa police left a message that I should report to them. I reported, but took along with me the secretary of Shirikisho, so that if something happened to me they would know and could act quickly.

The police wanted to know why I had made such statements. I said the reason was that the police were not doing their job. I said that this was highlighted in the evaluation workshop, and that in ranking, the police were given zero in efficiency. I explained that I was only voicing what people say. After long discussions, they agreed that they are having problems. In a way, it was getting difficult for them to perform their duties because the dynamite problem was an inside job. Then they said that it was the police commander who had instructed them to bring me to the police station. I said 'Yes, here I am. Try putting me in jail now and you'll see what happens. The people will retaliate.' I told them we knew much more about what was happening than the police, and if they wanted to get anywhere they had to work closely with us. The first agony was over, but I knew I was being monitored.

We decided to record the whole process on video, even the follow up of what happened six months after the workshop. We made a video documentary and organized trips to visit the regional commissioners of Lindi and Mtwara; the Ministers of Communication and Works, Natural Resources and Tourism, the Environment (both in the mainland and in the Isles); the Attorney General; Agricultural and Industries Supplies Company Ltd (AISCO); and other companies directly or indirectly related to the sale or keeping of dynamite and natural resources. During all these trips, video recording was done as a means of documenting the process. Many trips of the same kind were made to meet past leaders like the then Prime Minister and Vice-President who visited the area. In both of these cases it was hard for us to get a chance to show them our video or talk to them, as nobody took us seriously. But on all occasions we provided these leaders with a video documentary called *'Bahari Yetu Hatutaki'*, meaning 'Not in our ocean'.[2]

Meeting the Prime Minister

In February 1997, during the parliamentary session, four Sudi members and myself travelled to Dodoma to meet the Prime Minister together with Members of Parliament from the southern coastal area. To our amazement, they had talked to other MPs from the south and they had agreed that the problem concerned not only the coastal constituencies but the entire southern region, because that was their only source of protein – fish from the sea. So, the MPs received us as a team, and made plans for us to meet the Prime Minister, Mr Sumaye, the next day. In the morning, we attended the parliament session as guests, and in the afternoon we had a very fruitful meeting.

I went with the group from Sudi, not as a member, but to document the process. One of our aims was to document and make a video for the purpose of training and educating the masses and policy makers. So, our meeting started with the current Minister of Regional Administration and Local Government, an MP from Kilwa, introducing the team to the Prime Minister. He said, 'Mr PM, in front of you is a team of four members of the Sudi Committee and a group of southern MPs who have come to see you on this issue. Seeing us here as a team, you should understand that we are fed up with the situation...'. The Prime Minister asked, 'You have said four members, but I can see there is one other person. Who is she?' I introduced myself as a facilitator of the process, and said that I was only there to document what was going on using video and audio on behalf of the communities. During this meeting the Sudi Committee members gave the Prime Minister their video with documentation of the whole process and argued for him to take action – which he did. During this process we also asked for permission to film the meeting and he permitted me to do so. We explained to him that it was important for the association for this meeting to be documented so that our final video would be a document of the whole process. It should be noted that during this meeting, I did not contribute to the discussion in any way. I just documented the process. This group was so much empowered that they did not need an outsider to speak for them. Generally, the video had a big impact on making people come out and speak, because holding the microphone was a way of empowering them and giving them a voice. It draws people nearer, as they tend to believe more in what they say than in what we say for them.

After listening to the team, the Prime Minister reacted by asking them whether they knew these people who were involved in illegal fishing. They said yes. He asked whether it was possible for them to give him names of all those involved and they said they would do that in a month's time, that he would receive the names.

In his address to the team, the Prime Minister had the following to say:

In any war of this kind, without sincere and genuine co-operation and commitment from the communities, it will not be easy for the government to succeed. But the government also has its part, which it must play, which must be done fully. But we citizens must do our part. I am quite sure if we had had this awareness for many years, this would have without doubt been eradicated.

Action from the village

When we went back, the villagers, through their village environment committees, brought in over 200 names of potential dynamite fishermen from

Lindi and over 300 from Mtwara. On top of each list they wrote 'siri', meaning 'confidential', because of the sensitivity of the issue and the risks involved in naming these people. I compiled this list, printed many copies and gave them to the chairman and secretary of Shirikisho to sign. They gave them to the southern MPs, who took the list to the Prime Minister and to all the ministers and MPs concerned.

After a couple of months, the Prime Minister visited Lindi with his list of dynamite fishermen. Going into villages, he checked with the crowds as to whether the list was correct. The crowds roared that it was true that the people mentioned were doing dynamiting. Then the Prime Minister said that the regional commissioners would have to make sure that these people stopped dynamiting or they would be taken to task. And when he went back to his office he wrote back to them officially. One regional commissioner said to another, 'Hili li mama ndilo limetushitakia. Lazima tumshughulikie!', meaning 'It is this woman who has made us be taken to task, we are getting orders, we have to deal with her.' Another arduous journey began.

Professional battles

During the RIPS steering committee meeting the next day, the regional commissioner for Mtwara picked me directly. He said, 'I want Mwajuma to tell me, who told her to go to Dodoma with the group and how did they get the money to travel? I want to know who approved them to get that money. I hope they did not use the money from the project. I want to know also, why are they using the Lindi RIPS office address, who gave them authority? Do you think that you are going to stop dynamite fishing? After all this is a Mafia thing, how can you? That Mudhihir Mohamed who is helping you; he used to work in the president's office for a long time, why didn't he stop it? What is he going to do now?'

I don't think the programme co-ordinator expected him to talk like this in the meeting. He stood up to reply in my place, but I told him, 'I am going to take it myself, please sit down'. I told the regional commissioner that we went to Dodoma with RIPS money and that we followed all the normal procedures. The management committee, which comprises the two desk officers from the government side in the two regions, approved the trip, and so the government was aware of our intentions and our trip. I said that using their address did not mean that we own the address, as anybody could use the address of any other person till the Shirikisho gets its own address. I told him that I was speaking on behalf of the people and that I have a double role. I have a role to serve my organization as a facilitator of a process, but also I have a role as a Tanzanian to safeguard the interests of Tanzania. And when I am working, I am observing those interests. I told him that I was wondering why he did not react to our first trip in 1994. Was it that nobody took action and that now the Prime Minister took action, they feel embarrassed? I said, 'I have done it as a facilitator, and facilitation can bring negative or positive impacts depending on who is affected. And I did not regret that, and I take the responsibility.'

Personal costs

I am proud of working so hard and risking my life and my children's lives. My daughter, who was 14 years old at the time, was beaten up by thugs in front of the regional commissioner's residence – obviously organized by the same group who in the same night raided a dynamite armoury in Chipite, Masasi in Mtwara. It was done deliberately to derail my attention from them, and my daughter was hospitalized and has never returned to her normal self again. I was to lose my job. I decided then it was not time for me to work within the government system, until the time is ripe for change. But I am proud of all that happened, because the people were empowered to speak their minds. The government changed the policy and under the Civil Rights Ordinance the army is keeping patrol of fishing in collaboration with the village environment committee members, and is being changed every three months. This ends part of my story.

Lessons

I have given this example not because I want to accuse anybody, but because I want people, the government and the new generation to know that without changing attitudes and behaviour in our institutions, and without putting our own interests last, participation will be a dream. People's empowerment will remain rhetoric to the last days of this world (if there is any to come). For our governments are still the same. Same! Same! Same! And for women, they should know that working as a woman, you are looked upon as '*Hili li mama…*', meaning 'this woman'.

I have also learned that popular media is of vital importance in people's empowerment if their voices are to be heard. During this period we also used radio, especially during our meetings and trips. We asked for a radio reporter from Radio Kanda ya Kusini (Southern Zone Radio), and specifically for Mr Edward Kahurananga, who was one of our allies in this whole process from when we started. He used to air every activity that the committee was involved in or any information on dynamiting or dynamite victims that were reported to us during the whole period of the struggle. This also helped a lot in creating awareness in the community in other areas that had similar problems. This was used extensively and was the reason, if you recall, why I was called to the police station in Kilwa. The authorities heard us attacking them through the media, reporting the people saying that the police are ineffective.

The above experiences, and the many others which I have not reported here, moved me to look critically at the issues of empowerment, participation, rights and what are the processes – laws, policies and acts – put in place by the government for us (its people). To look critically at whether these processes are benefiting us in a way that helps people build up their capacity to speak out democratically to protect their livelihoods or/and to become empowered socially and economically. And to whether their voices are heard in the democratic process. Has the current system offered women and the poor what it is supposed to offer, according to what is stipulated in its policies and regulations towards any meaningful development, for their benefit and the country's benefit at large?

Notes

[1]First published in October 2000 as 'A Story to Tell: "*hili li mama*" meaning "this mama"' by Mwajuma Masaiganah in *PLA Notes*, vol. 39. 'Popular Communications', International Institute for Environment and Development, London, pp.38–41. Reproduced by kind permission of the publishers.

[2]The Sudi Committee was strengthened by removing unfaithful members who were said to collaborate with dynamiters and replacing them with other stronger members. Among the 12 members was a woman called Mwanashuru, who features a great deal in the video, and who proved to be very strong and maintained her position. The title of the video is derived from her words of wisdom.

CHAPTER 18

Jessica Nalwoga

To REFLECT or not to REFLECT?

In this chapter, I will explore the tensions between participatory ideals on the one hand and learners' expectations on the other. To illustrate this, I will use the example of a REFLECT programme carried out by a community-based organization (CBO) on the outskirts of Kampala, the capital of Uganda.

From my point of view as a PRA enthusiast, and from the point of view of anyone in this category, it appears that these learners' expectations are the opposite of the principles and ideals of participation. However, the difference in practice is not as clear-cut as it might first appear. The blur here arises from the learners' and their facilitators' selective use of participatory approaches to maintain a semblance of 'formal' education, something that they consider an important characteristic of any education process.

REFLECT in Banda

The Banda Community Development Programme (BCDP) conducts literacy programmes in Banda. This organization has organized seven literacy circles in an area with roughly 10 000 people. The method they use in this programme is known as REFLECT. This is a relatively new approach to adult literacy, which fuses the education ideas of the Brazilian educator Paulo Freire and the practice of Participatory Rural Appraisal (PRA). In this programme there is no use of textbooks, but rather the learners in each circle develop their own materials through the construction of maps, matrices, calendars and any other graphic/picture/diagram, as is done in PRA practice.

Circle composition

Banda, like any other urban slum settlement, is far from being a homogeneous, egalitarian community. With varied languages, norms and values due to different social, economic and cultural backgrounds, mounting an adult

education programme centring on communal interests poses serious challenges, especially because the extensive use of PRA graphics requires the participants to share at least some common interests. There are obvious
difficulties of language choice, finding appropriate places for learners to
meet, and catering for the different time constraints of participants. While
such challenges can be met, BCDP is struggling to integrate the different
interests of learners, who may be housewives, transporters, beer brewers or
market people, and who don't feel they have much in common just by
virtue of living in the same place.

Given that a common place of residence proved to be a non-viable uni-
fying factor, BCDP attempted to organize at least some of the REFLECT
circles so as to group members of the same professional backgrounds. This
too had its own difficulties. One difficulty that arose was that the facilitators felt out of their depth when it came to creatively adapting PRA tools to
the situation of their specific groups. Obviously, such an approach would
have required a fair amount of decentralized support. But this was not
favoured by the support staff, who felt it essential to retain control over what
was being learnt. Thus many of the activities in the circles have remained
standardized and the advantage of grouping together people from common
backgrounds was lost. Also, people of the same profession do not necessarily share common interests; market vendors, for example, face completely
different occupational hazards and risks according to which commodity
they trade in. This became abundantly clear when the fish ban (due to the
circulation of fish caught through poisoning) meant that the fish traders
almost ran out of business, although the *matooke* (banana) traders carried on
operating.

How do I come into it all?

I joined the Banda programme about a year ago as a research observer working for ActionAid-Uganda on research titled 'Literacy, Gender and Social
Agency', funded by the Department for International Development
(DFID). I joined ActionAid straight from university and began working on
this research. I did not have any practical experience with PRA, though I
had learned about it at school. I had also practised a little of it in two workshops. Apart from that, I had lots of theory and this is how I first became
interested in PRA. I had always wanted to have practical experience and I
got it with this research. When I say that I got it, I don't mean that it was
direct from the circles, because I was not a facilitator but rather a researcher
and observer. Because I was supposed to observe and judge, I had some
hands-on training that helped boost my interest in the approach. I won't say
that now I am fully experienced; I don't believe that anyone can have total

experience of the approach because it keeps changing according to the people who practise it. Also, the experiences that I shared at the Pathways conference in April 2000 helped, although I haven't as yet used it the way I would like. I believe in the approach and would like to get more experience, which I am sure I will with time.

To go back to the circles in Banda, however, let me talk about the way that the practitioners have forged their way around the problems of lack of homogeneity and PRA ideals. From what I said about the composition of the circles, one would almost think that the approach hardly works. However, what is most important to the Banda learners is that which they all desire irrespective of background. This, I realized as I conducted my research, was the desire to acquire an education. This is the only interest that all the learners share. The desire can be diffused and may include anything from being able to sign one's name to acquiring a masters degree.

Participation the formal way

Though it is an uphill task to construct circles based on common interest, so as to create a semblance of clearly defined communities, BCDP tried to do this in at least three circles: the stone crushers, the beer brewers and the market vendors. Ndenye is the facilitator of the market vendors' circle. She has been facilitating since 1996 and, as she told me, has taken part in three training workshops organized by the REFLECT Co-ordination Unit (RCU)/ActionAid. She proudly told me at one time that though she might still be lacking in some areas, she is good when it comes to facilitating discussion in the sessions. Ndenye is a middle-aged widow with five children, a local council vice-chairperson for her zone and has a busload of other responsibilities, but she still finds time to dedicate to her circle.

The circle is located about 200 metres from the market centre, a makeshift enclosure of iron sheets and wood. Sitting inside, one can almost touch the doorstep of the neighbouring houses and when it rains, the nearby sewage canal overflows and a foul-smelling soup seeps through the shelter.

Though any learning environment should ideally be in a quiet, secluded place to ensure concentration, it is next to impossible to secure such a place in Banda because it is a very poor settlement. And, if one was available, it would most likely be far from the market centre, thus posing access problems. The severe time constraints that the women face also make it imperative that learning takes place in the immediate vicinity of the market. At one point, the women had even suggested holding the sessions in the market itself, so that they could rush back to their stalls to conduct business should a client come by.

Ndenye, as many other facilitators in Banda, tends to fall back into formal teaching and most times her sessions would be hard to differentiate from primary school teaching. She writes words on a particular topic, for example 'dangers from the environment', on a large sheet of manila paper, cuts these words out, mixes them and then pours them on the ground. She then asks the learners to pick a specified word or she holds up a card for them to read. Her questions often run something like: 'Who can read this for us?' and when the learners start answering in chorus, she says, 'hands up'. If there are no hands up, she will pick a learner whom she knows was around the last time this topic was dealt with, saying something like, 'Jane, can you read this word for us?' If it so happens that Jane gives a wrong answer or doesn't know, Ndenye doesn't shun her, and the participants rarely laugh at each other's mistakes (though exceptions are made for obvious mistakes). Ndenye has strongly warned them against such action, saying that everybody in the circle is a learner and therefore liable to error. When an answer is wrong, she will accept it, but asks if there is anyone with a different opinion who would like to add it. This continues until she gets what she wants; it is only then that she writes down the answer on the board. Having thus validated the answer by writing it on the board, the learners are compelled to copy it into their exercise books. When Ndenye talks of being good at discussion, this is the process she has in mind.

Ndeye does, however, differ somewhat from the other facilitators in Banda in that she usually gives her class group work. Often this reduces competition between learners and helps create a comfortable group atmosphere, an asset not always encountered in the other circles. The only drawback is that Ndenye usually does group work last, as a kind of reinforcement of what has already been firmly established by her. Thus, what one would usually expect to be at the heart of a REFLECT circle, i.e. debate among the participants, turns into a mechanical repetition task. Participants might produce their own flip charts about a certain topic during group work but, more often than not, this results in exact copies of the text that Ndenye has previously written and proved. Nevertheless, such efforts are interpreted by Ndenye and her participants to be the result of 'discussion'. Participants enjoy this type of work and take it to be highly participatory because everyone will have contributed equally, therefore maintaining equality and respect for each other.

Apart from the process described above, I have never observed a graphic being constructed in the circle, though Ndenye informed me that before I arrived on the scene, an 'income-expenditure tree' had been constructed. The 'income-expenditure tree' is one of the few favoured graphics. When speaking to facilitators and participants about PRA graphics, this is the one they will mention most frequently. There are several reasons for this. First, the tree is straightforward and therefore easy for the learners to relate to. Second, the metaphoric use of a tree in the context of money management ties in closely with participants' perceptions of money as a natural good. Many of the terms Bantu speakers use when talking about money are connected with food – for example, a corrupt person 'eats' money. Also, given that this is a relatively simple graphic that can be done quickly and explained easily, many facilitators have dispensed with any attempt at adapting it to a common background of the learners. Instead, everyone is asked to construct their own graphic depicting their own personal money management.

It is real when written

So far I have, implicitly or explicitly, held the actions of Ndenye and her participants against the ideals of REFLECT (or, for that matter, PRA). However, what needs to be looked at is whether the learners realize their expectations. Regardless of the selective use of REFLECT, those participants who are still in the circles remain keen. As mentioned at the beginning of this chapter, the learners in Banda live in an environment that considers 'formal education' a great achievement, not least because in Uganda it comes with a huge cost in terms of both money and personal commitment. It is precisely this that renders it an important status marker.

So when the learners come to the circle, which they choose to call a 'class', they expect to learn like they would have had they gone to a formal school. The desire for formal education manifests itself in the way the learners interpret what they do in the class and what surrounds them while there. They call their facilitator 'teacher' or 'madam', and they treasure their exercise books. Often, the learners have asked me what will happen after they finish, i.e. whether they will get any indicators of successful completion, most notably certificates. Such clamouring for formalized recognition sits uneasily with the ideal of REFLECT. It is not the certified proof of what the participants have done in the circles which policy makers consider success, rather it is what issues participants have been able to bring out, debate and resolve through action. From my inquiries, it is evident that the desire to conform to the given standards outweighs attempts at challenging the norm. Therefore, the learners' efforts to copy down as much as they can during the sessions, and to be taught like in a formal school, fulfils an important function for them.

Reading and writing are perhaps the most 'natural' expression of the formal class atmosphere that participants aspire to. I have noticed that every time I ask learners what they learnt the previous week, they pull out their books, which are always handy, with great joy and proudly show me their work. These books are the only documentation they have of their long-term noble call and, in the end, it seems meagre to them, unworthy of the newly gained status. It is unfortunate that these documents tend to be of little prestigious value outside the class and it is often precisely because of this lack that participants start making practical use of their newly acquired literacy skills. Thus vendors will keep record books of their purchases and sales mainly to impress the woman at the next stall by displaying their own organized efficiency. Practical advantages of increased control over the running of the business are also noticed, but only as secondary to the status gains achieved.

A look at the future

To the learners in Banda, the REFLECT programme has given them the chance to have some literacy skills. They have been able to apply them and, from the way they see it, they have come a long way from when they were not able to write anything. They come together as members of the same class to do their homework. Above all, those who have participated actively have been recognized by friends, husbands and neighbours, and they feel that they have gained some respect.

However, due to the decisions made by the powers that be, the programme in Banda has come to a standstill because they no longer receive funding from ActionAid. Now, just as the learners were consolidating their skills, they have been abandoned by the programme. The future is rather blurred.

As for me, I learned many things that would have helped me in developing my PRA skills and perspective further, but since this programme came to an end I haven't done much with my newly acquired knowledge and the fire is dying down slowly. Hopefully, I will find a way of applying my PRA enthusiasm before I lose steam. However, I believe that once one has been hooked on PRA methods and the life it brings to education, research and any other programme where it is applied, it is rather hard to change to another approach.

The sustainability of PRA in any programme can pose serious drawbacks to the success of the approach. But what can be done when the interest of the small communities or the CBOs does not tally with those of the big international organizations and the funders?

Conclusion

From what I have written here, it appears that REFLECT is not really happening in Banda. However, this would be to ignore some of the gains that facilitators like Ndenye have realized through the REFLECT training. To many PRA practitioners, her approach to debate would represent a serious distortion of what it means to work in a participatory manner, but to Ndenye and her participants it still means a significant departure from the type of rote learning more commonly found in adult literacy classes. The point here is that even though one cannot expect facilitators to radically change long-learned attitudes and behaviours through occasional training workshops, they do pick up ideas from there and change in small steps.

Nevertheless, I have also shown that there are some limitations to participatory practice, which have their roots in the expectations of learners. Here, continued support and training for facilitators will obviously not have any effect. It is these expectations that REFLECT will need to consider and integrate more carefully, since participants will and should never be made to adapt to a participatory approach. Quite the contrary – participatory approaches should be adapted to meet the expectations of the participants.

CHAPTER 19

Koos Neefjes

PRA, poverty and livelihoods: reflections from inside the bowels of an international NGO

There are many Participatory Rural Appraisal (PRA) issues that are important for Oxfam GB, a large international development non-governmental organization (NGO). My view is one from within the beast, the bowels if you wish, where good food is turned into good energy and indeed constructive action, but where it is also a bit smelly, where things move all the time and where slopes are slippery. (In fact, after a while you think that sitting inside a tumble dryer is a pretty neat idea.) This chapter expresses personal opinions and is a reflection on my experience, and has no pretensions beyond that.

I came to Oxfam GB with several ideas and some experience in both using PRA (and Rapid Rural Appraisal, RRA) and training local staff in PRA, mostly in Africa. Before that, in the early 1980s, I attempted to assess local technical knowledge of farmers in Bangladesh through a mixture of qualitative data from interviews and some measurements of water and salt – but the term Rapid Rural Appraisal[1] had not yet been coined, to my knowledge. My introduction to the RRA methodology and later to PRA was through close friends and colleagues, who were talking about things that rang many bells. For me it was like bringing together my professional interest and experience on land and water management by poor farmers, and private exploits in amateur drama and the theatre world. I was hired to use my RRA/PRA experience in helping Oxfam GB further its work on environment and development, but met scepticism in many parts.

The three PRA issues discussed here are:

1 What are we learning about training in PRA and using PRA in Oxfam GB?
2 Is PRA about action?
3 Can PRA improve on poverty analysis, by involving lots of social actors and basing it on lots of different data?

Learning about PRA in Oxfam GB

Oxfam GB is large, with offices and programmes in well over 50 countries, thousands of staff, about £100 million turnover per year and more than a thousand grant-receiving partners per year, apart from so-called operational projects (i.e. managed by Oxfam staff).[2] Oxfam's programme is incredibly diverse, as it is responding to multiple realities and needs. The number of staff with high training skills in PRA have been limited to three or four at any one moment, and they were/are often based in the head office (i.e. removed from the country programmes and with multiple responsibilities in Oxfam's global programme).

My experience in Oxfam GB suggests that many managers and staff, most of whom are grant makers rather than project implementers, were and still are sceptical about the use of PRA (RRA, PLA). They are sceptical about its use in their own work and about its value in both project management and research for policy influencing. They will have read about it and may have had a few hours or a one-day course on it, or even have participated in a part of a field-based training, but many fail to appreciate the power of the approach in those different realms. They often give the feeling that they think PRA is a passing trend that they do not want to miss out on, but that they do not want to be identified with either. Scepticism has been strongest in Latin America, where the idea appears to persist (among Oxfam managers) that staff and partners have little to learn in this respect from Asia, the North or Africa. There are important exceptions to this.

The most common comment I have heard from managers is that 'PRA is important, but not very important for me'. This means that many managers and also several policy advisers are not alert to the possibility of using PRA in projects, while they are either critical of 'wishy-washy' qualitative methodologies, or not critical of flawed uses of RRA in research for policy influencing. Few are aware of the power of participatory behaviour lessons and tools in workshops, meetings and scheduled monitoring visits. In fact, there has never been a real debate about this in Oxfam outside a small circle of people who are knowledgeable about PRA.

There is still a large number of (frontline) staff who are interested, who use PRA tools and who have adopted PRA behaviour in their work with staff of national partner NGOs. Some have taken the step of becoming trainers themselves, not of (other) Oxfam staff but of staff of partners and other national NGOs, and of community leaders. These people tend to take part in national networks on the PRA approach and related matters, not in international ones.

I feel that the quality of the use of PRA in different stages of project cycles or research varies between extremely good to (actually) quite bad. In the latter case, staff may lack notions of cross-checking and trustworthiness (i.e. believe everything they heard), of facilitative behaviour (instead of 'handing over the stick' they keep their proverbial sunglasses on) and, in most cases, of what a learning process looks like. The weakest aspect, however, is reporting. There have been numerous bulky reports of workshops and participatory assessments that I have filed in the bin for recycling paper.

Hundreds (probably well over a thousand) Oxfam and partner staff have been trained in PRA (tools, behaviour and processes of sharing) over the past decade or so, by specialist staff and consultants. Many have received follow-up to this training in some form. A brief survey of a (biased)[3] sample of trainees was held in 1999 in order to understand more about the long-term impact of training in PRA and some related topics on the working practice of what we can call frontline staff (Neefjes and Woldegiorgis, 1999). It stands out that many interviewees feel they learned primarily from the behaviour lessons they took from the training. They have changed their own behaviour and they have improved their understanding of the behaviour of others. Less commonly, they claim to be using PRA tools regularly, and almost all limit themselves to using just a few tools, for example during monitoring visits, but more often in needs assessments. Frontline development professionals feel insecure about taking the lead in facilitating drawn-out learning processes, even where regular follow-up training has been provided. Perhaps stronger support from managers in applying learning from workshops by staff would have increased the impact of both training and follow-up.

PRA or PLA?

Some have tried to change the label from PRA to PLA, Participatory Learning and Action, because they have felt that it is not just about appraisal, it is not just rural, and it should be about learning and action. This has never really become accepted, and the acronym PRA has stayed. However, there are strong arguments for dropping it.

The little work that I have done with PRA in urban neighbourhoods in the South and in the North (which is largely urban or peri-urban) has shown that tools need to be adapted and that the learning process is totally different. People have less time, are more literate, have fewer spaces to gather spontaneously, move socially and geographically, and may not form a community with their neighbours. With experiences in urban areas, PRA is complemented and being enriched, and more and more of it is happening. Thus the 'R' is not appropriate.

I have been in reflective workshops with staff and partners who articulated the need to use participatory approaches in all steps in project cycles, not just the early ones (appraisal is a very early step in Oxfam, before grants can be made). However, to do this means that reports from early PRA events need to feed into later steps. Furthermore, tools need to be semi-standardized for monitoring and adapted, and new tools have needed to be devised for evaluation and impact assessment. For example, retrospective well-being ranking was an innovation that we found important for impact assessment, and we have adapted the matrix tool for finding out about relative attribution to social actors or organizations of certain changes in society and environment. Using participatory approaches in all steps also implies that more and more project tasks are to be done by beneficiaries, and that the notion of sharing between project and beneficiaries needs to be institutionalized (it should happen all the time, and not just in a PRA-based needs assessment). In fact, the boundaries between project and beneficiaries need to be blurred ever further. This challenges accepted practice.

To do this would take us into genuinely shared learning and action, as is the idea behind action research. Policy influencing happens mostly by the larger national and international NGOs, and good lobbying requires good information. Oxfam is heavily involved in this, and ever more so, internationally and at national and regional levels too (with national partners). The tendency is to extract data, notions and opinions from people and organizations, and use those in policy work, instead of pursuing the more cumbersome, slow and inclusive route of action research, in which objectivity of judgement is less important, and involving deprived people in changing policies and practices during the research process is the main objective.

Research that involves the social actors who are most important does happen, and possibly increasingly so – for example, on urban poverty in nine cities in India, which happened over a period of about two years with many partner NGOs. However, there rarely is a clear notion of 'social actors' in such research, apart from Oxfam and a few partners, who involve people who belong to certain 'social groupings'. This is also my criticism of how PRA is applied in projects, i.e. appraisals or evaluations. Interviews or dialogues and 'focus groups' are organized with, say, groups of poor women, or 'youth', or people who belong to a certain ethnic group, but these are not necessarily self-identified social actors, i.e. groups who operate as some sort of unit with a shared goal. Venn diagrams of local and less-local actors (including organizations) may be made and these may be cross-checked, but the social actors identified in this way are not necessarily invited to manifest themselves as a distinct participant in the learning and action process. I do not claim always to have achieved this in the processes for which I was responsible either.

Facilitating a process in which the social actors who are important with regard to poverty, social exclusion, deprivation and improvements in those conditions participate is, in fact, about negotiation and mediation between the powerful and others. This is extremely challenging in the most peaceful of cases. When we attempted this in a so-called 'complex emergency' in northwest Uganda, we were unsure whether we had opened Pandora's box or whether we were on the road to conflict resolution (Neefjes 1999). Nevertheless, for me the aim must always be learning and action, by all social actors who work to reduce poverty and challenge social exclusion.

PRA, analysis and livelihoods

One strand in the history of PRA (RRA, PLA) is agro-ecosystem analysis, another is the information need of external people (consultants, researchers, development workers), who wanted better information more quickly than was possible through conventional research methodologies. These two factors have remained: we are still struggling to understand the importance of environmental sustainability in the lives of poor people, and development professionals of all sorts still need good information for their reports, their lobbying and their support of the struggles of the excluded. This is important for making good analysis of problems and impacts of development programmes.

I have witnessed many events in which PRA has been used – appraisals, reviews, evaluations and monitoring visits – and they have gone in all possible directions. By applying all the tools in the PRA toolkit, answers to many questions were found, unexpected realities were uncovered and dialogues were established. However, it has been hard in the best of cases to draw clear conclusions, for example about impacts of project activities or policy changes, or to formulate prioritized and focused plans for development projects.

In Oxfam GB, we have used different incarnations of the so-called sustainable livelihoods framework since 1992, for formulating questions (at the start of a PRA-based assessment for example), for understanding basic causal relations between events and effects, and for assessing progress and impacts. The framework is primarily a tool for the outsider, the development professional who relates to deprived people and other stakeholders. The sustainable livelihoods framework has also been used by others, and has recently gained a lot of attention when the Department for International Development (DFID) started using it as a vehicle for refocusing development programmes and projects on poverty eradication (Carney et al. 1999).

As a tool in project appraisal, review or evaluation, the framework seems capable of providing the professional with a language and holistic concept that is compatible with that of ordinary people who are trying to survive, strengthen their livelihoods, educate their children and build up assets. Ordinary people think holistically and pursue multiple goals at any one time, unlike many scientists and development workers. Beyond that, the framework needs to help the professional to understand and discuss with different social actors what the critical triggers for improvement are in a specific situation. In this way, it is a tool that supports managing the learning process, or the 'process of sharing', that is seen by, for example, Robert Chambers as one of the three main aspects of PRA.

Much PRA training in Oxfam GB over the past few years has been accompanied by training in, or discussion of, the sustainable livelihoods framework, but with mixed success. Trainees (i.e. staff of Oxfam and partners) have found analysis of complex data from multiple sources an enormous challenge, and facilitating the analytical process more so. The framework itself is being seen as too abstract, and only comes to life by repetitive references to it in the course of several (contained) analytical processes (Neefjes and Woldegiorgis 1999). Furthermore, it has been seen as relatively ineffective in helping to improve understanding of the importance of environmental sustainability (in concrete cases), and when applied in a mechanical way one may miss out on the analysis of social differences. This does not negate the need for some sort of analytical framework, because making beautiful maps, drawing timelines and ranking well-being in a safe and honest environment, even if cross-checked with other sources, is no guarantee of trustworthy conclusions or well-targeted proposals for more learning and action.

I think we need better analysis in PLA processes, in Oxfam GB and elsewhere. We need to be more aware of the need for action based on learning at grassroots and other levels. And we need to ensure that development managers become more part of this process of sharing and improving. All who are interested in working to eradicate poverty and social exclusion should work to the true values of empowerment and learning.

Notes

[1]RRA: Rapid Rural Appraisal; PRA: Participatory Rural Appraisal; PLA: participatory learning and action. These terms for methodological approaches are often used interchangeably, but even though they are (historically) related in many ways there are big differences.

[2]I worked for Oxfam GB for over eight years. Oxfam GB is often known as Oxfam, which is used in the rest of the paper. However, all 11 members of Oxfam International are fully independent organizations – they include Oxfam Hong Kong, for whom I am now working in Vietnam.

[3]The sample was biased for training sessions in which I was a lead facilitator.

References

Carney, D.; Drinkwater, M.; Rusinow, T.; Neefjes, K.; Wanmali, S.; and Singh, N. (1999) *Livelihood Approaches Compared: a brief comparison of the livelihood approaches of the UK Department for International Development (DFID), CARE, Oxfam and the UNDP*, DFID, London.

Neefjes, K. (1999) *Participatory Review in Chronic Instability – the experience of the 'Ikafe' refugee settlement programme*, ODI, Uganda, London.

Neefjes, K. and Woldegiorgis, A. (1999) *Environments, Livelihoods and Staff Capacity: an assessment of impacts of training*, Oxfam GB, Gender & Learning Team.

CHAPTER 20
Bardolf Paul

PRA values:
how to become a true believer

The main purpose of this chapter is to explore certain aspects of the values that implicitly underpin the Participatory Rural Appraisal (PRA) movement and seek an understanding of how to kindle and foster the growth and sharing of these values. The assumption is that the more people are able to embrace these values, the greater the likelihood that the PRA movement and other similar manifestations of these shared values will be able to grow and spread.

I can remember reading some years ago a paper by Chambers entitled something like 'PRA is not a religion'. Having attended several of Robert's 'PRA revival meetings', which had the overt theme of converting the unbelievers, I found the title both amusing and ironic. It struck me at the time that there was an element of concern and discomfort regarding how to deal with the underlying values that are the cornerstone of the PRA movement. One concern was that we don't become fanatical proselytisers, but at the same time ask ourselves how do we foster the values that run through PRA?

For some years I have been reflecting on how to bring the question of values into a forum for discussion and exchange of experience. The opportunity that the Pathways to Participation project offered in April 2000 allowed me to put forward some thoughts and invite comments. In doing so, I would like to make a distinction between what I call the 'inner' and the 'outer' aspects of our being and experience. I believe we all have an inner dimension to our existence, something that goes on within our being that is separate and different from what happens in our outer life, where we are involved in worldly affairs. There is a constant interaction between these two arenas of existence, and although I believe that the ways in which we manifest our values are strongly affected by outer circumstances, the values themselves arise from our more permanent inner state or being. I have used these distinctions in describing my own experience with PRA values.

These parallel experiential processes – the external and the internal – if mutually reinforcing, make it possible to practise our values and behave accordingly, because our values and behaviours are rooted in an internal experiential and transformational reality. This brings me to the main question of this essay: 'Is it possible to affect and change people's externally manifested values if they don't have a corresponding internal transformational experience?' We all have special experiences, especially from activities like PRA, but how long do they last? Are we all able to spontaneously manifest the behaviour that is needed in the PRA process in other parts of our lives?

Personal background

I was first exposed to PRA in 1989–90, when working for a Canadian-funded project based at MYRADA, an NGO based in Bangalore, India. There was a lot of method development activity going on at this time involving MYRADA, other NGOs and Robert Chambers, who was based at the Administrative Staff College in Hyderabad. I was never directly involved in any of this activity, but was able to catch the flavour of it by proximity.

Towards the end of 1990, I attended a PRA training in Andhra Pradesh, which was facilitated by MYRADA under the guiding hand of Jimmy Mascarenhas. It was a seminal experience for me. Even though the methodology was still in a fairly rough stage, the exposure was sufficient for me to grasp the essentials, particularly the mechanisms for allowing people to do their own analysis and planning, and the use of visual media as a means of focusing and facilitating communication. The latter aspect was especially interesting for me at that time, as I had spent the previous 20 years working in various aspects of media production and communication design. So for me these were the 'external' attractions and interests related to PRA.

After India, I started working intensively with PRA in the north of Vietnam, and over a five-year period gained a great deal of first-hand experience in introducing and developing the methodology with government and NGO staff through field-level training and practice. This was followed by another five years working on institutionalizing participation and the use of PRA in the national education system for forestry undergraduate training.

As I gained more experience in working with PRA, another important dimension emerged – the intuitive element – a kind of faith in the validity of the process, and a way of being during the process. It took me a little while to fully recognize the fundamental importance of this element, but when I did, I realized that there was a significant convergence with another process that had been going on for some years in my life, an 'inner' development process.

Being open and letting go

'Being open' and 'letting go' are qualities closely related to having trust in the process of PRA. And by being open and letting go we affect and connect to our sense of values and being. This 'inner' dimension of PRA, and learning how to work with it, made my overall experience much more interesting and meaningful because of the connection to my own inner development.

Since childhood I had always felt a sense of incompleteness and an urgency to find something that would enable me to fully develop as a human being. Growing up in the 1950s and 1960s was a time when many young people began to question all of the accepted norms and look for direct experiential evidence upon which to establish and validate their values and beliefs. In my late teens and early twenties I began exploring various paths towards inner development, one of which was completely experiential. The experience arose by being open and letting go in an inner sense, and it brought about real changes within my self and my life.

One of the results of this ongoing internal experiential process was to become much more intuitive, to trust feelings more. And by the time I first encountered PRA I had been practising this other form of being open and letting go for 25 years, which is why I think I found it relatively easy to pick up the PRA approach and methodology. The capability to interact intuitively with people and situations is something that I feel is at the heart of good PRA. It makes it possible to be 'open', i.e. not have a personal agenda, and to 'let go', i.e. to trust the process and treat every situation like an exploration or adventure in which the answers and even the questions will emerge as you go along.

PRA values

The question of attitudes and behaviour has long been an essential element in PRA work – one of the 'three pillars' – but I have not yet seen much written about the values that drive attitudes and behaviour. Nor have I seen much in-depth examination of how to bring about fundamental change in attitudes and behaviour. Therefore, I would be interested in stimulating some discussion on the issue of how to change attitudes and behaviour, and include the question of values as essential to the discussion.

My perception of the 'ideal' combination of attitudes and behaviour in a PRA practitioner is someone who is able to be open to new ideas; accepts the opinions of others in a non-judgemental manner; approaches situations with a spirit of enquiry; is looking for the right answers and has no need for personal ownership of ideas; treats people in a kind and considerate way; etc. This list could go on extensively but, in essence, it reflects a set of values, many of which are commonly found in the heart of many religious and spiritual movements.

A key question is how do people acquire such a value system? For some it comes quite naturally and we can see this with newcomers to PRA, who very often just 'naturally' embrace the approach and methods. Then there are others who take some time to incorporate the principles and changes in their attitudes and behaviour. This transformation comes eventually after some exposure and practice. Finally, there are those who perhaps might never accept or take on the values and behaviour that are needed – they are unable to change.

What does this range and variation suggest, and what might the implication be for the spread of something like PRA? For me, it suggests that there are internal differences between people, but that these differences are not necessarily fixed – that there are possibilities for change. So if we think it is important to bring about inward changes in people, how to go about doing this? Is there anything we can do to help or is it something that an individual has to do themselves? Is this something PRA practitioners should even be concerned with?

How to change?

Changing the way people behave and think about something like rural development can in itself be a difficult task. Changing aspects of fundamental values within an individual that influence their attitudes and behaviour is a much more daunting challenge because it means bringing about an inner transformation or a kind of 'inner development' which very often is beyond the power of the individual themselves, let alone that of outside persons. So how to do it?

Many of us have experienced the change that comes about as a result of working extensively with participatory approaches, whether it is using PRA in natural resources or in other disciplines such as education or health. This surely can be an effective way to bring about change within our inner rural landscape, but it does take time and it is not always guaranteed. I can recall being in a session some years ago with a group of PRA practitioners, discussing how to change attitudes and behaviour, and some people expressed their frustration at being unable to change, despite being very aware of appropriate attitudes and behaviour for themselves. I wonder how widespread this experience is?

The implication is that, in some cases, something more than external experiential learning is needed to bring about effective personal change in one's attitudes and behaviour. I suggest that this 'additional something' might be worth looking into.

I have already briefly described my own experience, which has been the combination of work experience that fosters personal change in attitudes and behaviour, coupled with an inner transformational process that brings about deep changes in one's being. The latter was essential to achieve permanent personal change. This is a touchy area to get into because of the associations, and because it is personal. Nevertheless, I firmly believe that as we shift our focus more and more to the importance of human relationships, we have to enter into the realm of personal change, because the biggest obstacles to achieving successful results with approaches like PRA are the attitudes, behaviour and values of the people involved.

Conclusions

The question of attitudes, behaviour and values is fundamental to the successful future growth of participatory approaches in all fields. Some people are 'naturals' and can immediately swim with the tide, others have to go through transformational processes to be able to incorporate these approaches. A certain degree of personal change can happen through direct experience with participatory processes, but it may be only a short-term change, i.e. for the period of the event. Long-term personal change may require other types of transformational experiences, perhaps on an inner level, in order to achieve deep penetration and permanency.

Because of the fundamental importance of personal development and transformation, we should ask ourselves: is this not something that should be discussed and explored in PRA circles, especially if we believe in the need for more 'true believers'?

CHAPTER 21

Wilhelmina R. Pelegrina

Rediscovering a dream: reflections on PRA experience

This chapter is an account of a very personal journey through the many ups and downs of Participatory Rural Appraisal (PRA) practice and training in the context of strengthening farmers' role in agricultural development. It tells a story of how, at one point, there was much enthusiasm about it, how suddenly interest waned with experiences of misuse, and how disillusionment was overcome and PRA rediscovered.

Discovery

My own PRA pathway is like a love found, lost and found again. The journey is both happy and sad, fulfilling and frustrating, but at the end of it all, I could not have asked for anything better.

My first encounter with PRA came during my first year in community development work. I moved out of research and the university because of a personal dilemma. I was given the task of developing a protocol for the extraction of a chemical from a plant with insecticidal properties. Young as I was, I raised questions about the benefit of such research to farmers who could extract the chemical cheaply using traditional knowledge. Call it an inherent seed of rebellion, but I started questioning the research direction and the ethics of research. Little did I know that I was heading to my own extinction from formal research.

My questions found their way to a friend, who led me to discover development work. Two weeks after I resigned from the university, I found myself in another world where farmers' participation and empowerment are daily buzzwords. I soon had to unlearn and discover new methodologies to improve people's participation in community development.

We were in the process of reviewing our methods of work and improving our tools in community organizing to give us a better grasp of the community situation and effectively deliver our interventions when I stumbled upon PRA. I was given the task of developing a training module that would provide development workers with a toolbox or a collection of method-ologies to assist in planning and attaining that elusive community develop-ment agenda. The political scenario was ripe for introspection as non-governmental organizations (NGOs) in the Philippines were undertaking self-examination vis-à-vis their position and relevance within the newfound democratic space. The space demanded a shift from mere political to broader development concerns.

We looked at literature and it was through interactions with some friends that we stumbled upon *RRA Notes* No. 13, where some PRA tools were explicitly discussed. Devouring the information, extending our imaginations and seeking help from someone who has undergone Rapid Rural Appraisal (RRA), we included a three-day training on PRA with farming communities. The result was overwhelming, especially when we merged PRA with community organizing using an experiential learning process, and the action–reflection–action process to synthesize the whole experience.

The training was such a success that I soon found myself moving from one province to the other, giving PRA trainings using a three-day or two-week module. Introducing PRA was a touchy subject because development workers are offended, as if you are questioning their commitment to partici-pation. At that time, such a question was as lethal as the NGO community debate on politics and ideology. Such an uncomfortable situation was easily resolved by urging participants to experience the process, reflect and apply only those aspects that they thought were relevant. As a result, more con-crete plans were generated and interest from the communities heightened.

We used PRA as an appraisal tool, but from the start PRA was not a mere tool for rural appraisal for my co-trainers and me. It was never a stand-alone process and it was never neutral. We used it then as a mirror for develop-ment workers to see how true we are to our commitment to people's par-ticipation. That is why all of our PRA training sessions were emotional – either we kept the fires of commitment burning or we triggered discontent with organizations. There was an instance where we had to extend our train-ing because we elicited serious internal debates, complete with emphatic speeches among the staff. Those were the heady days of PRA.

Changes

Circumstances led me to pursue further studies. With much difficulty, I left the Philippine NGO scene and PRA training and practice for a while. I tried to continue and enrich the experience overseas, but I failed to find a good opportunity. I soon discovered that PRA is used differently in the Northern country I was in – there is less passion and less commitment. In most cases, PRA was used as a career move and done out of compliance. I thought this was solely a Northern phenomenon.

Having left the Philippines when PRA use was gaining momentum on the ground, I was not surprised to find a lot of changes when I returned. I was, however, not prepared for all of the changes.

Realities

What has happened to PRA in the Philippines after almost a decade? What have we got to show, in terms of people's participation and change? Whom are we sharing the information and our reflections with, in this day and age where information and knowledge is a means of production? Have we created our own PRA élite in the process? Instead of mainstreaming and sharing, have we grown into professionals routinely executing PRA and PRA training? Is our motivation to conduct training and PRA for consultancy or to satisfy the demand of a funding agency or to satisfy the demand of the participants or for genuine people's participation?

I have seen how some researchers use PRA tools to extract information. I have been a party to one such process. A small grant was made by an international organization to look at the role of children in agriculture in two Asian countries. I was given the task of assisting in the facilitation in one of the countries. Instead of working with the children of partner farmers, we went to the local schools and asked the teachers for volunteer students for this activity. The areas where we went were service areas of the local NGO and the NGO assured us that there would be follow-up. We did a focused PRA, went back to the office, analysed the results, produced the reports and presented the report to the funder. The funder was impressed with the results as they clearly showed that children played a significant role in agriculture and it signalled its intention to develop a programme to address this reality. That was three years ago. To date, I have not heard of any action from the organization, the funder or the local NGO in this area. I don't even know if the results of that study were presented back to the community. And we call this participatory?

I was also asked to assist in an international training course that involved a one-day PRA activity in the community where tenancy along the forest buffer zone was a major issue. I disagreed with the choice of location, as there was no clear purpose for our entry except to orient the participants on PRA. What happened was very memorable. I explained the whole situation to the participants and threw the challenge at them. They walked out of the room and demanded to know from the training organizers why a junior staff member was handling the PRA training. Still, we went to the community the following day. There was not much interest from the participants, not because of the timebomb of the previous day, but because at the first instance the community people bluntly asked us for the significance of the PRA activity and where the activity would lead. Would this support their cause, they asked? So we failed as facilitators at both the training level and the community level, but which matters most?

Decision

There was a time when PRA was used to elicit genuine people's participation, when the facilitator's aim was solely to assist the local communities to analyse and take control of their situation. What happened along the way? I wondered if this was the norm now. Am I too idealistic? Am I too much of a purist? Do I still believe in participation? Shall I move with the tide and satisfy the demand for PRA and PRA training? Or shall I stand firmly for what I believe in? What do I believe in? Am I the only one asking these questions? It was a tough choice but I was left with no other option. I soon decided to close that chapter of my life as a PRA trainer. I decided to step back, observe and seek other possibilities.

Rediscovery

One day I found myself in another organization, quietly observing how my younger colleagues grappled with suggested methodologies to enhance farmers' participation in agricultural development. After some prodding, they soon raised questions, issues and realizations. Are they really involving farmers in their research or are farmers merely respondents? What matters most? Is it the sound statistical design they need to implement for a good technical report or the fact that the farmers are actually doing their own research according to their objectives, criteria and preferences? Shall we follow the centre-based design of research or evolve our own? What are we doing? Where are we heading?

I could not leave those questions hanging, having triggered the self-examination in the first place. Slowly, I began introducing PRA in small talks, then in a training and then more. It was not an easy task. I met resistance and rejection along the way, but the reaction of villagers and the enthusiasm of a couple of my younger colleagues to try the process led me to resurrect and reinvent PRA in my current work. I used it again, as I used it before, as a mirror where my colleagues see their actions and the meaning of their work.

To be less controversial, I introduced PRA as a tool for baseline surveys. Not everyone agreed to use it. What proved its worth is the fact that the group that used PRA has completed its baseline and is now implementing programmes, while the other group, which opted for questionnaires, is still

143

in the process of analysing its data. From a baseline survey tool, slowly I linked PRA again to community organizing and to the core of our work on agricultural technology development and policy advocacy. With support from colleagues, we moved the reinvented/rediscovered PRA from the Philippines to two other Southeast Asian countries on a national scale, and we are slowly breaking into a lesser-known Himalayan country.

What was the reinvention? We are currently learning to use PRA in establishing the baseline for plant genetic resources conservation and development. The baseline information is gathered through PRA and the whole activity is part of a season-long Farmers' Field School. From baseline, farmers use PRA to set their own plant breeding objectives, secure the parent materials for farmers' crop improvement efforts, including securing base materials for crop selection, monitoring and evaluating crop responses, pest and disease environment, and more. The process is simultaneously being developed in 19 communities in 11 provinces in three countries by a multistakeholder group composed of national government agencies, research institutions, NGOs and farmer groups, with the objective of strengthening farmers' role in agricultural science and technology – an empowerment agenda. Slowly, and with care, we are also experimenting with using PRA to strengthen the role of farmers in local and national policy actions as part of consolidating their successes in their fields. For instance, we will try to use PRA tools to rally actions and argue against the passing of a bill on plant variety protection.

A happy ending? Not really. As early as now, I'm bracing myself for a lot of errors, rejections and misuse. I can only hope that the mechanisms we have set up and shall set up will be able to address these concerns. It took us almost three years to reach this stage and it will take us ages to perfect participation. But what is life without challenges?

To others, this may not be a reinvention of PRA, but PTD, PAR,[1] community organizing or whatever. To me, I don't care much about the label, as I never placed PRA in a box with set rules, guidelines or manuals for assembly and use. I've learned that PRA has a life of its own. It takes so many forms and never expires or rots if you allow it to grow, as long as the core is that elusive word 'participation'. As a trainer, you can only do your best and pray that you've planted a few well-selected, good seeds that will bear good, juicy fruits, and will quench that insatiable appetite for genuine people's participation. Idealistic? Yes, maybe, but it is worth a try. Then again, I may just be dreaming. Or am I?

Note

[1] PTD, Participatory Technology Development; PAR, Participatory Action Research.

CHAPTER 22

Kamal Phuyal

Sharing happiness through PRA

My introduction to PRA

I am from Nepal. I used to work for a development organization in a rural village, about 13 years ago. Some of my colleagues and I always tried hard to encourage the participation of the poor people in development activities, but with little success. At the beginning of 1991, the organization to which I was affiliated organized a ten-day Participatory Rural Appraisal (PRA) training for us. In those ten days' interaction, we could feel what we had lacked, which previously hindered us from increasing participation of the marginalized section in the development process. One of our realizations was about our attitude, or let's say our way of thinking about development, about poor people and also about our role in the development process.

Our organization conducted a mid-term evaluation of all our programmes using PRA. First, local people, including teachers, social workers, leading farmers and the representatives of local authorities, were oriented on the PRA approach. The evaluation helped both local people and our organization to realize that many of our programmes could not reach the poor people who were in real need. The evaluation work built up a very close rapport with the local people. It helped to change our 'mental map' of the development process. Since then, I have been involved in applying participatory approaches.

In my experience, knowing the process of applying PRA tools is not a big deal; the challenge is having the values – a participatory attitude, respecting diversity, giving people choices, facilitating rather than leading and always taking the side of marginalized sections. I have seen many people who have not even heard about participatory approaches but whose work is participatory. Even their thinking is participatory. Conversely, many PRA facilitators and even trainers have made PRA very technical, or they concentrate only on the application of tools for information collection. I think a participatory approach should be applied in our personal life. My learning is that 'only a good husband (or good wife, good brother, good son or a good human being) can be a good PRA facilitator'. So, I am trying hard to be a good husband in order to be a good PRA facilitator as well.

Here, I would like to share some of my personal experiences that reveal how we can share our happiness with community people, or how they can share their happiness with us, and how PRA can be helpful in this regard.

Development means sharing happiness

Once, one of my colleagues told me, 'What development means, in my experience, is mainly sharing happiness with others.' He explained his point using various cases he had experienced and I liked his idea of development.

I have had opportunities to visit many development projects, some spending millions of rupees and some only a few thousand. Once, I was in a village near Pokhara, within 200 km of Kathmandu. We were doing a participatory evaluation of a drinking water project. We had a very good time there; we could share a lot with the villagers and they were happy to have us in their village. Financially, it was a small project. The government's watershed district office and a Japanese organization implemented the project jointly. They spent about Rs35 000 to complete that project. The women explained their project to us:

> A *Didi* (sister) came to work in our village. We ignored her for a long time. You know, the villagers told her to go back as they had some bitter experiences with previous development workers, but she used to think about our problems for the whole night on the other hand. She was so nice. Ultimately, we liked her and worked together and completed many things. Now we have our own co-operatives. We did literacy classes. We did have a very nice time with her. We were very happy while working together and enjoyed it a lot. We get excited even now by remembering those days. We love our project very much and we never let it die as we recall our time with her.

Those villagers cannot even pronounce the name of the development organizations properly. The only thing they revealed repeatedly was that they were very happy to be with that *Bikase Didi* ('development worker – sister'). Unfortunately, we could not meet the *Didi*, but when we asked about her, what we found was that she used to be very happy to work with rural women. We came to know that her only motto was to share happiness with other people. All of them, the villagers and *Didi*, shared their happiness. The drinking water project was the means for them to share happiness and that happiness brought success to the project. The villagers do not care about the amount spent on the project, nor do they remember how much was spent. During the whole evaluation period, they recalled their happiness repeatedly. That happiness encouraged them to do many other things.

146

Now they have their own co-operative, they have formed a maintenance committee among the women. They have saving groups. 'We are happy to be in a group and we come there, we share our problems and in fact we can share our happiness there,' they said.

Money is not enough

To take a different example, one of the biggest multilateral organizations spent Rs1.5 million on *one village's* drinking water project in Nuwakot district, the northern part of Kathmandu. Yet one Village Development Committee (VDC), which covers several villages, normally receives only Rs500 000 from the government as their annual budget. In this case, there has been a large conflict between the project and the villagers. The villagers were not happy with the project, even though it had solved their problems with fetching water from a long distance away. In their evaluation of the project, the villagers said:

> The construction of the project is almost completed, but we do not even recognize the project people. They keep changing the staff members. We never see any people for the second time in the village. We do not think this is our project. We heard that they have formed a working group. We do not know who they are. They must be among the political leaders. The staff do not have an office here nor do they have any permanent place to stay. Most often they go back to Kathmandu or Trishuli [the district headquarters] in their vehicle after visiting the sites. One of the neighbouring village's contractors has taken responsibility for construction work. We once went to talk to the staff members, but they did not seem happy to talk to us.

The villagers have been fetching water from the nearby spring for many years and they can continue to do this in the future. The villagers were not asked about their desires, or what their real thinking was. The project was planned by outsiders and implemented with the support of a handful of people who did not have problems with water supply themselves. Here, we found that the project could not be the means of sharing happiness. The gap between the villagers and project people started widening from the beginning of the project's entry into the village. It seems that the staff took that project as just a part of their job. They think they are being kind to the villagers by bringing water to the village. They are not ready to take the time to talk to the villagers; if they do not talk to the people, how can they share happiness?

Motivated by happiness

In Nepal, our history tells us many stories regarding the participatory work done by the people themselves. We find that people have made many temples, roads, dug wells and ponds, schools and so on. They used to do all these things as if they were celebrating ceremonies. If you continue analysing, you will find that the main motivation behind all of these activities was to share happiness. They used to sing songs, conduct social work collectively, share food with each other at parties, laugh and enjoy, and complete their work. It seems that sometimes they shared their happiness by giving something to others, and sometimes by taking from others, and sometimes by sharing with each other.

Once, a big organization offered an important job to one of my colleagues. She thought a lot, discussed it with others and at last she refused the offer. She said:

> I am not sure whether I can find such a happy environment in the new place or not. I am very happy to work with my colleagues here with whom I can share my happiness. I am enjoying my work here. Yes, of course, they have offered me a doubled salary and better facilities. But, I am afraid of losing my happiness.

Sharing happiness through PRA

Recently, I reviewed 60 PRA training reports. I consulted the evaluations done by the participants. I didn't find a single report of people who said the PRA training was boring. I found statements like; 'Ten days spent like ten minutes', 'the learning process was like games', 'we did not feel bored', 'we laughed a lot, we shared a lot', etc. What you learn from PRA can be learnt in other ways as well. However, one of the main values of PRA, in my experience, is that it creates an environment for sharing happiness. The participants do not feel hierarchy there; they do not feel any disparities, whether in socio-economic, caste or gender terms. They all laugh, learn and share. Sharing happiness develops the sentimental attachment among the sharers, which is what PRA ultimately does either during the training or in the community. As a PRA facilitator said to me:

> While doing social mapping, the villagers move stones, sticks and make houses. They remember that they are making a village map, or an artificial map, for the first 15 minutes. Then they all forget that they are playing with stones and other local materials. They go to reality then. They shout, they laugh, they talk openly and sometimes they become angry too. Therefore, what I have felt is that after 15 minutes they start entering the live discussion and analysis, and the sharing of happiness starts. When the artificial moments end and sharing happiness starts, other villagers who are standing aside commence to participate in the exercise. Even the illiterate and the

marginalized people who normally hesitate to speak in public start to partici-pate. Sharing happiness makes the process easier.

But PRA without 'sharing happiness' becomes boring and very technical.

Dangerous PRA

Sometimes, PRA becomes dangerous as well. Once the chairperson of a VDC of Dhading district, a neighbouring district of Kathmandu, shared their experience of seeing a 'PRA gang' behaving like this:

> A team of PRA practitioners came, headed by four or five porters carrying their lodging and foodstuffs. They arrived in the village and some of them went to find the chickens, some went to cut the branches of trees for an evening campfire. A group of youths went to the water tap and started teas-ing the young village girls. In the evening they had a big cultural evening. They played *Angreji* (English) music and started to disco dance with alcohol. They shouted and the dancing stopped only when two dancing drunk guys began to fight. The next morning they gathered only seven or eight people, including three from the house where they had stayed, and 'did PRA'.

This kind of non-participatory PRA does not share happiness but steals the happiness of people. Moreover, such PRA exercises, with their vested inter-ests, also ruin the values of PRA itself.

Whatever we do through PRA can be done in other ways too. We can encourage the illiterate and marginalized section to participate in develop-ment processes by using other techniques. But, the main value or contribu-tion of PRA is that it holds the potential to create an environment of sharing happiness.

Wealth and happiness

I was observing villagers discussing a well-being ranking in a village of Sind-hupalchowk district, which lies on the northeastern part of Kathmandu. They categorized an old man in the 'lower (poor) rank'. He was there in the group too. He denied that he was in that category. Discussion took place for a long time. Others wanted to prove that he was poor by giving many exam-ples. Actually, they wanted to help him, as the project was going to provide some programmes for the poor people. The old man had nothing. It was even difficult for him to arrange two meals a day. He said, 'I do not have enough food, but I am happy. I am the happiest person in this village you know. Have you ever seen me being sad or depressed? How can you call me poor?' In fact, he was the one who used to be first to take part in,

149

or lead, any social work. Finally, the others put him in the 'middle rank'.

After that exercise we talked with the man at length. We found that he had a source of happiness within him. All the villagers feel his absence when he goes away for several days. The PRA team realized that of course basic needs (at least) are the right of all human beings, and hunger might create obstacles in the way of feeling happiness. However, economic well-being cannot be compared with emotional well-being.

Development and spirituality

Last month I had a discussion on development and spirituality with other development workers. Somebody asked: 'What about the empowerment of the marginalized section of society?' We concluded that, of course, we want justice, we do not want disparity, we do not want exploitation and we want 'the empowerment of the disempowered'. Therefore, we want the marginalized people or deprived people's participation in their development process. We want to listen to them. We want to be their friends in the process of their empowerment. We want this not because this is our job, but because we will be happier for this experience. We want them to 'rise' and the disparities to become smaller. We should let them feel that we will be happy to be their friends in their empowerment process. This is how we share happiness with them. Once they understand our desires, they will also start sharing their happiness with us. PRA can help us to share happiness with the marginalized sections as it removes all the formalities between us and it supports the process to go on as per their way of thinking.

Saving the table

A VDC chairperson shared his experience of using PRA for planning with me. He said:

> Before PRA, we used to collect demands from each ward member. Our table used to suffer a lot before – as each and every ward member tried to prove their demands were the most important by banging on the table! However, pair-wise ranking has saved our poor table these days. We do all the prioritizing happily.

I have learnt from my experiences so far that PRA helps us to share our happiness with the villagers as well as their happiness with us, and especially with those who are vulnerable and marginalized. I believe that reflecting on the positive aspects of anything can help us to go forward for development. Reflecting *only* on the negative aspects encloses us; we cannot go forward through concentrating on the negative alone.

CHAPTER 23

Michel Pimbert

Learning to live the politics of participation

My commitment to 'participatory approaches and development' initially grew out of a critique of normal science as well as an interest in
the interaction between society and technology, and the role of human
choice in this interaction.

I was trained as an agricultural ecologist and spent the first part of my
professional career doing ecological research in small farming systems in
developing countries. Much of my early work focused on the design of
locally appropriate pest management technologies. Repeated interactions
with small farmers in villages of Costa Rica, West Africa, South and Southeast Asia soon opened my eyes to the importance of rural people's knowledge and their ability to diagnose and analyse problems, experiment and
evaluate new agricultural technologies.

This phase in my professional life was also greatly influenced by existing
political debates on how the nature and design of technologies in any society encode the values of that society, or more precisely, the values of those
who make the decisions from positions of power. These insights gave me the
confidence to ask questions more openly, as a professional scientist whose
values and priorities count in the choice of research questions and the evaluation of their results and impacts on people's lives. Encouraging people's
participation in the production of knowledge, the design of technologies
and policies became central to my search for a more socially responsible –
and accountable – science.

My exposure to, and use of, participatory methodologies (AEA, Agroecosystem Analysis; PRA, Participatory Rural Appraisal; PAR, Participatory
Action Research) allowed me to further embed participatory approaches in
my fieldwork. During my association with an influential, and rather conventional, international agricultural research centre in India (International
Crop Research Institute for the Semi Arid Tropics, ICRISAT), I was able to
give more legitimacy to farmers' values and decision making in pest management research. Participatory processes created space for the inclusion of

farmers' priorities and knowledge in research and in the validation of technologies. The production of an educational video on 'Participatory Research
with Women Farmers' for National Agricultural Research Centres and non-
governmental organizations (NGOs) was an important part of my efforts to
spread and scale up PRA methods and approaches more widely among agricultural scientists dealing with complex, risk-prone farming systems in
semi-arid regions.

The use of PRA methods and dialogues with rural people in their own
ecological and cultural settings was a source of considerable personal learning. These experiences led me to shift my attention more and more from
farming systems per se to rural livelihoods, their complex internal linkages
and the many types of natural and other resources that sustain them. It was
at this time that I left agricultural research and joined an international conservation organization (WWF) to co-ordinate policy research on the conservation and sustainable use of biological resources in different
environments (forests, wetlands, rangelands...).

Throughout my association with WWF I tried to encourage an approach
that focuses on understanding the ways different groups perceive, value, use
and manage biological resources in diverse economic and ecological contexts. For example, participatory policy research with rural people affected
by protected area and wildlife management schemes led to new insights on
the types of conservation and land-use policies needed to better serve the
needs of the poor and to sustain diversity – both biological and cultural
diversity.

While with WWF I also directly experienced the difficulties of
mainstreaming people-centred approaches and participatory methods
in large bureaucracies. This gave me deeper insights into the inertia
associated with normal professional bias, the micro-politics of bureaucracies and the insecurity generated by open-ended, learning process
approaches that seek to change existing power relationships. At the
same time, however, this intellectual and painful emotional experience
strengthened my desire to better understand how, and under what conditions, participatory processes can be institutionalized in bureaucracies and
everyday life.

Some of the thinkers and activists who influenced me most during this
professional and personal journey include libertarian socialists and anarchists
(e.g. Peter Kropotkin, Paul Goodman, Lewis Mumford, Elisée Reclus,
Murray Bookchin, André Gorz), radical science and technology collectives
(in the UK and France), iconoclasts on development and needs satisfaction
(e.g. Ivan Illich, Robert Chambers, Ignacy and Wolfgang Sachs, Gandhi)
and educationalists (e.g. Paulo Freire, Budd Hall), as well as indigenous
peoples and farmers.

Dealing with corrupt participation language and practice

The variety of contradictory meanings projected into 'participation' by different social actors has been confusing and frustrating to me. The language of participation and token participatory dialogues is used as a fig leaf by a variety of organizations, from donors and government to NGOs and consultants. Genuine participatory processes have been/are often co-opted to promote the interests of the powerful at the expense of the disenfranchised. Emancipatory possibilities have been/are being neutralized by an increasingly globalized participation rhetoric that helps reproduce and legitimize 'business as usual'.

My *personal* response to this disorientation and tokenism is to be more open with others about where I am coming from and to where I am trying to travel. This basically means being more explicit about the meaning I give to participation, clarifying the values and beliefs which *bias* my own style of PRA/PLA (Participatory Learning and Action) work and the kinds of social relationships I see as desirable. Being clear about values helps me draw the line and side with coalitions of interest who want to move beyond corrupt participation language and practice, stressing instead social change for equity and the empowerment of those hitherto excluded from decision making and control over resources. How do other practitioners deal with these disturbing trends? Are any *collective* responses possible?

The need for more comprehensive learning for action

Much of the training in participatory methodologies and approaches could be made more relevant to the challenges ahead by stressing:
- experiential learning and the importance of values, ways of being and relating with others. Humanistic psychology may offer approaches and methods to deal with the difficult – and often taboo – questions of change in individual life orientation, attitudes and behaviour as well as growth in empathic understanding and concern for others.
- the quality of facilitation. All too often facilitation for PLA is equated with using appropriate methods to solve problems at the local level without taking into account the wider scale and questions of governance. Facilitating and encouraging individual and collective learning within the participation paradigm requires attention to the international, national and local institutional contexts that increasingly set boundaries on the spread, scaling up and mainstreaming of participation.
- the importance of cultural diversity and specificity as the basis for intercultural dialogue and action.

Do we have good examples or initiatives from which we can learn?

Walking the talk in our own institutes

A number of Northern-based institutes house individuals who have made remarkable contributions to the spread of participatory methodologies and approaches in development and environmental practice. These institutes have become world famous, attracting funds and new people eager to learn more about these approaches. However, I have often found that these institutes have done little to *transform themselves* into learning organizations that value experiential learning and participation. There may be a case for donors earmarking funds in their frame agreements to allow these institutes to experiment with and facilitate change within their walls. My hunch is that attempts to transform such organizations will have an enduring impact on the theory and practice of participation, an impact that may ultimately be far greater than using the same funds for one-off PLA/PRA trainings and networking. Are any donors and champions out there willing to take the bull by the horns?

Participation and the policy process

Despite public statements in favour of participation, there are few examples of organizations supporting, or learning from, processes of participatory policy research and formulation. This is partly due to lack of commitment to more *direct* forms of participatory democracy. But lack of familiarity with more inclusive forms of deliberation and appropriate methodologies is another possible reason for this. My limited experience suggests that citizen juries and scenario workshops could be combined with PRA/PLA methodologies to create more democratic styles of policy formulation. But we need to work out:

- what combinations of participatory methods and deliberative and inclusive processes (DIPs) are useful in bringing the diversity of local knowledge, priorities, policy analysis and location-specific definitions of well-being into the policy process. How can policy processes be grounded in these forms of deliberative democracy?
- how, and under what conditions, can the new communication technologies (digital video, Internet...) be used as a methodological complement to make the outcomes of local-level participatory policy processes and DIPs more visible to decision makers and civil society at the local, national and global levels?

Institutional transformation for participation

To facilitate PLA on a large scale, external support organizations such as government departments, NGOs and donors are faced with the challenge of transforming themselves: their professional style, organizational culture and procedures. This goes beyond tinkering with the system, although I would still maintain that changes at that level are worthwhile gains.

Institutional transformation for participation is ultimately about creating a culture of democracy: political, economic, technological, gender and cultural democracy. Many would agree that the enabling conditions necessary for the scaling up of participation and organizational change include decentralization, high-level government support, and in-country critical mass of people with relevant and quality training and experience.

In addition, we may need to pay more attention to – *and work on/with/ against* – two sets of contradictory trends that now influence the extent to which participation can be institutionalized, and on *whose* terms. Civil society organizations and indigenous peoples are increasingly seeking to reclaim more control over decisions affecting their lives and environments by rebuilding sustainable local economies and renegotiating their relationships with the state and the market. Yet at the same time, more opaque processes of globalization are taking place in which a small minority of powerful economic actors seek more control over markets, technologies, policies and institutions, imposing a one-dimensional homogenizing reality on diversity.

Perhaps more than ever before, the growth of democratic participation in the North and the South depends on expanding spaces for autonomous action by civil society as well as on a process of localization and reversals that regenerates diverse local economies and ecologies. It is not enough to view the institutionalization of participation as an expansion of *political* democracy to include more people and places in shaping the policy process and institutions. An analysis of how power is increasingly exercised and mediated today suggests that widening *economic* democracy is now a key, overarching condition for the mainstreaming of participation in this globalizing world. Levelling the economic playing field for participation calls for mutually reinforcing and radical structural reforms, such as: Tobin-like taxes on international financial flows and speculation; a guaranteed and unconditional minimum citizen income for all; a reduction of time spent in waged work and more equitable sharing of jobs and wealth; the introduction of anti-trust laws and policies for local competition; the re-localization of plural economies that combine both subsistence and market-oriented activities. Imagining and experimenting with these and other institutional transformations for participation remains a central challenge.

CHAPTER 24

Rajendra Prasad

PRA as learning and empowerment – for children too

My start in development

I did not choose the development field immediately after my graduation, but then I had a chance for employment in World Vision of India as the project manager of a sponsorship programme in Karnataka. During this period, I wanted to experiment with the strategies for development activities that I felt were right. I realized that all the people-based programmes were successful, but in those days, top-down planning was at its peak, and the development workers, even I, held the perception that people are ignorant and we need to teach them. My boss used to say, 'Do not go out of the planned programme. The donors would never agree.' But I believed in people, and in people-centred programmes. A few of my strategies backfired and I was cornered by my administrators for them, while the successful projects were not considered by my boss. Repeated frustration made me resign from the job.

John Devavaram and Erskine, my classmates and colleagues, also decided to come out of the organization, and to start our own organization so that we could try to do what we perceive as development. So SPEECH evolved, and I was introduced to Participatory Rural Appraisal (PRA). SPEECH is a community development non-governmental organization (NGO) working in the southern part of Tamil Nadu, India. The main focus of SPEECH's work is development and support of people's organizations, natural resources management, gender and development, child labour rehabilitation and child rights protection. Our main aims are to enable people in the villages to have access to services and facilities and to have control over local resources, in order to improve living conditions and social status of all in the community.

My introduction to PRA

During 1989, John Devavaram attended a PRA training at MYRADA, facilitated by Robert Chambers. After the workshop, John shared what he

156

learned with us, and we were somewhat impressed by it. But we asked lots of questions, about issues like transparency, people's expectations, etc. Since I already had the attitude of believing in the people, I took it very straight. I decided with John and Erskine, why not organize a few PRA trainings and invite Robert? We organized a few, and Robert facilitated the process. I became familiar with the tools and methods, and I wanted to try them on my own in the field. I found PRA to be very useful for knowing people's perceptions, and for planning people-based programmes. I started internalizing the process and realized its value in helping local people as well as development workers to be knowledgeable. It helps everyone to be successful together. I therefore decided for myself to become an effective PRA practitioner. I made it a point to listen, respect, share and plan with people, and to critically analyse issues with them and cross-check with others, like experts, also.

Facts are facts

For instance, during a PRA exercise, the people insisted on constructing a percolation pond. The place was decided, and my team members were happy that everything had been worked out positively. I was invited to finalize the project with the people. I visited the spot and the slope was fine, the inflow channel was fine, but the ground was hard rock. Since it was a percolation pond, the ground needed to be soft rock, not hard rock. I had to discuss it with the people, and they decided to make it a farm pond for animal and human use. My point is, even if it was the people's choice, the facts remain facts, and it wasn't suitable for percolation.

Learning to listen

I have internalized PRA by practising it. It convinced me many times that people's knowledge is important to a development plan. For example, during a PRA on health, the people drew a map with many water stagnation points and improper drainage systems. The map of the future or the 'desired situation' did not touch on the issue of the stagnant water points. I was rather frustrated and became impatient. I said to them, 'It's a healthcare progamme planning map. You have not considered that the stagnant water points should be levelled with mud so that they don't allow the mosquitoes to breed!' The answer thrashed me down. They said, 'Those are the two water points where our animals go and drink water. You want us to level those points so that our animals go without water?' Once upon a time I used to think that all the local beliefs, values, rituals and customs are superstitions, but when I realized the meanings and value of each practice through PRA, I felt I was ignorant. I started listening to them. Before, I thought that my respect and acceptance in society was at a high level whether I agreed with local people or not. PRA made me change.

SPEECH started to internalize PRA, and to use it for everything. The process helped us to plan programmes and mobilize the resources very easily. Handing over was very easy and smooth. We have seen many finished projects maintained and managed by people without our help. The learning was great through PRA. Our ideas and knowledge was easily transferred to people through this process.

Lessons from a child rights project

The particular SPEECH programme I will focus on in the remainder of the chapter, in the Periyapottalpatti Village, Sivakasi block, Virudunagar District, has a special focus on child rights as part of SPEECH's holistic programme. Statistics show that Sivakasi has a large proportion of children who drop out of school (Table 1). Many take employment in various industries. Sivakasi is known throughout India for its 2400 large and small match industries, and its 1200 firework factories. It is also home to 220 printing presses.

Table 1 The child labour situation in Sivakasi block of Virudunagar District

Total population (1991 census)	1 565 037	
Children aged between 0 and 14 years	547 919	(35.01%)
School-going age group between 6 and 14	331 037	
Children actually attending school	245 869	
Children working in match/firework industries	85 168	
School drop out rate (annual, %)	36.77	

We at SPEECH had decided that children would be one focus of our work, along with small and marginal farmers, landless agricultural labourers, rural artisans and women. During a field visit, John and Erskine witnessed a fire in one of the fireworks factories where many children died. They could see the parents beating their chests and crying. At that time, the district collector, Mr Sridar, invited SPEECH to do something about this problem. Although few of our staff members were trained in planning and implementing programmes to ensure child rights, Mr Sridar promised and mobilized funds from the Ministry of Labour. We view child labour as a cycle that is hard to break. In our district, the child labourer becomes unproductive by the age of 40, and then depends on their own children to go to work. All of this made us perceive child labour as a development issue.

We had already done an exploratory PRA in 13 of the villages where there was a high level of child labour, and we had already developed a relationship with the people. Later, we wanted to know the people's perception of the reasons for child labour. We held PRA sessions in a common ground in the village where most of the parents could come. Erskine, Mayandi, Bala, Sundar (the local non-formal education teacher) and myself were in the PRA team. The parents of child labourers used both a problem-and-cause matrix and pair-wise ranking to discuss what the reasons for child labour were (see Tables 2 and 3). These tables show that the participants were very sure that child labour was the result of poverty. But after these first two exercises, the SPEECH staff team and the village partners come to the conclusion that while poverty is one of the reasons, it is not the only reason.

Table 2 Problem-and-cause matrix on child labour

Problem	Causes				Score	Rank
	Caste differences	Political system	Fewer opportunities for economic activities	No investment		
Poverty	9	8	9	10	36	I
Illiteracy	8	4	10	5	27	III
Unemployment of adults	2	8	10	5	25	IV
Ignorance	6	7	6	8	27	III
Ill health	2	2	8	10	22	VI
No interest in agriculture	6	2	8	10	26	IV
Debts/bondage	6	5	9	10	30	II

Table 3 Pair-wise ranking on causes of child labour

	D	NIiA	IH	Ig	U	I	P
P	P	P	P	P	P	P	X
I	D	N	IH	Ig	U	X	
U	D	U	IH	U	X		
Ig	D	Ig	IH	X			
IH	IH	IH	X				
NIiA	D	X					
D	X						
Scoring	4	1	5	2	3	0	6
Ranking	III	VI	II	V	IV	VII	I

Key: D = Debt; NIiA = No interest in agriculture; IH = Ill health;
Ig = Ignorance; I = Illiteracy; P = Poverty; U = Unemployment of adults

After the matrices and pair-wise ranking analysis was finished, the SPEECH team further probed into the problem through a money-wastage map analysis. We looked again at the social and resource maps, seasonal diagrams and problem matrices we had drawn during our exploratory PRA.

The groups were facilitated to identify the entertainment points in the area, such as the liquor shop, lottery ticket sales points, cinema theatre and gambling centres. Then they identified the persons who go to the entertainment points by looking at the social map. Although looking at people's habits is a sensitive task, the process and the tools made it easy. The approximate daily expenses on entertainment of people from the village were calculated (see Table 4). The amounts were added up for 30 days, one year and five years (see Table 5). The final figures were shocking and represented previously unimaginable amounts of money for both the community and us. The people and the SPEECH team arrived at a consensus about the root cause of child labour: it is ignorance, not poverty. It is because so much money is spent on entertainment, rather than on other household expenses.

Table 4 Use of entertainment points in Periyapottalpatti Village

Entertainment points	No. of persons who go daily from the village	The amount of money spent every day (Rs)
Liquor shop	15	600
Lottery shop	22	220
Cinema theatre	25	250
Gambling	6	600
Total	68	1670

Table 5 Calculation of money wastage

Period	Total (Rs)
One day	1 670
One month	50 100
One year	601 200
Five years	3 006 000

Learning from failure

Following these analyses, we facilitated the community partners to plan a programme for the child labourers' rehabilitation. The parents gave emphasis to children's education; non-formal education centres were opened in all our working villages. Each day between 7pm and 9pm the children came back from the factories and attended the respective evening centres. However, day by day, the children's attendance gradually fell. Six months later, the centres were empty.

The SPEECH team had a discussion on the failure of the programme. Some of our team members even doubted the PRA process, because all our other programmes except this one were successful. It was very discouraging to the practitioners in our team. I felt sad and could not think any more about it that day. But when I was in bed that night, I realized that the children were never consulted. The next morning, I invited the PRA team to meet once again, and explained my idea. We agreed that the children are the primary stakeholders, and they have their own desires and wants. But we never consider them. We ask their parents' opinions and they decide for their children. Instead, we wanted to know children's perception on this issue. Everyone agreed to do PRA with the children.

Our team decided to conduct problem-and-need matrices with children, especially child labourers, in all our working villages. We brought together the child labourers, although they were hesitant, because once again they would be in the lifeless non-formal education centres. But we already had a good relationship with the children, and our organizers used songs and other cultural activities to bring them together. Slowly we facilitated the process of making an analysis of the child labour problem. We started with the things that the children like, such as games and food. There was great participation that we could not control. When we came to the village a second day, most of the children came running to us and we got down to business. The results of the children's analysis surprised us all. According to the discussion, the children's priorities from highest to lowest were as follows: recreation, sleeping (rest), good food, clothing, education. We realized that, unlike their parents, the children's priorities were not education – but recreation.

We asked the children to explain the reasons for child labour. They said that one reason was the education system. They said that our schools are not interesting, but factories are interesting. They said, we can talk while we work, laugh while we work, listen to music while we work, sometimes dance while we work, but in schools, our teachers tell us not to talk, not to sing, not to dance and it is boring. Another reason they gave was holidays. They said that during the school holidays, their parents tell them to earn some money in the factories. The children said that they see the opportunity for money, knowing they will be allowed to spend a little portion of their earnings on themselves, so they convince their parents to send them to the factories. During the peak agriculture season when the schools are open, their parents want the children to assist them in agriculture. When they are free during summer, the schools are closed. Finally, parents take huge advances from the factory owners, and then agents take the children to the factories to repay the advances. This cycle continues.

Based on the perceptions and understandings of children, the action plan was again redesigned to match the children's priorities. Our staff team, who are directly involved in the children's programme, the administrators and the team leaders were open to the changes and agreed to convince the donors. With the participation of children, a book was developed which is based on learning through a 'play' method, and it is going very well. The centres are fun places for children, where they can take up lessons only when they want, but otherwise they can use the centre for recreation. Most children eventually choose to study. Many communities now have child labourers' associations, through which the children get involved in community development activities and help to maintain their school buildings. SPEECH has also developed a programme through which child labourers can progress in the mainstream school system.

Conclusion

One lesson from this story is that it is necessary to practise PRA with direct stakeholders as well with the indirect stakeholders, accepting them as equal partners, even if they are children. Most of the time, we need to negotiate with different stakeholders while planning and before implementing the programme. Often, when we talk about 'participation' we are not very clear about exactly who within the community is participating in what way. In this case, at first we thought that the children would just be programme beneficiaries, not the ones to help with analysis and planning.

Traditionally, children and women are powerless in the community. They are ignored and most of them feel that they are incapable of doing anything for themselves or for their society. But given a chance, they have proved to the community that this is wrong. The programmes were planned, implemented and being monitored by children and women through a PRA process. PRA has enabled them to realize that they are competent, and they have gained respect from the community, especially from the men.

I have also learned from this experience that if we do not doubt the first information that people give during PRA, we are heading to disaster. Although we learn to respect people's knowledge as part of PRA, we need to analyse what they are saying and give them a chance to come up with new analysis themselves. In this case, we had a discussion that pushed them to reflect deeper on what the source of child labour was. Rather than just hearing what they had to say already, the PRA exercises allowed them to deepen their thinking, to expand and change their point of view. If we do PRA properly, we should expect this kind of learning process. If PRA is practised superficially and without changing our attitude and behaviour, it will backfire.

Many practitioners say that PRA increases people's expectations. I agree that it does, because a normal human being must have expectations. When you and I have expectations, like having a television or a car or a good job, nothing is seen to be wrong. Yet for some reason, we expect that poor people should not have any expectations beyond what they have already. They are human, not animals. If they have expectations, dreams and visions, people will thrive in reaching towards them. PRA helps everyone to understand and analyse whether the expectations are practical and realistic, whether the resources are available for fulfilling the expectations, whether their dream may come true or not. It can help to differentiate between needs and demands. All of this is provided that we practise PRA with sincerity and a total change in attitude and behaviour.

Attitude and behaviour are not one-time events. They are lived day by day as we ask ourselves, how did I behave today? Did I hurt someone by forcing my views on him? Did I block my own mind from learning? It is a lifelong process. So PRA does not end with exercising the tools, it begins with the tools. It is an empowering process, not a project that ends within a certain period. So let us realize the lifeline of PRA – empowerment.

CHAPTER 25

Garett Pratt

Discovering new faces of PRA

My route into PRA

My introduction to development was through six weeks of development tourism in Kenya and Zimbabwe when I was a high-school student. The Canadians leading the trip aimed to demonstrate the advantages of small non-governmental organization (NGO) development projects, while villainizing large-scale World Bank-funded development. After a year studying community development in the Philippines, and three years of a degree in political science, I joined a Canadian NGO as a student intern during my summer vacation. I was attached to a project in Sri Lanka that provided capacity-building to governmental and non-governmental organizations for vocational training. The programme was very successful on its own terms – but as a political scientist, I couldn't help but question why this programme was being funded and run by a foreign organization, and an NGO at that. Why wasn't government making this investment?

At that time, I also read *Rural Development: putting the last first*, by Robert Chambers (1983), and I was inspired by his powerful message about working to overcome the anti-poor biases of development programmes. I saw government programmes all around me working for the not-so-poor. I wondered what role in development there could be for a Canadian who thinks that governments should be 'doing development', and that the real challenge is to make government work for poor people. I realized that it was largely up to citizens to put pressure on their own governments to make services work for them. But I couldn't help but wonder if a foreign development professional could help to pressure Southern governments to open their decision making and thus the benefits of their programmes more to poor people?

The same friend who lent me Robert's book also suggested that if I were considering a masters degree, the Institute of Development Studies (IDS) at Sussex would be a good bet. A year later, I arrived at IDS to start one. I was lucky to have John Gaventa as my supervisor. His stories from his activist action research background expanded my view on what participation could mean. My reading and writing allowed me to start developing a more sophisticated view of what participation means in relation to knowledge and power.

My formative PRA experience

Along with four other interns from my masters course, I joined an IDS team providing 'technical support' to a Participatory Poverty Assessment (PPA) in the Shinyanga region of Tanzania. The Shinyanga Human Development Report Project was funded by the United Nations Development Program (UNDP), implemented by the regional government of Shinyanga, and supported with technical assistance from IDS. The project aimed to synthesize the findings of a PPA with several sectoral studies prepared by national consultants into a 'Human Development Report' (HDR) for the region. Unlike the conventional HDRs produced by the UNDP, it would aim to present local perceptions of poverty and well-being.

The researchers included government staff from the Shinyanga region, a team of university-based consultants who would also prepare sectoral studies, and us five IDS student interns. We had three weeks of training in PRA, with a little training on participatory theatre. We formed teams of four or five people and started three weeks of fieldwork.

I was in a team with one university-based researcher and three government officers, all practising PRA for the first time. The team had very mixed motivations. As a young, inexperienced student who was very keen on learning about PRA, I saw this exercise as a golden opportunity to gain some field experience. The motivations of the others on my team ranged widely: (1) disinterest in being a development worker in general and so definitely no interest in doing PRA; (2) wanting to do a good job to please superiors and protect their job; (3) wanting to maintain a standard of academic professionalism; (4) wanting to learn everything possible about PRA in order to work more effectively with people in future community work. These motivations meant we were willing to invest different amounts of effort and thought into our fieldwork and reporting. If everyone had been more motivated, I am sure there are days when we would have done a much better job, because we would have spent more time planning and more time on reporting while the discussion was fresh. What was the experience of doing PRA like for people who were forced to do it as part of their job? What was it like for the local people being facilitated by someone who felt forced into it?

When we introduced ourselves in the village, one of my team members managed to argue that it was a great privilege that the village had been chosen for the study, and so they should be proud to contribute as best they could. But we also had to explain that there was currently no funding available for follow-up. I realized how much time we would take from local people, and how uncertain the benefits were to them. The action planning we would do might have been useful to them in organizing their own local development efforts. We knew the document might affect development policy in the region, and particularly UNDP's decision about how and what to fund. There was a group of women who came day after day, and referred to the PRA exercises as 'school', because they felt they were learning something – that is the most tangible positive impact I saw in the community. I still wonder what did local people get out of contributing to the PPA, and were we honest enough about how uncertain and diffuse the benefits would be?

I didn't realize for a few days that the village committee had coerced people to turn up to the PRA exercises. One of the bylaws said that if households did not send a representative to official meetings, they could be fined. I questioned this arrangement with my team-mates, and I argued that it was up to us to convince people it was worth attending the exercises, but that it was wrong to coerce them into participating. They explained that the bylaw existed because the community had approved it – that they had decided that it was necessary to have that kind of incentive or people would not attend meetings. I think that this is the way that government has operated in Tanzania for years, and so three weeks of PRA training wouldn't lead people to see this practice as inappropriate. Was our experience unique? Does the current pressure to do PRA for 'our' purposes encourage practitioners to coerce people to participate?

It took me some time to understand the social positions of the people we met each day. Many were from the better-off households in the village. Our day-to-day reporting reflected little about the details of who said what, and who else was there when they said it. How much can we make of the views we recorded without that information? For example, I gained some very interesting insights into the negative way that not-so-poor people in the village perceived the poorest. But in recording their views about 'the poor', I worried that their views would be represented as the views of the poorest themselves, or perhaps as an accurate depiction of the poorest people. In recording findings, it was easy to slip into treating them as 'facts' rather than 'perceptions', especially as the synthesis process removed the original statements further from the hands of the people who understood the context in which they were said.

Many people in the village where we worked felt their government health worker, who would not provide free care or free medicine at the government clinic, was cheating them. He was taking the free medicine and selling it from his own private clinic. Some members of the community seized our visit as a chance to complain publicly and to threaten to take it up with the district authorities. During the action planning, the people present made a plan to have the health worker replaced. The health worker took this as a serious threat. He disappeared off to the District capital to argue his case with the authorities, before they heard from a representative of the village, or read our PRA report. What responsibilities did we have in this case? In the end, I didn't do anything to follow up this issue – I don't know whether my team-mates followed it through in any way.

The only direct provision for follow-up in the PPA design was an evaluation visit six months after the fieldwork. At that time a seasonal river cut off the road to the village where we worked, so a team could not visit. What happened to the conflict with the health worker? More generally, what was the impact of our intervention in the life of the community? I don't know, but I can imagine scenarios resulting from our work that could have made life worse in the village, or better. I lack the information to evaluate myself on the impact of what I did, and thus I cannot learn what I could have done better. I suspect this is a widespread experience in PRA. I wonder how many myths about PRA are sustained by practitioners who, like me, are enabled through their institutions to 'do PRA', but not to maintain any longer-term connection with the places where they worked?

Once back from the village, we were faced with the pressure of the development policy 'machine', which wants generalized, simple statements and recommendations, when all our fieldwork pointed to complexity and diversity within the region. We had designed the study to highlight diversity through the selection of field sites, and by talking to diverse people with varied perspectives within those communities. In the end, I think our report reflects existing development thinking as much as it reflects what people in the villages explained to our researchers. There was so much filtering necessary to make the things local people said look like a policy document that suits development organizations like the UNDP.

Accepting shortcomings

As I reflected back on the shortcomings of our team's work over the following months, I felt more and more comfortable about admitting to myself and to others the ways in which we could have done things better. To use a metaphor, the first time I baked a pie, the crust was like concrete and it was completely inedible. I don't feel bad about that – it is quite usual that when we try something for the first time, we make a mess of it. And doing PRA 'well' by even the simplest standard is far more complicated than making a pie! Why do we organize processes as if we can do PRA particularly 'well' based on only three weeks of training? I think that people's success at PRA in their first fieldwork following training had more to do with their character and values than anything they learned in the training. I find it hard to look back and to know that I did my best, but that my best, given our whole team's inexperience, wasn't that good.

What is even worse was that the UNDP never did fund a major development programme in the region. I was not placed to understand why. One reason could be that our 'innovative' exploration of poverty led to a proposal for the most standard cookie-cutter development activities one could imagine. But there must have been other reasons that I will never understand.

PRA in the big picture

For my masters dissertation, I travelled to India to trace the policy process that led to the adoption of a new national set of guidelines for watershed development, and then to see how these more participatory guidelines were being implemented in practice. This experience put PRA in a new perspective. Methods like PRA do little to shape the interactions between field staff and local people, given the constellation of ideas about knowledge and expertise, attitudes towards gender relations, the procedures of government institutions and the stretched resources that limit the ways in which government programmes respond to citizens' priorities.

I then began working at IDS on co-ordinating the Pathways to Participation project. Through interviews, informal meetings, workshops and reading, I started to discover just how nebulous PRA, our 'object of study,' is in the real world. This really struck me when I conducted a series of about 50 interviews with PRA practitioners in Nepal (Pratt, 2001). I found that with every interview, I would discover a different explanation of PRA: PRA as a tool for action research; as a tool for top-down development projects; as a way to avoid conflict; as a tool for raising critical consciousness about the causes of poverty; as a way of life. Some people told me the tools didn't matter, just the attitude and behaviour; others complained about practitioners doing PRA by having group discussions but not using visual tools. Some saw it is as a tool for mobilizing social movements through discussing the global structures that perpetuate poverty. However, one person I met saw PRA as insignificant in the face of global economic competition unless workers used PRA to formulate bids to attract international investment to their region. What is this thing called PRA?

My enthusiasm for PRA has gone through peaks and troughs. For example, there was a short time in which I was overwhelmed by the nauseating down-side of PRA's mainstream acceptance. Knowledge of PRA has become such a valuable and scarce 'commodity' in some places that it creates incentives for people to clutch their knowledge to their chests, to exaggerate their own skills, to try to undermine other practitioners and to smugly avoid any critical reflection on their own work. At other times, I have found what I have learned about PRA inspiring – stories about social action mobilized through the discussions accompanying PRA processes, or professional people's personal testimony about the way they have changed as people through the experiences they have had of PRA. I have also been lucky to meet people who have been through PRA who assert their solidarity with one another, their confidence in their own knowledge and their willingness to assert their rights against powerful people.

Where has this exploration left me? I see that PRA has been, and will always be, a collection of very loosely related practices. All the people who call what they do 'PRA' will possibly not agree on how to do PRA 'properly'. PRA will continue to be used by all sorts of people with different political values than myself, but I have also found friends through the Pathways project that make me proud to be associated in some small way with PRA. I have come to judge PRA by the political agenda behind it. I wish the best of luck to those using PRA to pursue positive social change, and I hope to do my own very small part to steer things in that direction too.

References

Chambers, R. (1983) *Rural Development: putting the last first*, Longman, London.

Pratt, G. (2001) 'Practitioner's critical reflections on PRA and participation in Nepal', IDS Working Papers 122, IDS, Brighton.

CHAPTER 26
Jules Pretty

What have we learned about participatory methods? Some thoughts on the personal and professional

Let a hundred flowers blossom and let one hundred
schools of thought contend *(Mao Tse-tung, 1957)*

Hindsight is always 20:20 *(Billy Wilder, American film director)*

A brief personal history

I began working with Gordon Conway at Imperial College in 1985, focusing on agricultural systems and their impact on environment and health. In 1986, we moved to the International Institute for Environment and Development (IIED) to establish the sustainable agriculture programme, which I later directed until late 1996. The programme ran field- and workshop-based training courses in participatory learning methods in more than 40 countries. In 1997, I went on sabbatical to the University of Essex in Colchester, which resulted in my setting up a new cross-disciplinary centre called the Centre for Environment and Society, which I now direct. Today, my focus is also on domestic contexts, mainly in East Anglia, close to my university.

On methods, packages and flexibility

A flowering of innovation initially occurred with the marriage of methods arising from Rapid Rural Appraisal (RRA) and Agroecosystems Analysis (AEA), along with some inputs from other important approaches, such as farming systems analysis. Somehow, the methods rapidly expanded in number – this was celebrated, while the overall 'package' never became fixed. In my view, this focus on principles rather than fixed packages was crucial.

Visualizations were vital too. As I recall, the early visualizations (maps, seasonal calendars, decision trees, historical profiles, Venn diagrams, transects) were developed in AEA to help professionals learn from one another.

They were then given a great boost when handed over to local people for them to engage in analyses of their own situations.

The critical period was 1987–98, as this was when things could have been set in stone – as occurred with some subsequent methodological packages. Some methodologies have even been trade-marked™, to the dismay of myself and many others. At this time, we were promoting, testing and trying new methods, and we did not know whether they would work. We had to push, we had to be determined. There were many sceptics who would have taken great pleasure from seeing this whole thing fail. There was much resistance within workshops and training sessions. Yet despite this, something clicked with large numbers of participants.

The methods acted like replicable viruses loaded with vital DNA – they could spread independently, but the whole/resulting/final organism always ended up being different/unique. Flexibility was always promoted, and the maxim became 'every context is different, and every package of methods must be designed to suit the circumstances'. I have had no reason, over the years, to change this basic principle: keep the principles, adapt the methods. Celebrating innovation was a vital core value – there is no right or wrong; indeed not knowing the 'rules' often led people to innovate unknowingly.

On two 'P' words – participation and power

In the early 1990s, I developed a typology of participation as I was worried about its multiple interpretations. Like sustainability, everyone says it is a good thing and that they are in favour of it. But it has different meanings to different people.

This is the trouble with participation – it can be passive, consultative, bought, interactive or mobilizing. It depends on what we want from a situation. Most professional agencies would probably like to keep things towards the consultative end of the spectrum, as it means controlling power. Making participation really work means giving up personal and institutional power, and we all know that this is very difficult indeed. Such power, I believe, often has to be taken – it is rarely granted.

On spreading the principles and methods

So why did RRA, Participatory Rural Appraisal (PRA) and all the participatory methods spread so quickly? In many ways, they should not have done – after all, they are just another set of methods among many antecedents and competitors.

I believe it was partly because something fundamental happened to the people involved – both the professionals and the local people. These methods were new, interesting, exciting, fun and above all empowering. They gave a sense of control. Of course they did not lead to changes in economic structures, or reformed institutions, or access to resources, but they did help people believe that they could make a difference.

Information was vital, and *RRA Notes* (beginning in June 1988), later becoming *PRA Notes* and then *PLA Notes*, did play a key role. The idea for *RRA Notes* was hatched at a meeting in the Institute of Development Studies (IDS) itself, and we always said from the start that *RRA Notes* should be like 'letters from the field', and so not be too polished or 'academic'. What we needed were the experiences of busy people close to the ground, who were also probably unaccustomed to writing. The core intention was to encourage learning and reflection, without being too heavy-handed. The Notes have always been free to people in developing countries – and clearly this made a difference to access.

This was laudable – but hard work. Each issue took a huge amount of editing. Perhaps one of the most significant issues was *RRA Notes* 13, the report of the February 1991 meeting in Bangalore, at which 35 (mostly Indian) practitioners from many different states came together in a most extraordinary meeting and series of exchanges. We worked hard on writing up the papers, and ensuring that key lessons and visualizations were fully represented (this was the first issue with photos). I believe that this was something of a watershed, as it reported innovation and diversity in both government and NGO settings, and showed a significant degree of impact. Financial support from the Ford Foundation in India was vital at the time – both for editing and mailing.

A danger of valuing spread is that it can look like proselytizing, selling a message. I can see no way out of this – if we want good practice to spread, then we have to seek to promote and sell it. But this can be tempered by making sure that innovation is continually celebrated. Local naming of methods is a key part – and this may go against the very notion of a core term like RRA or PRA. I have always said the more terms the better, especially if they help to promote local ownership.

On leading with a set of values

It is clear to me that the core values of RRA, PRA and other associated methodologies are progressive. Most people involved do care – about poverty and the environment, about people and communities, about making a difference. This seems to me vital. There is always a need to be objective and clear-headed, but if you are doing participation simply 'as a job', then I don't believe you care enough, and so are less willing to struggle and contend against existing forces. Obviously, this can be a problem, as it raises the question: whose values are correct?

In 1988 and 1991, I helped run two courses in northwest Pakistan and the Punjab. On both occasions, I made it clear that there had to be women members of the team, so that women's voices could at least be heard both in the field and the analysis. This was not easy, and we came under great pressure. Indeed, in 1991, we were told at the last minute that 'no women had been found' to join the government training course (no women were employed by the relevant agencies, so none could join the course…). I told the donor and the local contacts that we would have to refuse to run the training – whereupon, eight women from non-governmental organizations (NGOs) were invited to join the training. This led to productive NGO–government links as well as cross-gender ones. Many of these trainees have gone on to be outstanding international figures in their own right.

I did something similar in China at the end of the 1990s, where the donor wanted a project preparation team to be entirely European, but I held out for an equal representation of Chinese team members (all drawn from a university, and all with PRA experience). The team had two leaders, a Chinese professor and myself. This meant that when we got to the field, we had sufficient experience in the group to 'train' a wide range of people (including some of the other consultants) while preparing the project.

Over the years, others and I have been under massive pressure from time to time to accept assignments to 'do' or 'promote' participation with a very short lead-time. Even today, with my focus on East Anglia, I still get agencies calling me to ask if we can organize a public 'consultation' process beginning 'next week'. I still start by saying no. It seems to me that appropriate preparation and planning are vital – the training actually starts long before the formal training or community assessments begin.

An important issue is clearly how we are personally affected by 'PRA et al.' – how we are changed by it all, by caring about the processes and outcomes. A consultant gets information and goes away to do something. I have been part of several missions to set up projects when some team members (usually male, over 50 and divorced) have been utterly cynical and tired – 'nothing will change, it never does, why bother with all this nonsense?'. These kinds of attitude should no longer be acceptable.

By contrast, many of the places I have worked have left me feeling I have an intimate (though inevitably very partial) knowledge of places and people. This quality or depth of interaction, of joint learning, has been vital for my personal learning. It is all, I believe, quite different to much normal or conventional development. I believe that we should care enough to do something different, to be passionate, but at the same time objective and clear-headed.

On who can do it

So, are participatory methods for everyone? Clearly, not yet. Our early train-ings were intensive, often late into the evenings. It seemed that there was a job to do, and we all needed to get on with it. We felt that everyone present should be exposed and have the opportunity to engage. Like all teachers, I found that the weaker students took the most amount of time. Later, I learned not to worry so much, and to be much more relaxed. If some do not get it, don't worry. Provided they don't sabotage proceedings, then let them tread water, even go back unchanged.

My general rule is about a quarter of participants in any given context become active participants, capable of training others and significant sources of innovation. They are so good that they can spread the methods and principles to others. About a half of participants get components (a method or two) and can implement some in their own work context. The final quarter do not understand it at all (some deliberately). Following the rules of triage, the group to bother most about are the middle half – a bit of extra help and some can make it to the top group. But in the short term, forget about the bottom quarter.

One of my greatest pleasures occurred in western Kenya in 1993. I was part of a Ministry of Agriculture team involved with an evaluation of the catchment approach, which had begun in 1989 with the adoption of par-ticipatory methods for soil and water conservation. A local extensionist was taking me around the catchment, and he didn't know who I was. He told me about the various visualizations they'd used, how 18 different govern-ment agencies had been involved, how the plan had been implemented, and how food production had greatly increased, springs reappeared and tree cover increased. He particularly emphasized the participatory methods.

At the end, he said, 'you should try them some time'. It turned out he'd been trained by his divisional officer, who had been trained by his district officer, who had been trained by me three years previously. Enough of the principles and methods had clearly stuck, despite several different trainings and many different interpretations on what was correct and incorrect. This is important – if enough of the DNA can remain long into the future, then the opportunities for spread and transformation are indeed great.

On mistakes

Of course, there have been more than a few…. The early trainings were too intensive and so not replicable. I recall meeting someone who'd been at a training course in Indonesia three years previously – he said, 'excellent course, I remember it well'; I asked what had happened since, and he said, 'oh nothing at all'…. A good course with no long-term impact, and so largely a waste of time (except for those directly involved).

The early days were also too formulaic – balancing the need to push hard with something we simply didn't know whether it would be 'gone tomorrow' and the need to get it right, was difficult. Another mistake was the impression given to sceptics that the 'methods could change the world'. I don't think anyone ever said this, or indeed believed this, but somehow that impression came across.

Another was the impression that the methods were not grounded in theory. Perhaps this is why there was so much innovation, as methods were not tightly bound by theory. But it is my impression that many activists, protagonists, trainers, were deeply interested in theoretical aspects of learning, of ways of knowing, of alternative paradigms. But we clearly did not do enough to get this across to sceptics.

These days I am much concerned with the linkages between human and social capital – and how participatory approaches can help to build new relations of trust, to foster the emergence of new institutions, of reciprocal arrangements, of new rules and norms at local level. Social capital is an asset that can be built up, but it is also something that can be run down and destroyed. These are, in my opinion, a prerequisite to the accumulation and transformation of natural capital.

On a local agenda – and some more innovations

One of my aims on setting up the Centre at the University of Essex was to ensure we took every opportunity to work locally in East Anglia on participatory approaches. My colleague, Rachel Hine, and I have conducted a range of activities for different sectors, including community assessments for whole river-basin planning, health sector analyses for urban regeneration, stakeholder processes for estuary management plans and participatory appraisals for countryside management.

We have amended the notion of mapping, and now use pre-prepared and coloured maps on a polystyrene base, usually about one metre square, so that they can be carried out into the community. Some have been larger, filling whole village halls. We ask people to put different coloured flags (cocktail sticks and coloured paper) into the map to show: (1) special places or things; (2) problems; and (3) opportunities for improvement. We use a variety of other methods to encourage people to think forward to ideal futures (how would you like things to be in 20 years), and then work back to how to get there. We also use a range of other methods (social audits, common timelines, pyramids of action, seasonal calendars, etc.).

The special places component works nicely – it challenges professionals to see places through the eyes of local people. We did one week-long exercise in the summer of 1999 in a very poor and much-maligned community on the Essex coast (several hundred families living in ex-beach-huts, where running water and sewerage facilities were provided only in the mid-1980s). Jaywick has a reputation locally for trouble, yet the 250 people or so involved in the process came up with a huge number of things they said were special about their place – much to the surprise of many of the professionals involved. We also make sure that we always have local people on the team, and of course, they're not so surprised by such findings.

A common principle in all these contexts is the need to 'open the box'. The professional agencies involved inevitably have a narrow agenda – so our aim prior to the event/process is to get them to accept the need to open it all up. We completed a series of participatory activities with urban communities in east Colchester, a run-down area subject now to a regeneration programme. Professionals had designed an excellent regeneration plan, but as it was so good, the need to do more than consult was strong. We opened it up, saying we needed to understand what people wanted, then see how the plan fitted those needs. Some 320 people engaged in various elements of the process, and came up with 345 new ideas for improvements to the area. Professionals were simply astounded that there could be so many good ideas at local level. And in the end, this is where transformations can occur – radical changes in mindsets of both professionals and local people.

CHAPTER 27

Mallika R. Samaranayake

Tracing my participatory footsteps

This chapter shares the insights I have gained in the course of committing to a participatory approach in the development process. My experience relates to my role as a promoter, practitioner, trainer–facilitator, networker and researcher, bringing inputs to development projects and to policy research. I will begin with a sketch of my work experience, giving significant milestones. These experiences carried me through my pathway to participation, as I internalized Participatory Rural Appraisal (PRA) principles, both knowingly and unknowingly. My commitment and positive attitude towards 'hearing voices of the community' was, I feel, the key element that helped me to face challenges and to influence other actors to appreciate the human dimension crucial for development efforts.

My start in studies and teaching

From the mid-1960s to the 1970s I pursued a university and teaching career in geography. As a university student, I understood participation in terms of the community as recipients of social welfare. As volunteers interacting with poorer communities, we decided what was best – resulting in sewing classes, milk feeding centres and literacy classes.

In my teaching career, I interested students in geography and social studies by building in a practical component, which included sketching, mapping, modelling and interacting with the community in projects focusing on health and sanitation. This approach motivated them and helped them achieve remarkably good performance in their course work. I interpreted participation as active involvement of students in the learning process.

My experiences in government

From 1980 to 1985, I worked as a programme officer and planner in the Ministry of Education in Sri Lanka. I was responsible for activities connected with initiating and implementing the school cluster concept, which was an innovation for rational planning in the provision of school facilities.

We planners were engrossed with statistics and projections focusing on grade-wise rationalization of schools. As planners, we knew best and presented our findings to the community. I remember how one principal reacted to our suggestion to reduce the number of classrooms in the school, based on statistical computations that showed it was not economically viable to provide teachers for a small number of students. The principal said, 'I have only a few more years until my retirement. This is like cutting my throat. How can I face the community? They will blame me for downgrading the school from junior secondary to primary.' He was steaming.

After he calmed down we suggested he arrange a meeting with the parents. We explained that the children were being denied access to quality education, without the full complement of competent teachers. The principal agreed. Much to his surprise, the parents understood and commented on the poor results at scholarship examinations. Parents were willing to send their children to the next closest school for grades six to eight, even though children had to walk three kilometres. We realized that the impediment for positive change was often the intermediary who has no feel for people's perceptions. I learned that we could avoid conflict and misunderstanding by working with teachers and the community. We were only the facilitators.

Learning about ZOPP

From 1986 to 1990, I served as special projects director in charge of the Sri Pada College of Education Project, establishing a National Pre-service Teacher Training College supported by GTZ. It was during this period that I had my exposure to the Logical Framework Approach (LFA), also known as ZOPP (Objectives Oriented Project Planning). Expatriate and local project staff, representatives from the government and the donor participated. LFA/ZOPP analysis was useful for clarifying concepts between donor and government, but the beneficiaries did not play a role in planning. What matters is 'whose participation?' It was participatory only at the secondary levels, if not 'top-down', and left much to be desired. LFA/ZOPP made a framework available for monitoring and evaluation. However, there was hardly any flexibility to change the 'givens' in the log-frame once it was agreed. Looking back, I feel we could have made it more relevant to the direct beneficiaries if the opportunity provided by the mid-term review had been used for consultation and adaptation. I was still in the sphere of 'limited participation' – a long way to go on the pathway to participation.

Learning about and promoting PRA

From 1990 to 1996, I worked as the joint director of the Self-help Support Programme in Sri Lanka, supported by Swiss Inter-cooperation (SSP-IC). I enjoyed the opportunity to get exposure to the PRA methodology. It was introduced as an approach to enhance self-help capacities among communities served by SSP-IC's governmental and non-governmental partner organizations. As a promoter of PRA methodology, I had to convince partners conceptually to commit to a change in approach, build their capacities in PRA methodology and backstop field practice. It was not an easy task. There was resistance from non-governmental organizations (NGOs) and government institutions to changing their development approach to 'participation'. They were so comfortable with the established system. I remember the president of an NGO asking us, 'Why should we change the way we are doing things? We also discuss with people. We use social mobilization and the Change-Agent Approach. Why should we change to PRA?' We said, 'Having learnt about it you can decide whether it makes sense to adopt it.' It took some time for NGOs and government institutions to take to PRA. Perhaps if SSP-IC was not giving funding support to NGOs, they would not have taken PRA methodology seriously.

The outcome was worth the effort. The different partners adopted it to varying degrees. There was sensitivity towards 'participation' built during training. We stressed that what matters most is the way of conducting oneself, the behaviour and attitude that is reflected in the application of the methodology. Returning to one's 'habitual behaviour' when out of the training context appears to be normal. My experience shows that consistent follow-up and reflection with the partners is what answers the problem. At this time, SSP-IC programme also supported training of PRA trainers from different organizations.

It was during this period that Asia Regional and National training workshops were organized in collaboration with Robert Chambers (Institute of Development Studies, IDS) and John Thompson (International Institute for Environment and Development, IIED) in 1992 and 1994. These training workshops had their desired impact on the government and NGO sector that participated. As a result, the Regional Development Division of the Ministry of Plan Implementation requested PRA training for all their directors and deputy directors of integrated rural development projects.

A network of PRA practitioners/trainers and committed organizations was initiated during this period, to exchange experiences in using PRA methodology. It was initially sponsored by SSP-IC. It was also hoped that the forum would contribute to maintaining quality in this era of widespread use of PRA.

I enjoyed giving training to organizations in the country as well as outside. In 1993, I introduced PRA to a group of NGOs in Indonesia. In 1994, I trained British Voluntary Service Overseas (VSO) field officers and island chiefs of the Kuldufishi Atoll in Maldives. In 1996 and 1997, I trained NGOs of the SSP-IC NGO programme in Kerala. These events are considered significant milestones in contributing to the spread of PRA in the region. I had the opportunity to participate in several PRA experience-sharing regional and international workshops, organized by IDS and IIED.

Between January 1996 and July 1997, we passed a significant landmark in consolidating participatory methodology expertise in Sri Lanka with the establishment of the Institute for Participatory Interaction in Development (IPID), supported by SSP-IC. I was the pioneer chairperson and director. IPID faced the challenge of scaling up the methodology through government and NGOs. Some of the key organizations we supported were the Plantation Housing and Social Welfare Trust of the Ministry of Plantation Industries, Integrated Rural Development Program (IRDP) projects under the Ministry of Plan Implementation, the Mahaweli Authority and many NGOs, including Alliance Lanka and Save the Children Fund (UK). Today, IPID continues its role in providing services as a promoter, trainer, facilitator and backstopper. IPID also provides administrative services to the PRA network and the Resource Centre in collaboration with IDS and IIED. Participatory research and evaluation activities commissioned by donors such as the World Bank, Asian Development Bank (ADB), United Nations Development Program (UNDP), the World Conservation Union (IUCN), and United Nations World Food Programme (WFP) are carried out by IPID. The challenge is adaptation of participatory methodology to many sectors, such as poverty, health, education, energy, irrigation, the impact of small arms, etc.

Work for the World Bank

From 1997 to July 2000, I served a two-year contract with the World Bank country office as participatory development specialist. I was promoting integration of the social dimension into Bank-supported projects, particularly using PRA approaches at the design stage of the projects for obtaining people's perceptions. It was during this time that the 'Village Immersion Programme' of the World Bank was being conceptualized and operationalized. It was such a challenge, and a rewarding experience, to get the top and middle management of the Bank to live and interact with the local communities, and to learn from them using PRA. It resulted in some task managers advocating such a process for project identification, preparation and design. The village self-help learning initiative was an outcome of such a process. I consider this effort an important step in gaining commitment to participatory development because donors are in a unique position to influence their clients.

Lessons to share

Since I completed that contract, I have operated as a freelance consultant providing similar services and continue to support IPID as its honorary chairperson and technical adviser. I would like to share some of the lessons I have learned from my varied experiences.

Interpretation of 'participation'

The various levels of participation leading to empowerment are not easily understood. What does it mean? Whose participation matters? In project preparation, I have noticed that so-called 'consultation meetings' are sometimes general discussions which scratch the surface in an effort to legitimize ideas already conceived by consultants. Who participates is the key factor. Very often such consultations dwell on the secondary stakeholders or intermediaries. There are times when the same circle of NGOs and government officers, or at best farmer leaders, are being called on for consultation by various task teams. I found this to be common in the irrigation sector – so much so that once a technical officer remarked to a farmer, who pointed out some technical problems, 'Are you the engineer or am I?' The engineer realized his error only when he had to relocate the sluice in a small irrigation reservoir.

The exposure of technical staff to the PRA approach and their respect for the knowledge of local communities has improved. Community-level participation in analysis and diagnosis is currently gaining ground in donor-funded projects. The complaint still is about the time-consuming process of participatory analysis. But the benefits of using visuals in mapping the system by farmers or villagers, leading to the identification of problems and causes, has certainly justified time spent at the early stages. The local communities become committed to the process, as illustrated by my experience of the World Bank-supported Mahaweli rehabilitation project, and the ADB-supported technical assistance projects for protected area management and wildlife conservation.

Conceptual clarity about PRA

The relevance of PRA to the project cycle and the fact that 'the three pillars'

– methods, attitudes and behaviour, sharing/learning – are important in the process-oriented approach is slowly gaining acceptance. Yet many feel content compromising PRA to 'yet another way of data gathering'. This happens when the analysis by the community is not seen as part of the process and when people do not realize that 'the tools are only a means'. We often hear people say, 'We do PRA in our projects', but the way it is practised is another story. The challenge is to improve the situation by consistent dialogue, not sitting in corners, criticizing such limited interventions.

Quality assurance, training and ethics

The concern for quality in application continues in the context of a high demand for trainers. Requests for training of trainers for people without basic training and practice in the methodology are increasingly being made by government and NGOs – perhaps through donor pressure. It is a good aspiration to have a core group of trainers within organizations, rather than being dependent on outsiders and consultants continuously. The understanding that the team has to consolidate skills through practice before becoming trainers overnight with 'one-off' training sessions is missing. IPID continues to convince clients to commit to a training package, which includes 'backstopping' for those trained, and follow-up reflection sessions.

Our trainer network has developed a code of ethics, but who can ensure that it is adhered to? If organizations monitor training, performance becomes self-evident when there is commitment by the communities with which one interacts. Freelance trainers feel trapped in a conflict of interest, as they must do training for their livelihoods, maintaining a balance between quantity and quality. The advantage in working through institutions and networks can be seen as opening the possibility of sharing among trainers in the spirit of helping each other – with a commitment to quality.

Networking

Networking provides the means for establishing a constructive dialogue among trainers and practitioners to consolidate application of the methodology and to bring about quality assurance. Sharing and committing to a process is materialized through networking. However, success depends on who facilitates the process. Often networks are initiated by funding organizations that wish to promote participation. Experience has shown that organizational backing for the network is essential for continuing the process. If the network functions as a formal organization by itself, it may run only as long as funding is available. In networks that become a funding channel for various connected activities by other NGOs, we have seen breakaways and detours, which hamper the spirit of it all. The situation is not so bleak – a combination of the above scenarios may answer these concerns. We need to think of innovative ways of sharing and making networks work.

Research applications

We need to design the application of the methodology for research, carefully selecting the particular tools relevant to generate the information. Qualitative research has its limitations with regard to sampling and statistically significant numbers of participants. Economists sitting in judgement often put forward this concern. Recently, we experienced a PRA-type of research design being reviewed by a consultant on the same basis as a quantitative household survey. How representative is the sample? How many enumerators are there? How many households can be completed by each? It was quite a task to get them to appreciate the qualitative impact assessment using PRA methodology. The requirement was a purposive sample representative of different characteristics associated with farmer groups and farming systems and not a statistically representative sample.

Linking PRA with other methodologies

The issue of linking PRA methodology with ZOPP/LFA is coming up too often to ignore. My personal experience shows that information generation and analysis through PRA can be usefully linked to LFA/ZOPP. For example, drawing Venn diagrams can elicit the input for participation analysis, while the problems identified by the community can feed into the problem/objective analysis. Similarly, the information generated by the community on their own living conditions and lifestyles can be linked to the formulation of measurable indicators, both qualitative and quantitative. The result of such a linked analysis will lead to a meaningful action plan.

Institutionalizing the participatory approach

Absorbing a participatory approach has implications for the structure and working relationships within an institution. Our experience shows that success is dependent on the sensitivity developed among the different levels in the organization. The top management needs an orientation to the conceptual background, the middle management needs familiarization with the concepts and methodology, while the field staff require an intensive field-based training. Such a base would create an enabling environment for policy changes, procedural adaptations and, more significantly, attitudinal changes.

Linking micro and macro

It is often stated that participatory methodologies like PRA can be effective only at the micro level. Macro policy considerations, which have an impact on the micro situation and livelihood of communities, are lost sight of in the microanalysis. My experience shows that the linkages from the micro situation to the different levels of the area-based administrative systems need to be followed up as part of the rational planning process. In the Sri Lankan situation, this means while taking into consideration the micro-level diversity, linkages to wider coverage need to be considered at regional and national planning levels. We can look on the micro–macro linkage as a two-way enriching process. Community perceptions bring about insights that may lead to national-level policy changes, while micro-level analysis needs to be placed in the national policy context. Ensuring such complementarity, which allows for the voices of the underprivileged, disadvantaged and vulnerable to be heard in decision making that affects them is a goal to be reached on the pathway to participation.

CHAPTER 28
Tilly Sellers

Making waves:
a case for handing over PRA

I have worked with PRA in one form or another since 1992. Most of my experience has been related to health, specifically sexual health and HIV/AIDS. I have worked in Africa and the UK, and currently work in Cambodia helping to strengthen the non-governmental organization (NGO) sector response to a growing HIV/AIDS epidemic.

Through the years, I have often been reminded to reflect on my own practice, and to look at Participatory Rural Appraisal (PRA) within the wider picture. There was a point when I realized that PRA is so dynamic that even my own limited thinking and practice could in some way influence its direction. This dynamic quality has meant that PRA has thankfully resisted becoming a fixed model, but also means that visions of best practice require constant rethinking.

Principles and practice

As a PRA practitioner, using one's best judgement at all times is seen as the only 'rule'. This 'rule', however, means being able to recognize what 'best judgement' looks like, which is sometimes difficult. 'Facilitating' rather than leading requires a range of skills and also a level of confidence. Helping other people to 'do it themselves' in a way that means they seriously own both process and outcome requires enormous patience and commitment. I have learned through my mistakes, and there are some basic principles that have emerged for me as a result.

My own personal checklist would include being transparent about my own agenda and being clear, particularly about limitations and what will happen to, and as a result of, the information produced as part of the PRA process. More difficult is acknowledging the different dynamics created by myself as an outsider and finding strategies to use this effect in a way that will at least not impact negatively on the process. Finding strategies to address issues of power and social exclusion can also be time-consuming and involve complicated logistics, but this is probably the most important item on my checklist as a practitioner. I try to focus on my attitudes and behaviour, be self-critical and not rush people. I don't always succeed. I have discovered that using visual tools to maximize communication and understanding is vital, and that given encouragement, 'everyone can draw'. Using local materials is also important, as is encouraging invention and creativity so that people can discuss what is important to them, and not what I think is important.

Other issues discussed over the years in an effort to understand best practice in PRA have included whether it is right to 'use' PRA to extract information or for personal gain. An emphasis has also been placed on strategies to gain 'credibility' within the research community and with people in power. For a long while I felt that outsiders, including myself, were unnecessary, except perhaps as trainers and resource people. I felt the same about reporting PRA outcomes – who benefits from reports? I saw scaling up PRA as a process that would happen naturally and felt that it should not be contrived. I believed that individual understanding of PRA, including my own, develops over time and I have seen people change their attitudes radically over the space of a few years.

These issues of practice seemed vitally important at the time, but on only a few have I been able to make up my mind and take a definite stand. For the rest I waver according to the situation. I am beginning to suspect that these issues are just part of the whole 'PRA deal', wherever you are. I think everyone who encounters PRA for the first time thinks of it as 'foreign', and virtually the same issues have arisen for me as a practitioner in the North as well as in the South. I have found that the main difference with PRA practice in the North is that local people are less likely to participate in something they have not themselves initiated, and are less tolerant and even suspicious of those with 'good intentions'.

Although I know of many different successful applications of PRA, my experience leads me to believe that its major strength lies in facilitating communities to strengthen their own capacity for self-development. Given this, there are two issues for reflection that are current for me. The first concerns impact and the second is about compromise.

Making waves

I suppose, somewhat naively, I expected PRA to have a fairly radical effect on reforming development practices. Maybe I just haven't noticed it, or maybe it is still to come. Sometimes I think that things have in fact altered substantially and that I am too close to them to notice. Individuals have changed, usually through the 'seeing is believing' principle, but in my experience very few institutions have seriously been able to embrace

PRA principles and practice. In fairness, however, many do now talk about participatory approaches, research and training. Many subscribe in theory to the idea that local people can and should determine their own direction. We have more and better advocates for PRA than previously. Few people in positions of power, however, seem to genuinely respect local opinions and few accept that the decisions they make on behalf of others may not necessarily be the right ones.

This links to my second point, which concerns compromise. Maybe I'm the only PRA practitioner to have to compromise constantly, but I don't think so. I've heard people relabel this as 'being flexible' but I'm not sure that's right. Often when PRA work is organized, there are a number of different agendas to consider. The donor has criteria, there is limited funding, the focus has to be sectoral, the organization wants to own the information and outcomes, or there is a feeling that it needs to 'look more like research'. The PRA practitioner will also have their own agenda about community control of information and action and will be trying to negotiate for this to happen. Invariably some part of the PRA process is compromised as a result, and the outcome somewhat sanitized. In my experience, this will mean that most stakeholders are in fact satisfied with the outcome, but that this outcome falls far short of the potential. Compromise means making PRA seem easy, it means denying the real power of PRA to shake people off their seats, make them think in new ways and to seriously begin to challenge inequity. In my experience, PRA conducted from basic principles always, to a greater or lesser extent, makes waves.

Towards 'best practice'

The 'best' PRA experiences for me have invariably been when the practitioners are able to leave their various 'hats' at home and behave simply as concerned human beings. These are situations where there is no compromise, and where attempts at best practice are *de rigeur*. Well-organized fieldwork for training practitioners sometimes fulfils these criteria, and has many times been a better catalyst for action in the community than any number of donor interventions. Almost exclusively this has been successful when the agenda is set entirely by local people themselves, and when practitioners understand that they are invited merely to facilitate a process of analysis and make sure that all voices are heard.

I have been very fortunate to be part of the development of an extensive network of PRA practitioners in the north of England, which has grown purely as a result of training being made available. This network comprises mainly community activists, but also interested academics and other professionals. Since 1995, this network has carried out a staggering amount of work with those who are poor, vulnerable and powerless in the UK. Network members come from, and work with, communities where three generations of people may never have experienced employment. They have helped to analyse and solve problems that many had written off as impossible. In doing so they have been able to challenge the status quo with regard to power, particularly at local authority level, where decisions affecting everyday life are made. They have given a voice to those often not heard and who do not see themselves as part of mainstream society. Much of the focus in recent years has been with young people.

This particular network has a policy of members volunteering for PRA facilitation, which has enabled local groups to widen the scope and scale of their work and to draw on skills in advocacy, reporting and proposal writing. Where there is funding, members who are not in paid work can receive payment for facilitation. This opportunity to sharpen skills and become deeply involved has resulted in people from these communities being offered full-time paid work to continue to develop local institutions and services through participation. The network has now begun to provide training for relatively experienced PRA practitioners to tackle issues of best practice. There is also a programme for training PRA trainers.

Whose PRA?

Surely there is room for greater expansion of this kind of take-up of PRA by communities themselves? I know there are more such examples, but I also know that isolation and lack of funds often means that work by and for communities goes unnoticed. People involved at a local level like this are rarely invited to showcase their achievements – perhaps because conferences and workshops are seen as the domain of researchers and professionals. This can't, however, be the only reason why there are still only a few individuals and organizations actively engaged in encouraging natural diffusion of PRA at a local level.

PRA is still associated with academia, with professionals and development theory. Perhaps we have not yet seen significant impact because PRA has not yet become a widespread tool for community use. Maybe the strong focus on PRA having credibility with those in power has not been sufficiently balanced by attempts at institutionalization from the bottom up. Why? Could it be because we can't let go – do we use issues of quality as an excuse to control who 'does' PRA? It often feels as if there is too much analysis and not enough doing. We talk about 'handing over the stick' to local people, but what of handing over PRA? I suspect that we will see the true potential of PRA only when it becomes a tool used and owned by those very people whose lives current practitioners, including myself, claim to want to improve.

CHAPTER 29

Meera Kaul Shah

The road from Lathodara: some reflections on PRA

Lathodara: the beginning

In 1988, we at Aga Khan Rural Support Programme, India (AKRSP), a non-governmental organization (NGO), invited a consultant to help us introduce Rapid Rural Appraisal (RRA) methodology in our programme. Lathodara, a village in Junagadh district of Gujarat, was the first village in which we tried to use RRA for village planning. Just two or three days into the process we realized that we were making a mistake. While the maps and diagrams that we had drawn on the basis of our discussions with the villagers looked very good to us, the villagers had problems making sense of them. When we insisted that it should be the villagers themselves who should be presenting the analysis at the wrap-up meeting, we had a problem. The villagers were not able to interpret what we had done to their information on seasonality or the section diagram representing the transect walk.[1] These were soon discarded and the village representatives presented their information their way. We made sure that the process would be different from the very outset in the next village and that the local people would prepare and analyse their own maps and other visuals. There was no point in mystifying simple information. Besides, these visuals would be of little help if the villagers were not able to use them. What we did not know then was that we, along with the people of Lathodara, had contributed to the process of a significant paradigm shift.

At the time of our ten days in Lathodara, Gujarat was facing a third consecutive drought year. Successive crops had failed, cattle were perishing, drinking water was in short supply, foodstocks were depleted, many people had to migrate to other locations and people in many places had to go without a wash for a long long time. It was while we were in Lathodara that we saw the first good rain in three years. We were having a small group discussion on the verandah of one house. We were so busy with the discussion that none of us noticed the first few raindrops. But then we caught the

189

wonderful smell of first rain on a parched ground. We sang and danced in that heavy downpour. Who cared for seasonality analysis, trends, maps and other diagrams? The moment was far more important.

Although we at AKRSP moved fast on evolving what we then called Participatory Rural Appraisal and Planning (PRAP), it was the rains that we were more excited about for a long time. How were we to know that the Lathodara experience was just the start of a long path of discovery, innovation and a change in our thinking and development practice? I don't think those eight men and two women from Lathodara who had looked with dismay and frustration at our RRA diagrams are aware to this day of how they have contributed to this significant paradigm shift.

Moving beyond appraisal

From then on the participatory process evolved very fast. The timing was perfect. We at AKRSP had been struggling with making the programme more participatory. A new micro-watershed development project was also initiated at approximately the same time. Participatory appraisal was a perfect way to start a new project. It clicked.

New methods were improvised and old ones adapted to meet new requirements. Introducing participatory planning in watershed management design was a good starting point. Mapping of individual fields led to village resource maps. Villagers prepared sequences of maps showing run-off, land use and ownership patterns. They also had irrigation management maps, underground acquifer maps, and planning maps that were also used for implementation and monitoring. Sequences of social maps analysed social hierarchies, infrastructure, indebtedness, consumption patterns and wealth/well-being ranking. Subsequently, many of these maps, along with other diagrams, were used by the villagers for decision making, and analysing project coverage and project impact (Shah 1995).

The feeling was that any new idea could easily be explored by the community themselves. There was no dearth of new ideas. The villagers loved it. No one had ever before consulted them so much and had given them the opportunity to prepare and implement their own projects. Once several appraisals were carried out, we felt that it was only logical that the villagers translate them into action plans. So the participatory process began expanding beyond appraisals to planning and implementation. Village institutions revived and strengthened. People started owning the process and their projects. Having long waited to see such positive changes, we lapped it all up very fast. The excitement was intoxicating.

As the process evolved there was discomfort among some of the AKRSP staff. People felt threatened, as there was the fear of our becoming redundant in the process. So it was time to revise our roles. From managers and 'doers', we realized that we were to become the facilitators of this expanding participatory process. This role too was questioned in due course, as local facilitators turned out to be far more effective than us. Now we gave ourselves the role of trainers and back-up support resource. It did not take long for some of the local representatives to outshine us in this field as well. The real essence of PRAP was to work towards 'our' redundancy in the process.

This process did not evolve overnight. We had no model to follow. Every step and every agricultural season brought new challenges and new ideas. It was not smooth sailing at all times. And it was not easy. Local power balances shifted and had some repercussions in some villages (Shah and Shah 1995a). This led to both positive and sometimes negative impacts. The process developed faster and more smoothly in some locations than others. Village institutions had to devise their ways to overcome local differences and factions. Women and landless households were often marginalized from the initial decision-making processes, and special efforts had to be made for the process to be more inclusive (Shah and Shah 1995b; Shah 1998).

We have often been asked what made it possible for AKRSP to innovate, adapt and institutionalize the participatory process so effectively. On reflection I feel several factors contributed:

- a young multidisciplinary team of professionals, who were willing to innovate and try new ideas
- institutional flexibility, and flexible funding to some extent, that allowed for such innovation and trials
- emphasis on process and outcome (we often asked ourselves the question 'Will this lead to an improvement in peoples lives?'), rather than mere methods
- working with, and strengthening, local institutions, which were able to take over and sustain the process
- a cadre of trained village extension volunteers, who took over 'our' facilitation and training roles.

New challenges and frontiers

We were taken by surprise when many projects and development practitioners, both from India and abroad, started showing interest in our experience with PRAP. This was largely due to the efforts of Robert Chambers, who not only encouraged us and shared our experience with others, but also made it possible for them to get in touch with us. In early 1992, AKRSP was host to the first South–South Roving Workshop on Participatory Rural

191

Appraisal (PRA), along with two other Indian NGOs.[2] Participants from 11 countries observed a participatory planning process in the village of Kabri-pathar in Bharuch district, which was facilitated by men and women from a neighbouring village. An international training workshop facilitated by village volunteers!

By the early 1990s a lot of interest had been generated internationally in the PRA methodology. Of course, there were many sceptics. Many felt that what was possible in Indian villages would not work in Africa or other parts of the world. One by one these apprehensions were dispelled. Not only was it possible to adapt the methodology in almost all contexts and locations, but new methods emerged from every new experience. PRA was being adapted for use in urban communities, in post-disaster and post-conflict resettlement, in countries in the North, and in non-natural resource-based projects such as health and education. It was not long before the PRA methods were adapted for research purposes as well. I myself had the opportunity to work in several different contexts and projects over the years.

The warning bells

The speed with which the use of PRA methods spread around the world was amazing. I wish I could say the same for participatory processes. Soon it became fashionable to say that 'we have done a PRA' or that 'we use PRA'. In many ways, I feel this spelt the death of PRA. What actually spread was the use of diagrams and maps. These visuals happened to be the easiest to pick and to train others in. The feeling was that if you managed to get communities to carry out visual analysis, you could rest assured that participation is achieved. The more difficult issue of sustaining a participatory process was overlooked.

Although there are many projects and programmes around the world that have adapted the PRA methodology well in their work, there have been stories of misuse and abuse and poor-quality PRAs since early in the life of PRA. There have been numerous examples of projects carrying out participatory appraisals, only to be followed by a very top-down design of activities. Somehow the point that there are no short cuts to a participatory development process was often completely missed. I myself have witnessed examples of top-down and 'quick fix'-type of approaches being called PRA. One of these was some time in 1994, when I met a fieldworker in India who informed me that he had recently learnt a new methodology called PRA, and was now using it in his work in the villages. Pleasantly surprised, I asked him to share his experience. He pulled out a 24-page household questionnaire and said, 'This is the PRA we are doing'. In another instance I overheard a conversation between two women at a table behind me in a restaurant in Lilongwe, Malawi. They were preparing plans for a two-day training workshop, which included PRA as a topic. They discussed how much time they should keep for the 'PRA training'. One of them mentioned half a day. The other responded 'That is too much, two to three hours is enough to train them in PRA.' They settled for two hours. I did not turn around to look at the women. I did not want to recognize them.

As stories like these became known, concerns about quality, rigour and ethics of PRA were voiced. In the mid-1990s, the Insitute of Development Studies (IDS) organized a series of workshops on themes related to PRA. One of the first things discussed was the need for a clear definition of 'PRA'. All those present at a workshop in 1994 agreed that PRA refers to 'a family of approaches and methods to enable rural people to share, enhance, and analyse their knowledge of life and conditions, to plan, and to act' (Absalom et al. 1995). Despite this widely used definition of PRA, I think the unfortunate emphasis on 'appraisal' in the label has led to undermining the emphasis required on 'action'. There is much more to a participatory process than the use of some visual methods. Changing the label more recently from PRA to PLA (Participatory Learning and Action) has been a positive move. However, rather than focus on the rhetoric, it is important to ensure that the practice moves in the right direction.

The disillusionment: who has 'handed over the stick'?

The rapid spread of PRA led to several problems:
- short and poor-quality training, with a heavy focus on methods
- lack of trainers with hands-on practical experience in the field[3]
- emphasis on methods, at the cost of process
- a fixation with methods – maps, matrices, diagrams, etc., to such an extent that diagrams are seen as an end in themselves. Participation is seen as synonymous with visuals drawn by local communities
- impatience of funding agencies with process, and projects that yield late results
- easy adaptability of the methods for one-off research projects and studies
- 'taking over' by academics, especially in the North.

I think it was mainly two things that went wrong. First was the inadequate focus on process and outcome, and the fascination with methods. Numerous projects trained their staff in PRA methods. Many 'PRAs' were also carried out. Most of them never went beyond appraisal, and did not result in action based on the appraisals. PRA became a mere cosmetic addition to project proposals and annual reports. The second problem arose from the lack of a clear distinction between the use of methods for research, and their use in a development process. The biggest damage to the ethics and rigour of PRA came from the use of PRA methods in research. While I don't have anything against the use of PRA-type methods in research, and in fact I have myself used them this way a number of times, I do have a problem with calling a piece of research a PRA, no matter how participatory it is.[4] PRA rightly places a lot of emphasis on learning, especially learning by outsiders from the community. However, this learning is only the beginning. If this learning is used only to publish papers and build careers, we have got it completely wrong. Visiting a community for two days or a week in order to understand their lives and situation, and never to return or follow-up is not how I understand PRA. For me the AKRSP experience remains the benchmark for quality and rigour in a participatory process.

Much of the damage to, and criticism of, PRA stems from these short-term engagements in a community (Shah and Shah 1995a). Unfortunately much of the debate and discourse on PRA also involves academics, researchers and short-term consultants, mainly from the North, who get to spend very little time at the community level. Much of the writing on this methodology, which evolved in the field and in the South, has also been by observers, academics, short-term consultants and armchair critics. Problems of language, the supremacy of the written word, articulation skills and lack of opportunity, as well as creating models of dependency rather than working towards 'our' redundancy, have ensured that the 'stick' is yet to change hands in a big way.

These shifts in the practice and understanding of PRA led to a lot of resentment and anger within me. I realized that the concerns that surfaced early while trying to globalize PRA at breakneck speed have remained the same over the years. Every time some of us meet we end up discussing the same concerns. I think the damage is done. There are many different ways that the term PRA gets used and interpreted. Many arguments and bouts of anger later I felt it was time to move away from the label – PRA. I prefer to differentiate between a participatory development process and participatory research, and not to bundle them together under one label. I also insist that training in participatory processes cannot be achieved in three days, nor is the introduction to some methods a complete training on the process.

Looking ahead…

The road from Lathodara has been long. It has had its bumps and potholes, but there have also been some really magnificent stretches. The learning curve that took off in Lathodara is still looking upwards for me. Personally, I feel lucky to have had the opportunity to work in so many diverse contexts, on so many different issues, and to meet so many wonderful people along the way. I don't call the process PRA any more, but that does not matter. The pleasure and satisfaction from seeing others learn the participatory methodology and enjoy using it is immense. The joy of witnessing communities gain confidence to carry out their own analysis and take ownership of their development process is even greater. Years later to hear from village institutions that have not only withstood the test of time but have, on their own initiative, moved beyond their initial mandates – well, it is impossible to describe that feeling in words.

Notes

[1] I have personally never liked the transect (section) diagram, and have never used it since that day in Lathodara. Whenever we have asked the local people to present a visual on the basis of a transect walk, they tend to prepare a detailed single-dimension map.

[2] If I recollect correctly, it was at a review workshop held at AKRSP in late 1989 or early 1990 attended by two other NGOs in India – MYRADA and ActionAid – that we unfortunately decided to shorten the term PRAP to PRA.

[3] The lack of experienced trainers has been one critical bottleneck in the spread of good practice. Many feel that academic and textbook knowledge of methods is enough to train others in the methodology. This issue came up for a rather heated debate at one of the early workshops held at IDS. While some Southern practitioners emphasized the need for practical experience in the field before becoming an 'expert' and a PRA trainer, some Northern academics and researchers argued that it is good training skills that are more important.

[4] Whenever I use PRA-type methods for participatory research I insist on not calling it a PRA (e.g. Participatory Poverty Assessments or the Consultations with the Poor studies).

References

Absalom, E., Chambers, R., Francis, S., Gueye, B., Guijt, I., Joseph, S., Johnson, D., Kabutha, C., Rahman Khan, M., Leurs, R., Mascarenhas, J., Norrish, P., Pimbert, M., Pretty, J., Samaranyake, M., Scoones, I., Kaul Shah, M., Shah, P., Tamang, D., Thompson, J., Tym, G. and Welbourn, A., 'Sharing our concerns and looking to the future', *PLA Notes*, vol. 22, 1995, pp.5–10.

Shah, M.K., 'Participatory reforestation: experience from Bharuch District, South Gujarat, India', *Forests, Trees and People Newsletter* 26/27, 1995.

Shah, P. and Shah, M.K., 'Participatory methods: precipitating or avoiding conflict?' *PLA Notes* 24, 1995a.

Shah, M.K. and Shah, P., 'Gender, environment and livelihood security: an alternative viewpoint from India', *IDS Bulletin*, vol. 26, No 1, 1995b

Shah, M.K. (1998) 'Salt and spices: gender issues in participatory programme implementation in AKRSP, India', in Guijt, I. and Shah, M.K. (ed.), *The Myth of Community: gender issues in participatory development*, ITDG Publishing, London, pp.243–53.

CHAPTER 30

Marja-Liisa Swantz

My road to Participatory Action Research

I came to use participatory research through a felt need to learn more about the people with whom I lived and worked. Development of those people was not foremost in my mind nor was it their primary concern either. Later, when a research institute employed me in the University of Dar Es Salaam, I could not think that development research could bring results if the people concerned were not involved in it also. I started a long struggle to develop a participatory approach to research, which combines action with a scientifically respectable and academically approved way of doing research.

In the end I have come to the realization that it is not important for good results to have an academic stamp on the research. It is enough that it produces relevant and adequate knowledge, useful for the people who are engaged in it for their own benefit. I have also realized that the question is of much more than certain methods for gaining useful results. It involves important political principles, which deal with human rights and incorporate a participatory world view. This, in turn, raises some basic issues in the philosophy of science.

Starting out on my path to participation

I first came to Tanzania (Tanganyika) in 1952, holding a masters degree in Finnish language and culture and English philology. My initial training had made me believe that instrumental use of science, which I considered to be American pragmatism, cheapened the concept of science. Science for the sake of science was comparable to art for art's sake. I responded to the challenge to go to teach in Africa, because I was told that there was a great need for teachers there. I thought that I had chosen the road of practical work and it foreclosed the possibility of pursuing an academic career. I could serve humanity better that way than by doing research on some morphological detail of a language. I came back to scientific work in a roundabout way with a new vista.

196

I taught first-generation women teachers in a teacher training school on Mount Kilimanjaro for four years. After three years in England I returned to Tanganyika just before the country became independent, this time as the wife of a missionary. After another three years, as the mother of three four- to seven-year-old girls, I started to upgrade my theoretical knowledge in order to penetrate deeper into the culture of the people with whom we were working. My starting point was my life situation and inner need to understand and know more. We were living on the outskirts of Dar Es Salaam, from where I found my way into the villages in the hinterland of the growing city. I immersed myself in village life, built and shared a local house with a small local family, and did participatory research for five years, including the time of writing my PhD thesis.

Research was not to me an academic exercise, a one-way process. I had to recognize the ownership of people's knowledge, to respond to their expectations towards me, towards my research and knowledge, and to serve them in the ways possible for me in the given circumstances. It meant, at their request, teaching a group of women to read, and getting a nurse friend to come with me now and then to treat sores and ailments. It also meant getting the co-operation of the Water Department to come to assist the people in digging a shallow well, helping people with transport to the nearest health facility, and getting the Government to start a clinic in the village.

At the request of the elders of a circumcision camp, we were called into the camp to treat the infected wounds of the boys, although it broke the taboo against women entering this space. As an adopted daughter of a local medicine man, I assisted in the ritual of rebuilding his spirit hut and visited his patients with him. I attended divination sessions of a woman healer friend and drove her 100 kilometres to her spirit shrine. I also mourned with the bereaved and paid homage to my adopted relatives. I invited a group of 17 to visit my city home and show them the sites of the élite city folk, defying the doormen of a luxury hotel. I did these things as a member of the village.

Developing a new approach: Participatory Action Research

Having defended my thesis in the University of Uppsala, Sweden, and taught general ethnology in the University of Helsinki for a year, I returned to Tanzania. I was hired locally as a senior research fellow in the Bureau of Resource Development and Land Use Planning (BRALUP) in the University of Dar Es Salaam for three years from 1972 to 1975. Having had such close contact with village people, it was natural for me to think of doing research in co-operation with them and for their benefit. I was inexperienced and simple enough to believe that there was nothing more to it than to write a plan and start a research project. My proposal of studying the school leavers' situation in the coastal area was acceptable to the Institute, but when the plan was sent to the Research Council for approval, difficulties began. We had already been implementing the project for several months when my approach was found to be too different from the usual mode of research and it could not be approved. In fact, only with a push from the highest authorities, which found the approach to be beneficial for national politics, were the obstacles removed.

There was questioning also among my colleagues. I formulated the main principles of what I called Participatory Approach to Research and presented them in a short paper in a seminar in order to gain their understanding of my thoughts. In that paper I spelled out the basic principles of Participatory Action Research (PAR). Soon other writers adopted and expanded them. I discovered that adult educators had been acquainted with Paulo Freire, who had visited Dar Es Salaam before my arrival, but of whom I had never heard. I received support from the adult educators interested in Freire's approach and later I became part of the network of the Participatory Research group of the International Council for Adult Education (ICAE) in Toronto, Canada. As experience grew, the principles could be expanded. My first version was:

- Research conducted in a community should be planned so that part of it directly benefits that community. It should have a participant- and action-oriented role in the community.
- It should involve the people for whose benefit it is carried out in the process of research, both in formulating the immediate problems and in finding solutions to them.
- Research should incorporate into itself as many as possible of those working locally towards development of that community, whether they are village leaders, administrators, educators or extension officers. Development research requires an interdisciplinary approach. This would lead to research planning in large units rather than piecemeal projects.
- The educational and motivational potential of such an engaged research method should be fully utilized for the benefit of all involved in it (Swantz 1973, 1975).

I introduced PAR into the research projects I undertook, first on youths and then on women. Altogether 50 students of social sciences and education joined the research on their long and short holidays during the three years. They stayed in villages and learned to work with youths and families while being engaged in what I called Participatory Approach to Research. We proposed then to the Manpower section of the Ministry of Development Planning, which was planning a skills survey with International Labour Organization (ILO) support, that we implement it in a participatory way. A team was formed from different sectors of government and our institute for planning and carrying out a pilot project in three districts. Villages held meetings of self-analysis and members of villages of different levels of learning did the survey and preliminary processing of the results with some guidance from the team. The results were excellent, not statistically accurate, but providing an enormous amount of information and giving the villagers an opportunity to do self-examination and identify their unused resources and capabilities.

It makes me very sad to read those early plans and results of the projects. It seems to me now that for 35 years I have been repeating the same things over and over again. Much of what I have to say after all the experience was already stated in the beginning. We still have to convince the boards and councils that grant research funds, that the approach has its merits. The results and the self-criticism of the way of implementing the research have not changed a great deal. The impact of the approach is not in its theoretical insight; the results become evident in practice. The actions that follow are not always enduring, sustainable, but the reasons why this is not so become evident. Action research does not always end in action, but rather in self-reflection, in greater understanding of one's situation. Many times reasons for not succeeding are circumstantial and cannot be changed in a year or two, but people are better equipped to face the future.

Putting PAR on the map: the Jipemoyo project

In 1975–79, I shared leadership with the director of research in the Ministry of National Culture and Youth of Tanzania in a four-year PAR project, referred to as Jipemoyo. I had been asked to work for the Ministry, which I could not do, but proposed a Tanzanian–Finnish participatory research project instead, which got full support of the Ministry. Even then, individual bureaucrats tried to prevent the work, which covered a large part of Bagamoyo district. They feared that the researchers would find out hidden secrets of the local situation, which might cause them difficulties. It required again a word from the highest level to deal with the case. The possibility of bringing permanent results was enhanced because of the status of the project in the Ministry and its long duration.

The civil servants' and fellow villagers' prejudices against the Maasai pastoralists were changed considerably because the Parakuyo Maasai turned out to be people of quick action, eager to participate. The conflicts between the pastoralists and the sedentary farmers were dealt with, and the geographer helped the village development officers to draw maps of their areas and to make a survey of the village settlement patterns with both groups. In fact, during my visit to former BRALUP, now called the Institute of Resource Assessment (IRA) in 2000, Professor Kikula of the Institute showed me the underlined and worn-out book of Taimi Sitari on the village settlements. He said he has found it to be very useful indeed. Kemal Mustafa wrote a critique of the approach in relation to the Maasai, while he also was a proponent of PAR.

Jipemoyo made PR/PAR known in Tanzania and its researchers became the continental co-ordinators of the PR global network, first co-ordinated from ICAE, Canada. Jipemoyo researchers produced five doctoral dissertations and a couple of lower degree theses, articles and research papers. A continuous cultural interaction has been cultivated between Finnish and Tanzanian local musicians and cultural institutes.

Applying PAR in new contexts

In the 1980s, I was engaged in several major research projects in which PAR was used to different degrees. In co-operation with the Centre for Educational Development for Health (CEDHA) and Ministry of Health, we applied Participatory Research Approach in training teachers from institutes of all grades of health workers for participatory health work in villages. Another project was TECO, the theme of which was Research into Finnish Development Co-operation in Transfer of Technology in Tanzania and Zambia. Other projects in which PAR was applied in a limited sense were Grassroots Dynamics and Directed Development (GDDD) and Local Actors in Development (LAD), both in Tanzania. I led a lengthy participatory evaluation project to assess how development work has affected or incorporated women. Most recently I was employed by the Rural Integrated Project Support (RIPS) programme in Mtwara and Lindi regions as a senior sociologist and worked there on and off from 1992 until 1998. A research aspect was integrated into participatory development policy whereby Participatory Rural Appraisal (PRA) and Participation–Action–Reflection (PAR) were used in training local people and officials from different levels of local government in participatory planning and implementation.

TECO researchers had a participatory long-time presence in the research sites and close communication with the project staff and workers in each place. They did not, however, incorporate the staff consciously to study and evaluate their own situation, other than through interviews and seminars for self-assessment. The Tanzanians in the LAD project did research in their own home district. They were doctoral candidates or university teachers who had only a small amount of time for genuine long-time participation and could do little teamwork. On the positive side, the project initiated a local non-governmental organization (NGO) of largely women entrepreneurs and continuing action with the assistance of other materially more resourceful NGOs. It resulted in interactions between Finnish women entrepreneurs and Mtwara women, both through exchange visits and running common training seminars.

GDDD had to have extensive research plans presented to both the United Nations University World Institute for Development Economics Research (UNU/WIDER) and the Academy of Finland, as well as approval from the Ministry for Foreign Affairs, Department of Development Cooperation. LAD also had to be approved by the last two. The institutional demands and the wide spectrum of competencies of experts who review the plans discourage the application of participatory research approaches. Invariably the plans differ from the actual application. In true participatory research, the plan cannot be made in detail beforehand, if the researched community is to participate in the formulation of the problems and in the manner research is carried through. If the community is involved in extensive planning of a research project they expect implementation, yet one cannot guarantee that funding will be granted.

PAR and PRA: the RIPS experience

The RIPS programme is an extensive participatory development programme, integrated in the government system, in co-operation with numerous actors and organizations. It runs no projects, only supports local initiatives, which operate in a participatory way. It has also provided a forum for interactive programmes in an effective way. It was initiated as a result of previous PAR experience (TECO). In implementation it has incorporated PRA training extensively and it has generated and supported a national NGO forum for organizations and individuals using PRA, which is called upon by the government to act nationwide. My role as a 'sociologist' has given me an opportunity to immerse myself fully in the situation, sharing with people from all levels of everyday life, and not to differentiate 'research field', 'informants', 'research methods' and other such categories from everyday life. This I consider to be the ultimate achievement of PAR. I do not think that any of my friends with whom I have had lengthy discussions have thought that I have been 'researching' them. We looked together into the factors affecting their lives and reflected on the possibilities they had for solving their problems. I found it to be a great delight. I have written several research papers and studies based on the 'data' I gathered there. As a research result, I wrote a study 'Community and

Village-Based Provision of Key Social Services. A Case Study of Tanzania'.[1]

In RIPS, it has become very obvious that the use of PRA has to be deepened and the various tools used when applicable. In real life, the same tools cannot be used in the same places over and over again. Ideally, the drawn maps and recorded histories should be returned to the communities in which they originate, but it becomes impossible in a large programme in which many communities are being worked with simultaneously. The facilitators have to use imagination to develop the approach further, but they also need more training in analytical and historical thinking. Little research groups of villagers and extension officers – and researchers when available – have come up with very good studies. I think that PAR, if it is systematically applied as a continuation from PRA, digging into the reasons and meanings of the particular state of affairs, is an excellent step forward towards a deeper analysis. It gives a broader exposure to specific problems, which first become identified by PRA. PAR is good both as an introductory phase and as continuation after the PRA tools have been applied in different ways.

Challenging the separation of science from practice

In conclusion, experience taught me as soon as I came into contact with concrete situations that scientific work does not need to be separate from practice. I moved from an objectifying positivist concept of science to an interpretative, phenomenological and hermeneutic search for meanings. I also understood that the first result of participatory research is action or deepened understanding, not theory. I still think that PAR also has theoretical consequences but I do not believe theory should be the starting point. My own line of thinking has brought different forms of knowing into contact with each other. There do not need to be clear lines of difference between scientific and everyday knowledge, nor in the pursuit of them.

Note

[1]In *Research for Action* 41, UNU/WIDER, Helsinki. An edited version in Mwabu, G., Cecilia Ugaz, C. and White, G. (eds) (2001) *Social Provision in Low Income Countries. New partners and emerging trends*, UNU/WIDER Studies in Development Economics, Oxford University Press, Oxford.

References

Swantz, Marja-Liisa (1973) 'Participant Role of Research in Development', unpublished paper, Bureau of Resource Assessment and Land Use Planning, University of Dar es Salaam.

Swantz, Marja-Liisa (1975) 'Research as an Educational Tool for Development', *Convergence* Vol.8, No.2, pp.44-53.

CHAPTER 31
John Thompson

Learning from mistakes: reflections on improvisational participation

It was when I found out I could make mistakes that I knew
I was on to something. *(Ornette Coleman)*

The intro: harmolodics, participation and all that jazz[1]

Rarely does a musician emerge who dramatically changes the way we listen to music, but such a man is Ornette Coleman. Since the 1950s when he burst on to the New York scene, his artistic vision has expanded musical boundaries. Most people think of Ornette Coleman as the revolutionary saxophonist who created 'free jazz', but his music has always defied simple categorization.

From the 1950s onwards, as he explored, extended and fused honky-tonk, blues, funk and bebop, Coleman created a musical vocabulary free from the conventions of harmonic, rhythmic and melodic structures. Out of this fusion, he developed a theory, which he refers to as 'Harmolodics'. Coleman outlined the objective of the theory as trying to encourage the improviser to be freer, and not to obey a pre-conceived chord pattern according to a set of ideas of 'proper' harmony and tonality. The musician following this theory plays around the basic chord structure and possible intervals by using multilayered melodies and polytonal and polyrhythmic textures.

Over the years Coleman has gained, lost and regained favour among fans, critics and fellow musicians. As his 'style' became more defined, he was seen as an innovator and influenced many jazz musicians and composers around the world. How was Coleman able to handle criticism and still develop his visionary style of music? As he put it, 'It was when I found out I could make mistakes that I knew I was on to something.'[2] Coleman recognized the difference between making a mistake and failing, between pushing the boundaries and letting others set the rules.

Coleman's philosophy mirrors my own approach to what I will call here 'improvisational participation'.[3] I can say that my personal pathway to participation has been a journey of constant searching, endless experimentation, frequent improvisation, occasional innovation and many, many mistakes. But like Ornette Coleman, it was when I found out I could make those mistakes that I knew I was on to something...

The head: 'imitate, assimilate, innovate'

During the 1980s, I worked mainly in East Africa, first as a water technician and project manager, and later as a research fellow at the National Environment Secretariat (NES) of the Government of Kenya, Clark University and the World Resources Institute (WRI) on a programme entitled 'From the Ground Up'. The aim of the programme was to assess effective local-level approaches to sustainable natural resource management. As part of that work, I conducted my own PhD research on what led poor farmers to co-operate to manage their scarce land and water resources effectively and equitably.

I encountered significant methodological difficulties with my attempts to use structured surveys. My informants appeared uncomfortable when asked a structured series of questions on their individual and joint decisions and actions related to their resource management activities. I discovered through cross-checking that people were either withholding pertinent information or telling me half-truths. Their discomfort and wariness caused me to reflect on the nature of survey research itself. They led me to view an 'interview' as a discourse between actors, a 'speech event' where meanings of questions and responses are contextually grounded and jointly constructed by interviewer and respondent. All answers depend on the way a question is formulated – and by who asks the question. Too much can be inferred from answers taken at face value to questions of dubious merit.

By the late 1980s, the From the Ground Up team, myself included, had become deeply disenchanted with large-scale surveys.[4] We were sitting on mountains of data that we had painstakingly collected, entered into databases and analysed over many months. We had hoped to use this information to help the study communities to improve their resource management, but the time-lag was so long and the process was so disconnected from local people's own realities that the information was practically meaningless to them.

These frustrations led us to seek alternatives to the survey. We borrowed the principles, concepts and adapted methods from Rapid Rural Appraisal (RRA), Agroecosystems Analysis (AEA) and Participatory Action Research (PAR), which we learned from the work of Robert Chambers, Gordon Conway, Paolo Freire, Somluckrat Grandstaff, Terry Grandstaff, Peter Hildebrand, Neil Jamieson, Robert Rhoades and others.[5]

'Imitate, assimilate, innovate', is how the jazz trumpet master Clark Terry describes the creative process. I would say that sums up the early experiments the From the Ground Up team conducted with RRA. RRA gained popularity among rural development specialists in the late 1970s as a means to quickly mobilize resources to mitigate the problems of the rural poor. We did not follow the standard RRA procedures, which generally rely on outside specialists to apply the techniques, analyse the findings and select the proper course of action. Instead, we attempted to involve actively the farmers in the diagnostic process, working with them in the critical analysis of their own resource management problems and opportunities, and supporting them in their efforts to generate and implement viable plans. Thus, we decided that the methods could be better termed 'Participatory Rural Appraisal' or PRA, as it sought to involve local people directly in the research, to make the findings relevant to their lives, and to link analysis and reflection with action.

During the trials of the PRA approach in three districts, we had amazing 'eureka' moments. We made numerous mistakes, but we knew we were on to something almost immediately, such was the positive response we received from the study communities. The visual aspects of PRA, combined with its flexibility and iterative nature, made it useful for conducting action-oriented research with poor farmers. Most of those who took part in that early work remarked on how much they learned from the process and how much they enjoyed it. That was something no one ever said during our survey research.

The PRA approach encouraged the farmers to reflect critically on their own situation and on the obstacles hindering the attainment of their priorities. This was one of the major differences we witnessed between the survey and PRA approaches. People took ownership of the information generated through the participatory research process and used it to inform their decisions and actions.

The solo: jammin' on a world stage

While in Kenya, I crossed paths with Jennifer McCracken, from the International Institute for Environment and Development (IIED). We soon realized that we had been living in parallel participatory universes. She had been working closely with Gordon Conway at IIED and Robert Chambers at the Institute of Development Studies (IDS), UK. Jenny was also collaborating with the team at Aga Khan Rural Support Programme (AKRSP) in India, including Anil Shah, Meera Shah and Parmesh Shah, where they were developing an approach they referred to as 'Participatory Rapid Rural Appraisal' (PRRA).

Robert Chambers, at Jenny's request, invited me to a workshop at IDS on RRA in the summer of 1989, where I presented some initial lessons from Kenya. There I met a diverse range of researchers and practitioners who were grappling with many of the same questions as me. I left inspired, and felt I was part of a small but growing network of people who shared a common set of concerns and interests in participatory approaches.

That event was a turning point for me, as a year later IIED invited me to join their Sustainable Agriculture Programme in London. When I arrived in 1991, interest in RRA was growing exponentially. *RRA Notes*, an informal journal produced by IIED to share experiences as 'letters from the field', was gaining readers at a rapid rate. Our team at IIED, including Jenny, Irene Guijt, Jules N. Pretty, Ian Scoones and I were regularly asked to conduct field-based trainings in RRA and later PRA by governments, non-governmental organizations (NGOs) and international agencies around the world. The travel was nearly constant, the innovation was continuous and the learning was non-stop.

With colleagues at IDS, we organized numerous workshops, brainstorming sessions and exchanges, where we brought together remarkable groups of individuals from across the planet, who were also pushing methodological boundaries to see how far they could 'hand over the stick'. These events were 'jam sessions' where ideas were tossed around, pulled apart and reassembled to create new ways of approaching methodological challenges. As in Coleman's Harmolodics, we combined multilayered melodies and polytonal and polyrhythmic textures to create intricate syncopations; some of them were discordant, but others were rich hybrids that proved remarkably resonant.

I facilitated training programmes and applied participatory approaches in over 20 countries, from Estonia to Sri Lanka. I felt like an itinerant musician, travelling with my instrument from place to place, sitting down to jam with this group or that, showing them a few new riffs I'd picked up at my last port of call, adapting my style to suit the local musical vernacular. Looking back on it, that constant interaction and swapping of melodies with masters and novices alike was to be the best training a participatory performer could have.

Within a few years, ideas and approaches related to all things participatory were all the rage. Robert Chambers and other leading lights in the field were speaking in front of packed houses that would have been the envy of any performer. At IIED, we were deluged with requests for advice, support and information. *RRA Notes* subscriptions and sales quadrupled in a matter of 18 months. We had gone from humble street musicians, 'busking' on the corner in order to be heard, to headliners. Everyone wanted to be in on the act, from local NGOs to the World Bank, and everyone claimed to be 'doing' participation. It was the new wave.

The head out: participation, populism and power

The early 1990s was a time of tremendous methodological innovation and experimentation related to participation. In recognition of the proliferation of participatory research and development approaches, we renamed our informal journal *PLA Notes* – notes on Participatory Learning and Action, and saw subscriptions continue to grow. My colleagues and I also produced *A Trainer's Guide to Participatory Learning and Action* (Pretty et al. 1995), which has become the biggest-selling publication in IIED's history.

Large government agencies and major international organizations proudly boasted that they were designing and implementing participatory programmes that would affect the lives of millions of poor people. Donors frequently made the use of participatory approaches a condition for providing financial support. No self-respecting NGO could undertake research or development work without adopting the 'participation' moniker.[6]

Despite – or perhaps because of – this rapid spread and wide acceptance, participatory approaches were soon implicated in some very shoddy fieldwork. These unsatisfactory outcomes resulted not because there is anything inherently wrong with the approaches, but because of the way they were applied. We commonly heard reports of insensitive or biased interviewing, an emphasis on technique over process, the mistaken belief that the approach is 'value neutral', and the misguided search for methodological short cuts. Participatory approaches soon gathered a vocal set of critics from both the academic and development communities. I counted myself among them.

At IIED, we grew alarmed at how frequently organizations and individuals portrayed their work as 'participatory' when it was nothing of the sort. Control of the research or development process remained firmly in the hands of external agents, leaving local people as passive respondents or informants. Although we held deep reservations, we did not feel it was IIED's place to act as participation 'watchdogs' (though we discussed the issue repeatedly). Our philosophy remained, 'Let a thousand flowers bloom', as we sought to foster multiple points of innovation and to encourage good practice where we could.

Ornette Coleman once said, 'Improvisation is the only art form in which the same note can be played night after night but differently each time.' The same can be said for improvisational participation. Every time you use participatory approaches, the experience, the process, the outcomes are different – and they are never error-free. Participatory work, with its dynamic interplay between actors, the testing of ideas, the surfacing of different points of view, the frisson of anticipation as one player picks up the beat from another, leaves open the possibility that mistakes will happen. When those mistakes are acknowledged and embraced, new, mellifluous sounds can come out of the experience. When they are made repeatedly or become institutionalized, however, the whole thing can collapse in a cacophonous mess.

The poor practice and sham 'participatory' programmes we witnessed worried those of us at IIED enough to produce a joint statement in 1995 with colleagues from about 15 different countries (Absalom et al. 1995). We expressed our apprehensions and called for more attention to be paid to issues of quality and personal and professional attitudes and behaviour.

These concerns also led me to undertake research on a number of different fronts that aimed to challenge populist notions of participation and consensus-based approaches to research and development, and concentrate on addressing fundamental issues of the access, control and power through the analysis of difference. That work, informed by critical and social theory, resulted in numerous field reports, journal articles and a book (Scoones and Thompson 1994), and a PhD from Clark University (Thompson 1997).

My apprehensions about the apparent 'bastardization' of participatory approaches also spurred me to examine the challenges of 'going to scale'. I was concerned with understanding how bureaucracies can institutionalize participation (the principles, concepts and methods), become 'learning organizations' and apply people-centred approaches on a large scale (covering entire regions or countries) without a loss of quality. To date, that research has produced a book that looked at the institutionalization of participatory watershed management in different settings (Hinchcliffe et al. 1999), and a number of articles (e.g. Thompson 1995). It also helped to spark a joint initiative with IDS and other partners on 'Institutionalizing Participation for Natural Resource Management'.

Coda: the journey continues

As we moved into the 21st century, a time of rapid economic liberalization and global restructuring, worries about quality issues and the mechanistic use of participation have given way to broader concerns about democracy, governance and empowerment issues. This trend has caused many of us involved in participatory research and development work to focus our efforts on confronting disparities in power at all levels (not just within communities and between 'insiders' and 'outsiders'). We recognize that if significant advances are to be made there needs to be much greater attention paid to the political economy of participation, as structural political and economic factors matter as much as human agency.

All mainstream development agencies, both public and private, now use the language of 'participation' and 'empowerment'. Increasingly, however, great emphasis is also being placed on 'partnerships' (including those between corporations and communities) and 'stakeholder engagement' (including interactions between poor people and international development agencies who wish to listen to 'the voices of the poor'). Of course, some of this language remains mere window dressing, but some of it provides opportunities for disadvantaged groups to empower themselves or work with others to gain greater control over the forces affecting their lives. Nonetheless, I believe that there needs to be much greater acknowledgement of unequal power relations and conflicts in such partnerships. Moreover, we need to recognize that in some parts of the world, economic and political liberalization work in contradictory ways, as economic inequalities and levels of material deprivation may prevent poor people from taking up or making use of political spaces that may be opened up by these stakeholder dialogues.

To help participation work from the bottom up, we need to work increasingly from the top down. We need to help agencies such as government departments, NGOs and donors to transform themselves – their institutional norms, organizational cultures and operational procedures. This transformation must be reinforced by a real shift towards participatory democracy. We must also work from below in order to change things at the top. Increasingly, this will involve civil society organizations and social movements seeking to challenge authority and reclaim control over the decisions affecting their lives by rebuilding local economies and renegotiating their relationships with powerful public and private actors.

The guitarist Pat Metheny, a collaborator of Ornette Coleman, has said, 'I have to admit that more and more lately, the whole idea of jazz as an idiom is one that I've completely rejected. I just don't see it as an idiomatic thing any more... To me, if jazz is anything, it's a process, and maybe a verb, but it's not a thing. It's a form that demands that you bring to it things that are valuable to you, that are personal to you. That, for me, is a pretty serious distinction that doesn't have anything to do with blues, or swing, or any of these other things that tend to be listed as essentials in order for music to be jazz with a capital J.'[7]

Much the same could be said for participation. It too is a process, a verb, a way of approaching and transforming the world – no matter what acronym we chose to label it.

It ain't the notes, man, it's the way you play 'em.

Notes

[1]Most jazz since the bebop era is based on a form that is actually quite similar to the sonata form from classical theory: an optional introduction, the exposition or theme (possibly repeated), the development section and the recapitulation, possibly followed by a coda. The introduction, if present, sets the tone for the piece; the exposition is the main melody; the development section is where the composer extends the ideas of the exposition; the

recapitulation is a restatement of the theme; and the coda is an ending. In jazz terms, these sections of a piece would be called *the intro*, *the head* (possibly repeated), *the solo* section, *the head out*, and possibly a *coda* or *tag* ending. In this article I use these jazz terms to label the main sections.

²Reported by Martin Williams in *Jazz*, December 1963.

³Some recommended Ornette Coleman recordings are: *Something Else* (1958), *Shape of Things to Come* (1959), *Change of the Century* (1959), *Free Jazz* (1960), *Skies of America* (1972), *Body Meta* (1975), *Dancing in Your Head* (1975), *Song X* (with Pat Metheny) (1986) and *Sound Museum – Hidden Man/Three Women* (1994). A good place to start is: *Beauty is a Rare Thing: Ornette Coleman, The Complete Atlantic Recordings* (six CD box set), Rhino Atlantic Jazz Gallery (R2 71410) (1993).

⁴The 'From the Ground Up' team included: at NES – Amos Kiriro, Isabella Asamba, Charity Kabutha, Florence Kariuki, Julius Muinde and Eliud Ngunga; at Clark – Richard Ford, Barbara Thomas-Slayter and Sharon Lezburg; and at WRI – Peter Veit.

⁵We found a number of early texts particularly useful, including: Khon Kaen University's (1987) *Proceedings of the 1985 International Conference on Rapid Rural Appraisal*, Khon Kaen, Thailand, Rural Systems Research and Farming Systems Research Projects; Conway, G. (1985) *Agroecosystem Analysis for Research and Development*, Bangkok, Thailand, Winrock International Institute for Agricultural Development; Chambers, R. (1985) 'Shortcut methods for social information gathering for rural development', in Cernea, M.M. (ed.), *Putting People First: sociological variables in rural development*, Oxford University Press, World Bank, Washington, D.C.; Rhoades, R.E. (1982) 'The Art of the Informal Agricultural Survey', Social Science Department training document, International Potato Center, Lima; Hildebrand, P., 'Combining disciplines in rapid appraisal: the *Sondeo* approach', *Agricultural Administration*, vol. 8(6), 1981.

⁶As a result, we estimated that by the mid-1990s there were over 60 known approaches, each with its own acronym, bearing the label 'participatory' or 'participation'.

⁷Quoted in the *Toronto Globe and Mail*, 4 October 1997.

References

Absalom, E., Chambers, R., Francis, S., Gueye, B., Guijt, I., Joseph, S., Johnson, D., Kabutha, C., Rahman Khan, M., Leurs, R., Mascarenhas, J., Norrish, P., Pimbert, M., Pretty, J., Samaranyake, M., Scoones, I., Kaul Shah, M., Shah, P., Tamang, D., Thompson, J., Tym, G. and Welbourn, A., 'Sharing our concerns and looking to the future', *PLA Notes*, vol. 22, 1995, pp.5–10.

Hinchcliffe, F., Thompson, J., Pretty, J., Guijt, I. and Shah, P. (1999) *Fertile Ground: the impacts of participatory watershed management*, ITDG Publishing, London.

Pretty, J., Irene Guijt, I., Thompson, J. and Scoones, I. (1995) *Participatory Learning and Action, A Trainer's Guide*, International Institute for Environment and Development, London.

Scoones, I. and Thompson, J. (eds) (1994) *Beyond Farmer First: rural people's knowledge*, Agricultural Research and Extension Practice, ITDG Publishing, London.

Thompson, J., 'Participatory approaches in government bureaucracies: facilitating a process of institutional change', *World Development*, vol. 23(9), 1995.

Thompson, J. (1997) Cooperation on the Commons: collective action and reciprocal altruism in small-scale irrigation systems in Kenya, PhD dissertation, Clark University, Worcester, Mass.

CHAPTER 32

Andreas Wilkes

Rewriting the mass line: an outsider's reflections on participatory approaches in southwest China

The question 'is participation really possible in Communist China?' is one of the most common responses when I describe my work to foreigners. 'That's really what Chairman Mao was talking about years ago', is a typical response from Chinese people when I explain participatory approaches.

My Chinese colleagues have been exploring the possibilities for participation in practice in rural China since the early 1990s. With the economic reforms in the 1980s, and more recently institutional reforms, there are in fact many new spaces of opportunity. But like a window, each opportunity is surrounded by challenges that frame the space within which participation occurs.

In a recent review of experiences with participatory approaches in southwest China,[1] PRA practitioners discussed the innovations of recent years and the challenges they currently face. This chapter highlights the main issues raised, but views them through my personal window as a British citizen who has been working with PRA practitioners in southwest China since 1997. After describing my understanding of participation prior to arrival in China, and giving a brief description of the SW China Reflection project, I discuss several issues that are of concern to the Chinese PRA practitioners involved in the project and to myself:

- practitioners' livelihoods, interests and ethics
- influencing institutions
- enhancing villagers' self-management
- culturally appropriate training methods
- power and communities
- ethnic culture in development processes.

My discussion of these issues reveals how my own understanding of participation is developing.

A British understanding

In 1996, while working as a research assistant at the Institute for Development Studies, I had the pleasure of reading the hundreds of documents on Rapid Rusal Appraisal (RRA), Participatory Rural Appraisal (PRA) and other participatory approaches. At that time, I had a vision of participatory approaches as a route to realizing democratic decision making independent of the formal political structures that I saw as tainted by all sorts of perverse interests and other inadequacies. In 1997, I worked on a participatory needs assessment in London, in which we tried to generate enthusiasm among community members for taking actions on their own. I saw the dialogue with officials only as a by-product of the community process.

Later that year, I accepted an invitation from the Yunnan Institute of Geography in China to work with them on strengthening training capacity and management of the Yunnan PRA Network, which the Institute hosts. The attraction of living and working in China was for me the opportunities it presents to be more reflexive about the assumptions I have about the world.

Although I could already speak Chinese, I spent the first six months learning more about the context in which my new colleagues were operating than I did in making any contribution to their skills. The ideas that I introduced to my colleagues were often dismissed as inappropriate to the Chinese context, but gradually I saw how some of them were adopted, adapted and applied.

The SW China Reflection Project

In 1998, a small group of Network members and myself began to see that skills in the application of PRA were improving among members. Indeed, some were billing themselves as experts and declining to exchange experiences with other members. So in order to deepen understanding of PRA in the Chinese context, and also to promote a culture of sharing and continual learning within the Network, we initiated a process of personal reflection on past experiences with PRA.

Our Reflection project began with a small group of PRA practitioners drawing up a set of rough guidelines for reflection. These guidelines were then used by about 70 PRA practitioners in the Chinese provinces of Yunnan, Sichuan and Guizhou, for each to reflect individually on their experiences. Each province then held sharing meetings, and in January 2000, a three-day regional sharing meeting was held, which some of the discussion below draws on.

Issue 1: Practitioners' livelihoods, interests and ethics

Most PRA practitioners in China work in research institutions. PRA has not yet been accepted in mainstream research or government spheres. Most research institutions measure employees' performance in terms of length of published articles, so many practitioners feel the conflict between their superiors' demands to undertake conventional and less applied work, and their own desires to be personally involved in more practically oriented participatory development work. Since around 1996, providing PRA services to international organizations has become a main income source for some practitioners, and an attractive potential income source for many others. This has led to conflicts of interest among practitioners, mostly centering on the equality and mechanisms for distributing consultancy opportunities. For some practitioners, the pursuit of personal financial interest above other concerns is seen as being in conflict with the values of participation.

Thus, one set of emerging concerns is about the relationship between practitioners' conflicting roles as researchers, sellers of services, promoters of a set of values and as people who live by the set of values or ideals they promote. The current dominant discourse among practitioners recognizes the validity of interests and dismisses values except in so far as they can be tied to interests: 'don't try to change people's basic nature'. As an Englishman with some ideals, this makes me uncomfortable, but I continually strive to understand the history embedded in my colleagues' lives that has led to this situation.

Issue 2: Influencing institutions

When PRA was first introduced to SW China in the early 1990s, it was seen primarily as a survey tool. Even where research was the primary motive, most needs assessments were either directly or indirectly related to the operations of government agencies. Some practitioners soon realized that if the results of PRA are to go anywhere, practitioners must find ways to influence the relevant government institutions. I, too, came to acknowledge that the fact that government's presence can be felt everywhere from Beijing to the smallest village, and that relatively high levels of technical skill are available almost everywhere in government, should be seen not as a threat but as an opportunity. If this capacity of government can be further enhanced and linked to local realities and villagers' desires, the benefit to villagers could be enormous. So, unlike in many other countries, my colleagues and I often devote our efforts to enhancing government's capacity rather than creating space for villagers' autonomous decision making.

The whole Western concept of the project cycle is new in China, and we often give greater priority to improving officials' project management skills than to participation: even with the most participatory needs assessment, it will be the villagers who lose out if follow-up support by government is misdirected. As more practitioners get a grasp on project management, there is rising interest in how to apply institutional analysis in project work. Without this, it can be difficult to align the incentives of government staff in such a way that they can support villagers' actions.

The majority of PRA practitioners, coming from research institutions, lack experience of 'politicking' with government officials and manipulating their systems in the ways officials are used to. It is commonly perceived by practitioners that a necessary step is to convince ('brainwash' is commonly said in jest) the leaders at whatever level in order for space to be created to introduce, adapt and develop participatory approaches within government. But in the past two to three years some practitioners have developed considerable experience with undertaking institutional analyses in order to find ways to link the needs of farmers to institutional interests. They have sought entry points which may lead to the acceptance (and hopefully institutionalization) of PRA methods (or at least participatory ways of thinking) by agencies.

Issue 3: Enhancing villagers' self-management

Precisely because the role of government is so important, as PRA has moved beyond appraisals and planning, a major emphasis of recent innovations has been on developing mechanisms for community-based self-management. This allows government to reposition itself to provide support in the areas in which its comparative advantage lies. Often these approaches have involved setting up farmers' groups or facilitating villagers to devise customary laws. Examples shared during the Reflection workshops include the following.

- Caohai Nature Reserve in Guizhou province has developed 'community trust funds' in which groups of villagers are given a lump sum, and they decide their own management rules, interest rates, loan repayment periods, etc. Over two to three years, this appears to have had significant impact on community capacity to make collective decisions about other issues, such as infrastructure improvements and natural resource management.
- In Sichuan, Mr Tan Jingzheng found that collectively owned forest in one village was not being managed, owing to limited acceptance by villagers of the management rules. He facilitated villagers to first create an acceptable procedure for devising management rules, then facilitated them to make the rules, and finally to decide on their acceptance. The impact on forest management was immediately recognizable.

214

- In Yunnan, one institution (RDRC) has developed different forms of farmer mutual-help groups to enhance the effectiveness of agricultural technology extension. Voluntarily formed groups can mobilize existing communication channels among villagers, enhance villagers' roles in decision making, and reduce the transaction costs for extension agents in providing services.

These, and other cases, have led to a shift in the understanding of participation among practitioners. Whereas before, in the days of 'PRA = tools + villagers' voice', 'empowerment' was often seen as either 'the villagers can have a say' or 'villagers' capacity has been enhanced through this new way of allowing them to express themselves and collectively make decisions'. 'Villagers should be the main actors in development' was understood as respecting their views and decisions (in so far as they don't conflict with those of officials). Now, through the sharing of these recent experiences, many PRA practitioners place more emphasis on developing organizational mechanisms through which to allow villagers to decide their affairs more effectively on a day-to-day basis. Increasing attention is being given to participation beyond the discrete stages of the project cycle.

Issue 4: Participatory training with Confucian traditions

PRA training is almost always associated with participatory training approaches. However, it is unanimously recognized that participatory training methodologies need to be adapted to Chinese (educational) culture. But how to go about this remains a subject for debate in China. Some go for traditional lecturing, which all participants will be used to, but the majority of trainers realize that this is ineffective. Others are experimenting with mixed traditional lecturing and participatory methods, felt to appeal to learners' expectations of the trainers' role while also allowing time for learners to talk and think for themselves. I myself have felt that the key is not whether to lecture or not – mutual role expectations can always be discussed with participants. The biggest challenge for a Briton is to present key concepts in the conventional logical order which participants have internalized from their experiences of formal education and government propaganda. Once key concepts are grasped, learners are happy to learn with each other. It is interesting to note that satisfied trainees often refer to PRA as 'scientific', while unsatisfied trainees refer to PRA and the whole training experience as 'Western'.

Issue 5: Power and communities

My colleagues and I try to work as closely as possible with government at all levels. But this inevitably presents us with issues of power. It is most common for PRA to be intentionally used within existing formal power structures (e.g. convening group and village discussions through the village leader). In keeping with textbook principles, the voice of marginal groups is often heard, but this mostly disappears due to lack of influence in decision-making processes. I have observed several cases where it leads to the further marginalization of already marginal groups, such that these groups would be relatively better off in the absence of the PRA-guided project.

I have found that most of my colleagues are not too concerned with this issue, and many (good?) reasons are given for this. The most common reason is the need to obtain political support for post-PRA project implementation. In many cases (especially where PRA is seen as a tool to enhance project delivery) this is a valid concern, and the constraints of the external environment must be considered. Second, it is often said that for benefits to reach the majority of villagers at all is a significant improvement on past practices. Third, power is not a mainstream subject of discussion in Chinese social sciences, and is even somewhat sensitive, so many practitioners lack a background training that would point to issues of power in practice.

In revisiting some of my own previous work recently, it is also becoming apparent that many interactions between villagers, officials and facilitators (such as myself) are essentially strategic in nature. Group discussions that take place within the context of a 'project' (villagers all know that 'project = money') and within a short period of time, are a platform for different parties to enrol others in their strategies to reap short-term economic benefits. The current phase of the SW China Reflection project involves supporting 15 practitioners to return to projects that had previously used participatory approaches and interview different parties about what happened, and how the outcomes resulted. I hope that this will reveal more to us about what goes on inside this thing we call 'villager participation', and help place the power issue on the agenda in China.

Issue 6: Ethnic minority culture in development processes

SW China is home to more than 40 national minorities (elsewhere called 'ethnic minorities' or 'indigenous peoples'). While many of China's national minorities have beliefs and cosmologies that are difficult for outsiders to understand, they are also used to interacting with outsiders within the dominant paradigm. PRA processes are mostly outsider-driven, through the choice of tools, questions and activities. Thus, the outputs of PRA activities are almost universally understandable within the 'mind-worlds' of outsiders.

I believe this issue to be of concern, since I observe PRA being used within wider development processes that contribute to the erosion of the vitality of indigenous/non-mainstream cultures. I have now become aware of the need to re-examine the basis on which communication takes place in participatory processes. My own work in the coming few years will focus on developing ways to engage people from different cultures in inter-cultural dialogue as part of the participation process. I hope the terms and scope of communication can be redrawn to allow more room for both villagers (as well as their subgroups) and outsiders to take indigenous cosmologies more seriously when working together to enhance villagers' livelihoods.

Changing understandings

Looking back, I see my own understanding of participation as one that began as antithetical to government, and then became closely linked to capacity-building of government. With more attention to the way in which participatory processes occur, I now see the need for a more dialogical approach to participation, in which the cultures of government and villagers are recognized as important inputs in processes of participation. It is perhaps inevitable that a Briton working in China would move in this direction, as it will surely help me focus on more of my own personal and cultural assumptions about the world and the people in it.

Notes

[1] The SW China PRA Reflection Project has been funded by IDS and Oxfam Hong Kong.